Related titles from Palgrave Macmillan

S. H. Burton, *Mastering English Grammar*
Peter Collins and Carmella Hollo, *English Grammar: An Introduction*
Dennis Freeborn, *A Course Book in English Grammar*, 2nd edition

English Grammar for Today

A New Introduction

Second Edition

Geoffrey Leech
Margaret Deuchar
Robert Hoogenraad

First edition published 1982
Second edition published 2006 by
PALGRAVE MACMILLAN
Houndmills, Basingstoke, Hampshire RG21 2XS and
175 Fifth Avenue, New York, N.Y. 10010
Companies and representatives throughout the world

PALGRAVE MACMILLAN is the global academic imprint of the Palgrave Macmillan division of St. Martin's Press, LLC and of Palgrave Macmillan Ltd. Macmillan is a registered trademark in the United States, United Kingdom and other countries. Palgrave is a registered trademark in the European Union and other countries.

ISBN-13: 978–14039–1641–9   hardback
ISBN-10: 1–4039–1641–1   hardback
ISBN-13: 978–1–4039–1642–6   paperback
ISBN-10: 1–4039–1642–X   paperback

This book is printed on paper suitable for recycling and made from fully managed and sustained forest sources.

A catalogue record for this book is available from the British Library.

Library of Congress Cataloging-in-Publication Data
Leech, Geoffrey N.
  English grammar for today: a new introduction / Geoffrey Leech, Margaret Deuchar, Robert Hoogenraad.—2nd ed.
      p. cm.
  Includes bibliographical references and index.
  ISBN 1–4039–1641–1 (hardcover)—ISBN 1–4039–1642–X (pbk.)
  1. English language—Grammar. I. Deuchar, M. (Margaret) II. Hoogenraad, Robert. III. Title.
PE1112.L426 2005   2005050382

10 9 8 7 6 5 4 3 2
15 14 13 12 11 10 09 08 07 06

Printed and bound in China

100472U788T

Contents

Foreword to the Second Edition

The well-deserved success of the First Edition of *English Grammar for Today* among a wide audience of students and teachers has occasioned its timely publication in an updated and expanded version. Perhaps more than ever, with the internationalisation of English and the expansion of its literatures, all scholars of the language require a clear and knowledgeable guide to the complexities and nuances of the grammar in both its spoken and written forms. There can be no better introduction than this; no authors more expert and practised in delivering a clear and authoritative account of the language.

Cognisant of the needs of the reader, the authors have added a chapter with an exemplary explanation of the roles and terminology of English grammar. The clarity and detail of Chapter 2 makes it a landmark in accessible introductions to grammar. In addition, taking into account the numerous significant changes in the evolution, employment and functions of English throughout the world, the authors have incorporated new and useful discussions of the globalisation of English and its usage in electronic forms of discourse. These accounts will prove invaluable for assessing the role of English in current-day communications. Throughout the book, examples employed in illustrating points, and references given, have also been thoroughly revised, making this one of the most valuable and pertinent textbooks available.

There can be little doubt that this edition of *English Grammar for Today* responds superbly to the requirements of contemporary students and scholars alike, and is of very significant value in understanding, describing and appreciating English in all its varied forms. The English Association is delighted by the book's publication in this revised version, and is immensely grateful to the authors for their achievement in enhancing this already excellent book for new audiences worldwide.

PROFESSOR ELAINE TREHARNE
President of the English Association

Preface

After being in print for over twenty years, the first edition of this book was beginning to lose its entitlement to be called *English Grammar for Today*. It was time to prepare a new edition, bringing the book up to date, and taking account of what we have learned over the intervening decades. The result is a thoroughly revised and updated book that is proud of its title once more!

It is interesting, though, to trace what has been happening to grammar education during this period. While the teaching of English grammar has remained in high demand, students and teachers have continued to have a 'love–hate' relation with the subject. As David Crystal argues:

> In the past few years, the study of grammar, in an educational context, has come of age. From being a topic of marginal interest, beloved by a few, hated by many, and ignored by most, it has moved into the centre of pedagogical attention. You may still love it, or hate it, but you can no longer ignore it. (Crystal, *Making Sense of Grammar*, 2004)

In the UK, grammar has become part of the National Curriculum for primary and secondary education, whereas back in 1982 it was a neglected subject. In his preface to the first edition of *English Grammar for Today* Geoffrey Harlow of the English Association made clear the feeling many educated people had at that time: that a whole tradition of grammatical knowledge was on the wane and that grammar had to be reborn. There was a musty, dry-as-dust tradition, which in our preface we described as a spectre haunting 'our collective consciousness in the form of a Victorian schoolmaster instilling guilty feelings about split infinitives and dangling participles'.

That tradition has now largely disappeared: it has passed into history, along with the Victorian schoolmaster. There has emerged instead a new consciousness of the importance of grammar as a key part of language education. Yet many students and, indeed, teachers still find it difficult to engage seriously with the intellectual content of grammar. It is often felt to be too analytic, and 'difficult' in the way mathematics is assumed to be.

In contrast, our feeling, based on years of teaching, is that the intellectual challenge is part of what makes grammar rewarding. The important point is that the analytic part of grammar education cannot be separated from the study of its communicative function.

Again, as Crystal puts it, 'Grammar is the study of how sentences mean', or more explicitly, 'Grammar is the structural foundation of our ability to express ourselves' (Crystal, *Making Sense of Grammar*, 2004, p. 9). In this book we take care to provide an overall treatment of grammar in the context of communication, and especially the ability of grammar to *explain* and *promote* the successful and effective use of language.

The purpose, structure and content of *English Grammar for Today*

This book has a multiple purpose. It is primarily designed as a coursebook for students at the top secondary levels and the initial tertiary levels (especially first-year university students), but it is also adapted to the needs of teachers interested in applying an up-to-date approach to grammar, or of anybody keen to catch up with a subject taking on new importance in the educational system.

Ironically, although this book originated to meet a specific need in a British educational context, it was found to be more in demand in countries outside the UK, including countries where English is a second or foreign language. In the new edition we have taken care to address this wider international educational audience.

Some of the book is devoted to the correcting of preconceptions. Part A (Introduction) is meant to provide a fresh orientation: dispelling myths, and seeking to justify a new recognition of the value of grammar in present-day education. Here, also, in the second chapter, as a gentle introduction to grammar for the student unfamiliar with the basic concepts, we introduce some of them by applying them to the structure of words: morphology. Part B (Analysis), the main part of the book, presents a method for describing the grammatical structure of sentences. Part C (Applications) shows how this method of analysis can be used in the study of discourse and style in their broadest senses, including the development of written language skills.

The system of grammatical analysis introduced in Part B is based on that found in Randolph Quirk et al., *A Comprehensive Grammar of the English Language* (1985), and its adaptations for student use in Greenbaum and Quirk, *A Student's Grammar of the English Language* (1990) and Leech and Svartvik, *A Communicative Grammar of English* (3rd edn, 2002). It is a framework that has been widely adopted in the study of English around the world: it makes informal use of modern developments in linguistics, but does not depart without good reason from traditional terms and categories that we can consider a common cultural heritage. Naturally, at this foundation level, the framework has to be considerably simplified. 'Grammar', for our purpose, is defined in a narrow sense for which nowadays the term 'syntax' is sometimes used. It means roughly 'the rules for constructing sentences out of words', but it takes account of how words are structured, what words and sentences mean, and how they are used in communication.

We provide exercises at the end of each chapter, but their function in each part is somewhat different. For Part A the exercises are meant to encourage students' interest as well as some new thinking about grammar. In Part B the exercises are much more fully integrated into the learning process: students need to test and consolidate their understanding of the system by doing the exercises as they progress. In Part C the exercises in Chapters 9–13 invite the student to try out the system of grammatical analysis on different varieties and uses of English. Here grammar is related to other levels of language, such as meaning and vocabulary, as part of the total functioning of language as a communication system.

The book is designed to be used as a coursebook: each chapter providing one or two weeks' work, though the exercises are varied in form and purpose. Most of the exercises consist of problems with more or less definite answers, and in these cases answers are given at the back of the book (pp. 209–27). But some exercises – mainly those in chapters 9–11 – are open-ended tasks to which no answers can be given. The exercises which have answers provided are recognizable by 'answers on p. ....' alongside the heading. Students using the book for private study will gain considerable feedback, while teachers using the book as a class book will find enough material for week-by-week preparation and discussion, in addition to the exercises which students can check for themselves.

Following the answers to the exercises, we list books and articles for further reading (on pp. 230–2). The list is alphabetical but the publications are also listed by topic.

Although the book does not include a glossary of technical terms, the function of a glossary can be matched by careful use of the index, where technical terms of grammar are listed alphabetically, together with the pages on which they are introduced and explained.

Changes from the first edition

Those familiar with the first edition of *English Grammar for Today* should have little difficulty adapting to this new edition. Here are the main areas of change:

■ To ease the introduction to grammar for those unfamiliar with the subject, we have added a new Chapter 2, 'Getting Started with Grammar', incorporating some of the material from Chapter 1 of the original edition. One consequence of this is to equalize the length of the chapters: all the chapters in the book are now roughly of equal length, a major advantage if it is being used as a classroom coursebook. Another consequence, less fortunate, is that the numbers of all the chapters following Chapter 2 are increased by one. Thus Chapter 2 of the first edition becomes Chapter 3 of the new edition, and so on. The subsections of each of these chapters, however, remain the same, so that (for example) section 2.5 of the first edition becomes section 3.5 of the new edition, section 7.3.4 becomes section 8.3.4, and so on. In this way, it will be easy to match chapters and sections of the old edition to equivalent chapters and sections of the new edition.

■ The language of explanation has been simplified where possible.

■ We have used many new examples, often from authentic sources in spoken and written corpora of the language. These examples have been simplified or adapted where necessary.

- While the system of grammatical analysis remains almost entirely the same as that of the first edition, we have simplified notation to some extent, and have made more use of tree diagrams, which students tend to find easier than labelled bracketing notation. In two cases we have made a change of terminology. We have used the term TENSED instead of FINITE and the term TENSELESS instead of NON-FINITE, with reference to verbs and verb phrases. This change is made because 'finite' and 'non-finite', although traditional, are not transparent terms for a student today. 'Tensed' and 'tenseless', on the other hand, are increasingly used, and have the merit of naming the major defining criterion of the classes they refer to. The other change is to replace 'transformation' in Chapter 8 by 'structure-changing rule'.

- We have updated some of the extended passages and accompanying discussions of register varation in Chapters 9 and 10 by substituting more recent passages. We have also given some attention to new electronic modes of communication, such as e-mail.

- Chapter 12, on problems of usage, has also been adapted to changing habits and issues of English grammatical usage. For example, the debate about *I will* and *I shall* referring to the future is largely irrelevant today, as the use of *shall* has become increasingly infrequent.

We hardly need to add that the final sections of the book – the answers, further reading and index – have been thoroughly revised, to match the needs of the new edition.

Acknowledgement: Geoffrey Leech records his gratitude to Mick Short, his colleague at Lancaster, for his comments on the first edition; and to first-year students at the University of Wales, Bangor, in 2003 and 2004, for following this coursebook with apparent enthusiasm in trying out new materials in preparation for the second edition.

Lancaster, England

GEOFFREY LEECH
in association with
MARGARET DEUCHAR
and ROBERT HOOGENRAAD

Symbols and Conventions

The sections where the symbol or convention is first introduced, and where the grammatical category is most fully discussed, are here shown in brackets.

Labels

Function labels

A	Adverbial (4.2.4; 6.1.3)	Mv	Main verb (3.5.3; 5.5)
Aux	Auxiliary verb (3.5.3; 5.5)	O	Object (3.5.2; 6.1.2)
C	Complement (4.2.3; 6.1.2)	Od	Direct object (6.6)
Co	Object complement (6.6)	Oi	Indirect object (6.6)
Cs	Subject complement (4.2.3; 6.6)	P	Predicator (3.5.2; 6.1.1)
		S	Subject (3.5.2; 6.1.1)
H	Head (3.5.3; 5.1)	Voc	Vocative (6.6)
M	(Pre- or post-)modifier (3.5.3; 5.1)		

Form labels

ACl	Adverbial clause (7.1.1; 7.2.2)	N	Noun (3.5.1; 4.2.1)
		NCl	Noun clause (7.1.1; 7.2.1)
Aj	Adjective (3.5.1; 4.2.3)	NP	Noun phrase (3.5.1; 5.3.1)
AjP	Adjective phrase (3.5.1; 5.4.1)	p	Preposition (3.5.3; 4.3.4)
		PCl	Prepositional clause (7.2.5)
Av	Adverb (3.5.1; 4.2.4)	Ph	Phrase (3.2; Chap. 5)
AvP	Adverb phrase (3.5.1; 5.4.2)	pn	Pronoun (4.1; 4.3.2; 5.3.2)
CCl	Comparative clause (7.2.4)	PP	Prepositional phrase (3.5.1; 5.3.3)
cj	(Subordinating or coordinating) conjunction (4.1; 4.3.5)	RCl	Relative clause (7.2.3)
		-'s	Genitive marker (5.1; 5.3.4)
Cl	Clause (3.2; Chap. 6) (for Cli, Cling, Clen, see below)	SCl	Subordinate clause (6.2; 7.1)
d	Determiner (4.1; 4.3.1; 5.3.2)	Se	Sentence (3.2)
		V	Verb (3.5.1; 4.2.2) (used for full-verb or operator-verb)
e	Enumerator (4.1; 4.3.3)		
GP	Genitive phrase (5.1; 5.3.4)	v	Operator-verb (4.1; 4.3.6)
ij	Interjection (4.1; 4.3.7)	VP	Verb phrase (3.5.1; 5.5)
MCl	Main clause (6.2)	Wo	Word (3.2)

Composite labels

Cl, ACl, CCl, NCl and RCl combine with i, ing, en to form composite labels for tenseless clause types:

Cli	Infinitive clause	
Cling	ing-clause	(6.8; for AClen, NCli, etc., see 7.4)
Clen	en-clause	

V combines with o, s, ed, i, ing, en to form composite labels for tensed and tenseless verb forms:

Vo	Present tense or base form	
Vs	Third-person singular present tense form	(4.2.2, 4.3.6, 5.5.1)
Ved	Past tense form	
Vi	Infinitive (5.5.1)	
Ving	ing- (or present) participle	(4.2.2, 4.3.6, 5.5.1)
Ven	en- (or past) participle	

Specialized labels

The following symbols are used, mainly in 5.5, for subclasses of *Aux* and v:

Aux:
Mod	Modal (5.5)
Pass	Passive voice (5.5)
Prog	Progressive aspect (5.5)
Perf	Perfective aspect (5.5)

v:
be	Primary verb *to be* (4.3.6; 5.5)
do	'Dummy' verb *do* (5.5; 5.5.2)
hv	Primary verb *to have* (4.3.6; 5.5)
m	Modal verb (4.3.6; 5.5)

The following particles (4.3.8) are used as their own labels:

it	'empty' subject *it* (8.7.1)	there	'existential' *there* (8.7.2)
not	clause negation marker (4.4)	to	infinitive marker (4.4)

Brackets and other separators

[ ]	around clauses	(3.3.1)
( )	around phrases	
—	separates word constituents (3.3.1)	
⟨ ⟩	encloses two or more coordinates (7.7)	
{ }	encloses an optional constituent: one that can be omitted (3.4.4)	
⌐⌐	links interrupted constituents of a unit (6.1.3): e.g. *(Is (he) kidding)?*	

Labelling

An asterisk (*) precedes an ungrammatical construction (3.5.1).

Form labels (3.5.1) have an initial capital for open classes, and lower case for closed classes. They are written as subscripts before the opening bracket or before the word: NP(pn *You!*).

Function labels (3.5.2) are in italics in the text; when writing them, use underlining: e.g. use $\underline{S}$ for **S**. They are written as superscripts before the opening bracket or before the word: $^{Voc}(^{H}$**You!**$)$.

Function plus form labels (4.2.1, 4.3.8): the function label is written above the form label: $^{Voc}_{NP}(^{H}_{pn}$You!$)$.

Skeleton analysis (7.6)

The plus symbol + stands for the coordinating conjunction in linked coordination (7.7).

The comma is used between coordinates in unlinked coordination (7.7.1).

Tree diagrams (3.3.2)

See 6.9 on how to build up a fully labelled tree diagram.

Use of italic, bold and capitals

Italic type is used for examples of language quoted or cited in the text, as in: 'The single word *Fire* can be a complete sentence'. Italics are also used for the titles of books, and for drawing attention to particular words or expressions in a displayed example, e.g. 'The *early* train arrived *early*'.

CAPITALS are used for technical or grammatical terms, where these are introduced and/or explained, as in: 'The smallest units of grammar are known as MORPHEMES.'

Bold type is used for other kinds of emphasis, with the aim of drawing your attention to particular words or expressions which are more important in the context than others, as: 'Which of the following nouns are **count nouns** and which are **mass nouns**?'

When a sentence is quoted in italics, ***bold italic*** is sometimes used to highlight particular words in the sentence for your attention, as in: '*The cook doesn't actually **cook the meal***'.

Acknowledgements

The authors and publishers wish to thank the following for permission to use copyright material: British Broadcasting Corporation for extracts from *Newsbeat*, BBC Radio 1, 13.8.04 [bbc.co.uk/radio1/news/main_news/main.shtml] and BBC Sport, Radio 4, 13.8.04 [news.bbc.co.uk/sport1/hi/olympics_2004/; Church House Publishing for the Confession from *Common Worship: Services and Prayers for the Church of England*; Copyright © The Archbishops' Council, 2000; IATA for extracts from the IATA Passenger Ticket and Baggage Check; NI Syndication Ltd for an extract from 'Robbie Dumps Rachel: Superstar "too paranoid"', the *Sun*, 13.2.03; Oxford University Computing Services for extracts from the British National Corpus; Pet Mate Ltd for an extract from information supplied to purchasers of a pet door; Sony UK for an extract from an advertisement for the Sony Cybershot digital camera; Trainline.com Ltd for an extract from a telephone dialogue between a customer and a railway ticketing service; Vauxhall Motors Ltd for extracts from 1980 press and television advertisements for the Vauxhall Chevette car; David McKee for the letter on p. 157.

Every effort has been made to trace the copyright holders but if any have been inadvertently overlooked the publishers will be pleased to make the necessary arrangement at the first opportunity.

Part A

Introduction

What Grammar Is and Is Not

1.1 Grammar and its role in language

It is important from the outset to be clear about what we mean by the term GRAMMAR in this book. Many people think of grammar as a rather boring school subject which has little use in real life. They may have come across the concept in learning languages like French or Latin, in English composition, or in the explanations of teachers as to what is 'good' or 'bad' grammar. So grammar is often associated in people's minds with one of the following ideas: a dead language such as Latin, learning how to write 'properly', or learning what 'good English' is. None of these ideas about grammar is completely wrong, but collectively they give quite the wrong picture of what grammar is about and what grammar is for.

In this book we use the term 'grammar' to refer to the mechanism by which language works when we communicate with other people. We cannot see grammar concretely, because it is represented rather abstractly in the human mind, but we know it is there because it works. One way of describing grammar is as a set of rules which allow us to put words together in certain ways, but not in other ways. At some level, speakers of a language must know these rules; otherwise they would not be able to put words together in a meaningful way.

Even if they have never heard of the word 'grammar' all native speakers of English (i.e. those who have learned English as their first language) know at least unconsciously that adjectives are placed before nouns in English. You would get unanimous agreement among English speakers that *The blue book is on the table* (where *blue* is an adjective, *book* a noun) is a possible sentence, whereas *The book blue is on the table* is not.

If we study the grammar of our native language, then we are trying to make explicit the knowledge of the language that we already have. We might do this out of pure curiosity as to how language works, but we might also find the knowledge useful for other purposes. We might wish to teach English to foreign language speakers, for example, or work out how a foreign language is different from our own. Or we might want to work out how the language of poetry or advertising makes an impact on us, or learn to criticise and improve our own style of writing.

So far we have said crudely that grammar is a way of putting words together, but we have said little about sound or meaning. We can think of grammar as being a central part of language, which relates sound and meaning. The meaning of any message conveyed by language has to be converted into words put together according to grammatical rules, and these words are then conveyed by sound. The term PHONOLOGY is often used to mean the system of sounds in a language, and SEMANTICS, the system of meaning. However, in this book we will be concerned mainly with the central component of language, GRAMMAR, which relates phonology and semantics, or sound and meaning. The relationship between the three components is represented in Figure 1.1.

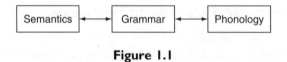

Figure 1.1

So meanings are conveyed, via grammar, in sound; but what about writing? One of the ideas which many people have about grammar is that it has to do with the written language. The word 'grammar' in fact goes back to the Greek *grámma*, meaning 'something written, a letter of the alphabet', but although statements about the origin of words such as this may be interesting historically, we cannot rely on them to tell us the current meaning of the word, as meanings change in time. Traditionally, grammar did have to do with the written language, especially the Latin language, which continued to be studied and used in its written form long after it had ceased to be generally spoken. But the written form of a language is really only secondary to its spoken form, which developed first. Children learn to speak before they learn to write. Whereas they learn to speak naturally, without tuition, from the language they hear around them, they have to be taught to write – that is, to convert their speech into a written or secondary form. Yet writing performs an extraordinarily important function in our culture (see Chapter 9), and in this book we view grammar as a mechanism for producing both speech and writing. We can now modify our previous diagram, as shown in Figure 1.2.

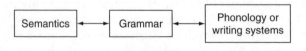

Figure 1.2

1.2 'Good' and 'bad' grammar

The value terms 'good' and 'bad' do not apply to 'grammar' in the way in which we are using that term in this book. If we view grammar as a set of rules which describe how we use language, the rules themselves are neither good nor bad, though they might be described well or badly in a description of how the language works.

Linguists who write grammars are concerned with **describing** how the language works rather than dictating, or **prescribing**, how it should be used. So if it is common for people to use sentences such as *Me and Kim are good friends*, then descriptive grammar has to allow for this type of sentence in its rules. People concerned with prescription, however, might consider this to be an example of 'bad grammar', and might suggest that *Kim and I are good friends* would be a better sentence. But what is considered better or worse is of no concern to a descriptive linguist in writing a grammar that accounts for the way people actually use language. If people are communicating effectively with language, then they must be following rules, even if those rules are not universally approved. So the role of the linguist is similar to the role of the anthropologist who, if asked to describe a particular culture's eating habits, would be expected to do so without expressing a personal opinion as to what they should be like. The latter would be a prescriptive approach. It is probably more difficult, though, to avoid being prescriptive when dealing with our own culture. As speakers of their native language, many people have ideas or prescriptive notions about how it should be used. Nevertheless, we should be able to separate the expression of our own or other people's opinions from the activity of describing actual observed language behaviour.

Although the focus of this book is to be on descriptive grammar, we have to recognise the existence of prescriptive rules, such as the 'rule' that says we should avoid phrases beginning with *Me and* at the beginning of a sentence. (This 'rule' was broken in the example quoted above – *Me and Kim are good friends*.) Prescriptive rules are clearly not grammatical rules in the same sense as descriptive rules, so it might be appropriate to call them rules of grammatical **appropriateness**. Then we can see that what some people call 'bad grammar' is something like 'bad manners', i.e. it is something you might want to avoid doing, if you wished to give a good impression. Some people consider it bad manners to put one's elbows on the table while eating and yet, from a descriptive point of view, it occurs rather often. All the same, people who eat regularly at home with their elbows on the table might avoid doing it at a formal dinner party, simply because it would not be fitting behaviour in such a setting. Similarly, there are occasions when being on one's best linguistic behaviour means obeying rules (e.g. saying or writing *Kim and I* rather than *Me and Kim*) which one would not normally adhere to in private conversation.

For a moment, let's go back to the anthropologist studying social customs. In some societies it is famously considered 'good form' for an invited guest to burp appreciatively after eating. But in other societies a burp, whether appreciative or not, is avoided as a faux pas. The anthropologist would not try to judge which of these two habits is the 'correct one'. Instead, his or her job would be simply to describe such different attitudes and patterns of behaviour. Hence anthropologists can even be **descriptive** in giving an account of **prescriptive** norms. And the same is true of grammarians.

This leads to the point that, as well as knowing the grammatical rules of a language, its speakers also have to know how to use the language appropriately, and this often involves a choice between different options associated with different LANGUAGE VARIETIES.

1.3 Variation in language

1.3.1 Introduction

Taking a rigidly prescriptive approach to language, we might suggest that there was just one, 'correct' form of the language that everyone should use. We might recognise that not everyone speaks this 'correct' form of the language, but we would describe any other form as simply wrong.

If, however, we take the descriptive approach explored in this book, we cannot dismiss any forms of language in regular use as incorrect: we have to be prepared to describe all varieties of language.

A descriptive approach recognises that there are many varieties of a language such as English. We can identify Americans as speaking in a different way from British people, northerners from southerners, young from old, white-collar from blue-collar workers, and men from women. So language will vary according to who its USERS are. A user's speech might well reflect several of these characteristics simultaneously: for example, a young woman will speak differently from both a young man and an older woman.

So language can vary from user to user, depending on the user's personal characteristics. This does not mean that each person speaks a uniform variety of language which never changes. Of course, speech can change as personal characteristics change: as a young person becomes older, a northerner moves south, or social-class membership changes as a result of education, for example. In addition, a person's language will vary according to the USE it is put to in different situations. For example, the way you talk to a friend will be different from the way you talk to a stranger. The way you talk on the telephone will be different from the way you talk to someone face to face, and you will use yet another variety in writing an e-mail or a text message. Your language will also vary according to what subject you are dealing with, e.g. sport, politics or religion. The variation of language according to its use means that each user has a whole range of language varieties which he or she learns by experience, and knows how to use appropriately. If you talked in the classroom as you would in the pub, you might be considered poorly educated (you might be using 'bad grammar' from a prescriptive point of view), and if you addressed your friend as you would your teacher, you might be laughed at.

Let's now consider variation in language according to **user** and **use** in more detail.

1.3.2 Variation according to user: dialect

The characteristics of the language user which can affect language include the following: regional origin, social-class membership, age and gender. A useful term in connection with these characteristics is DIALECT. This is often used to reflect regional origin – as in, for example, New England dialect, Cockney (London) dialect – but can be used to refer to any language variety related to the personal characteristics listed above.

Regional variation

We can often tell where a person comes from by the way he or she speaks. Depending on how familiar we are with the variety of a given region, we may be able to identify, for example, Cockney, Glaswegian (Glasgow), Scouse (Liverpool) or Geordie (Tyneside) speech. On an international level, we might be able to identify dialect features of (say) Australian, Canadian, Caribbean or Singaporean English. We can identify speech on the basis of its pronunciation, vocabulary or grammar. For example, in Yorkshire dialect, as in some other northern England dialects, the words *put* and *putt* are pronounced alike because the vowel found in the standard or southern pronunciation of words such as *putt*, *bus*, *cup*, etc. is not used. Regional dialect traits of pronunciation are often referred to as REGIONAL ACCENT. Yorkshire dialect also has its own vocabulary, for example the use of the word *happen* to mean *perhaps*. Finally, on the level of grammar, the dialect has *were* as the past tense of the verb *be* in all its forms, so that, for example, *he were* is commonly heard instead of *he was*. So dialect can be identified on the levels of pronunciation, vocabulary and grammar.

At this point we should emphasise that the term 'dialect' does not imply an incorrect or deviant use of language: it is simply used to mean a variety of language determined by the characteristics of its user.

As standard English has become the best-known variety of English, and is habitually used in public, especially written, communication, we will use it for analysis in Part B of this book.

Social stratification

The extent to which we can identify social-class dialects is controversial, but the social stratification does certainly affect the variety of the language used. In Britain there is a very noticeable relationship between social stratification and the use of standard and non-standard speech: the 'higher' you are up the social scale, the less likely you are to use non-standard or regionally identifiable speech. This means that it is not usually possible to identify the **regional** background of, for example, an upper-middle-class speaker educated at a public school. To make this clearer, imagine that you travel from one end of the country to the other, talking only to manual workers, and tape-recording their speech. Then, on the way back, you take the same route, but record only the speech of 'professionals' such as doctors and teachers. On

---

SPECIAL NOTE ON STANDARD AND NON-STANDARD LANGUAGE

Sometimes, however, the term *dialect* may be used to refer to varieties of the language which are not STANDARD. Thus the expression *he were* mentioned on page 7 is considered to be an example of non-standard grammar.

The standard language is in fact just another variety or dialect: in English use throughout the world, there are similar 'standardized' varieties widely accepted as the most suitable for public communication. Beginning in Britain more than five hundred years ago, standard English became established as that variety which was generally used by southern British, educated speakers of the language, and in writing and in public usage including, nowadays, radio and television. It is sometimes known as 'BBC English' or even 'The Queen's English'. A similar standard (with some differences, for example, in spelling and pronunciation) exists for American English. Standard English is not inherently better or more 'grammatical' than non-standard English – all varieties are grammatical in that they follow rules. Clearly, standard English gained prestige for social rather than linguistic reasons. It was ultimately based on the usage of educated people living in the south-east of England, where the important institutions of government and education became established.

---

comparing the recordings you would expect to find more variation in the speech of the workers that in that of the professionals. The speech of workers would contain a higher proportion of features which are not found in the standard language. Several of these features would be found in more than one area: for example, *done* as the past tense of *do* is found in both Liverpool and London among working-class speakers (who might say, for example, *Who done it?* as opposed to *Who did it?*).

Age

Less is known about the effect of age on language variation, but there are grammatical features which distinguish age dialects to some extent. For example, the question *Have you any money?* would be more likely to be asked by an older speaker of British English than a younger speaker, who would be more likely to use the construction (normal for American English): *Do you have ...?* Younger speakers in both American and British English are more likely to use *'s like* as a substitute for *said* in utterances like *She's like, "Who put that there?"*

Gender

Differences of language behaviour between male and female have been a focus of great interest in recent years, but it is difficult to come up with firm conclusions on grammar, because most research results could be influenced by situational factors, such as the kinds of dialogue in which speakers are engaged. But the following are examples where **typical** linguistic differences have been claimed between female and male speakers on the basis of convincing evidence:

- Female speakers show a tendency to use more prestige pronunciations than men. For example, men tend to use more pronunciations of -*ing* as /ɪn/, as in *gettin'*, *flippin'*, etc., whereas women are more inclined to use the standard pronunciation.
- Males show a stronger tendency to use non-standard grammar, as in *I ain't done nothing. I didn't want no trouble.*
- Males also show a stronger tendency to use taboo words and 'rude' expressions.
- Another difference is a tendency among males to use less polite language, such as plain imperative forms, e.g. *Sit down*. Female speakers, on the other hand, show a preference for less confrontational strategies, such as *Let's sit down, Would you like to sit down*, etc.

It should by now be clear that personal characteristics of the language user can combine to influence the variety of language used. The term 'dialect' has been used for convenience to identify the effects of these characteristics, as in, for example, 'regional dialect', 'social-class dialect', but these factors are not really separate. All the characteristics interact with one another, so that any individual will speak a language variety made up of features associated with several 'dialects'. Taboo expressions, for example, are associated (a) with males rather than females, (b) with lower social strata rather than higher, and (c) with younger people rather than with older. You may well find these associations unsurprising!

1.3.3 Variation according to use

As was pointed out in 1.3.1, no user of language uses one uniform variety of language. Language also varies according to the use to which it is put. While the term 'dialect' is convenient to refer to language variation according to the user, REGISTER can be used to refer to variation according to use (or 'style' in a general sense). Register can be subdivided into three factors of language use, each of which affects the language variety. These are: TENOR, MODE and DOMAIN.

Tenor

This has to do with the relationship between a speaker and the addressee(s) in a given situation, and is often shown by greater or less formality. For example, a request to close the window might be *Would you be so kind as to close the window?* in a very formal situation, compared with *Shut the window, Jed* in an informal situation. Formality also has the effect of producing speech which is closer to the standard. For example, a witness in court might be careful to say *He didn't do it, Your Honour*, rather than *'E never done it*, which might be said to Cockney-speaking friends outside the courtroom. A speaker has to know which is the right kind of language to use in which circumstances, though sometimes the wrong choice may be made deliberately, for humorous or ironic effect.

Mode

This has to do with the effects of the medium in which language is transmitted. Spoken language used in face-to-face situations relies on many 'non-verbal' signals such as gestures and facial expressions. On the telephone, however, the visual channel is not available so that, for example, *Yes* or *Yeah* has to be substituted for head-nodding. In writing, only the visual channel is available, so the effect of intonation, or 'tone of voice', cannot be conveyed, except, in part, by graphic means such as exclamation marks and question marks (!, ?). Written language usually involves addressees who are not present and so cannot respond immediately, and this has an effect on the language. For example, in letters or e-mail messages, direct and shortened questions tend to be less common than in conversation, so that you might be more likely to write something like *Let me know whether you are coming* rather than *Coming?* The key category difference of mode is the distinction between written and spoken language, and recently a fascinating merger of these modes has been taking place in electronic communication, using the internet. These matters will be given further consideration in Chapter 9.

Domain

This has to do with how language varies according to the human activity in which it plays a part. A seminar about chemistry, for example, will involve a wider range of vocabulary, more technical terms and possibly longer sentences than a conversation about the weather (unless by meteorologists!). Similarly, the language of a legal document will be different from that of an advertisement, and the language of a religious service will be different from that of newspaper reporting. We can thus refer to domains of chemistry, law, religion, and so on.

As with dialect variation, the categories of register variation have a combined effect, so that we cannot really identify discrete registers any more than discrete dialects. Further, dialect and register variation interact with each other since both the dimensions of user and use are always present.

To summarize what has been said in this section, language varies according to both user and use. While certain personal traits and dialect 'settings' will characterise the language use of a given person, that person's language will also reflect a range of registers appropriate for various uses.

1.4 English and other languages

1.4.1 What is a language?

So far we have shown that a language such as English has many different varieties, which result from a combination of factors.

We have not questioned the assumption, however, that a language made up of such varieties can be clearly distinguished from all other languages. It is true that we have separate labels for different languages, e.g. English, French, Chinese, but the existence of labels should not delude us into believing that these are linguistically well-defined entities. One criterion used to define a language is MUTUAL INTELLIGIBILITY. According to this, people who can understand each other speak the same language, whereas those who cannot do not. But there are degrees of comprehension. For example, southern British speakers of English may have difficulty understanding Tyneside English, and American English speakers may find it virtually incomprehensible. There is even less mutual intelligibility in the group of 'dialects' referred to as Chinese: North Chinese speakers of Mandarin, for example, cannot understand Cantonese, though both use the same written language. On the other hand, in Scandinavia, speakers of Norwegian, Danish and Swedish can often understand one another, even though they speak what are called different languages. If Scandinavia were one political entity, then these languages might be considered dialects of just one language. So the criteria for defining languages, rather than being strictly linguistic, are often political and geographical.

1.4.2 Grammatical rules in English and other languages

If a language variety is viewed as a standard language rather than as a dialect (usually for non-linguistic reasons), then it has more social prestige. This partly explains, for example, the recent proliferating official recognition of distinct languages in Europe, where previously these had been 'officially' disregarded as dialect varieties: Catalan, Galician, Ulster Scots, Macedonian, Croat, to mention a few. When a language variety does not have social prestige, its grammatical forms are sometimes condemned as uneducated, as 'bad grammar'. This is true of the rule of multiple negation in some English dialects, for example. This rule allows sentences such as *I didn't see nothing* ('I didn't see anything'), which do not occur in the standard. The high prestige of standard English leads people to claim that multiple negation is wrong because it is illogical or misleading. However, we have never heard French speakers complain about multiple negation in standard French, which has *Je n'ai rien vu*, containing two negative elements *n'* and *rien*, as a translation of the English sentence. Also, Chaucer had no qualms about the matter when he wrote (in the *Prologue* to the *Canterbury Tales*):

He *nevere* yet *no* vileynye *ne* sayde
In al his lyf unto *no* maner wight.

('He *never* yet *didn't* speak *no* discourtesy
in all his life to *no* kind of person'.)

In fact, not content with double negation, Chaucer uses four negatives in these two lines! Multiple negation was perfectly acceptable in the fourteenth century.

It is important for English speakers of whatever variety to realise that other languages or varieties can have their own grammatical rules. We cannot assume that other languages or varieties will fit the framework of the one we know well. This kind of mistake was made in the past by classical scholars who tried to describe English in the framework of Latin. For example, the prescriptive rule that *It is I* is right and *It is me* is wrong comes from assuming that the distinction between *I* and *me* must be the same as the distinction made in Latin between *ego* and *me*. This rule is not at all descriptive, since *It is me* occurs often in English.

Many of us first encounter grammatical rules different from our own when we learn a foreign language such as French, German or Spanish. We find that, for example, the rules of word order in these languages are different from those found in English. In French a pronoun like *le* has to precede the verb rather than follow it. So, for example, *I see him* is translated as *Je le vois* (literally, *I him see*). In German, certain forms of the verb must be placed at the end of the sentence, so that, for example, *I will go tomorrow* is translated as *Ich werde morgen gehen* (literally, *I will tomorrow go*). In Spanish a subject like *usted* comes after a past participle in a question rather than before it, so that, for example, *Have you forgotten the word*? is translated as *¿Ha olvidado usted la palabra*? (literally, *Have forgotten you the word?*). However, French, German and Spanish still show considerable similarity to English in their grammar: all four languages belong to the INDO-EUROPEAN family of languages. In all four, for example, you can form questions by changing the order of words in the sentence. This is not true of all languages, though: in Japanese, which is not an Indo-European language, questions are formed by the addition of a particle (*ka*) at the end of the sentence. So *Suzuki-san wa ikimasu* means *Mr/Ms Suzuki is going*, while *Suzuki-san wa ikimasu ka*? means *Is Mr/Ms Suzuki going*?

These examples serve to show that we need to avoid preconceptions about the form which grammatical rules will take in a given language or language variety. Instead, we can find out what these rules are by observing the way people speak or write in different situations. Once we have done this, we can return (as this book does in Chapter 12) to questions of appropriate usage.

1.5 Grammar and effective communication

The main function of language is to communicate with other people. We said in section 1.2 that in the language itself there is no such thing as 'good' or 'bad' grammar. It is reasonable, however, to distinguish between good and bad **communication**. In other words, language use should not be evaluated according to what kind of grammatical rules it follows, but according to whether it conveys its message effectively. It is quite possible, for example, to speak or write according to the grammatical rules of standard English, and yet to produce language which is unclear or difficult to follow. This can be described as 'bad style', and the following examples from written English illustrate the point:

(1) This is a picture that a girl that a friend of mine knows painted.
(2) I saw it in a book that a former teacher of mine thought of at one time setting us some exam questions out of.
(3) If a bomb drops near you, don't lose your head – put it in a bucket and cover it with sand.
(4) For sale: a piano belonging to a lady going abroad with an oak case and carved legs.
(5) The problem of what contribution the public should make to the swimming pool arose.
(6) She has given that part-time job in San Francisco up.

There is little doubt that these sentences are grammatical, according to the standard rules for constructing sentences in English. But it is interesting to consider why these sentences strike us as being 'unhappy' in their construction. In (1) and (2) the sentences are put together in a way which makes them difficult to unravel and understand. For example, in (1) who painted the picture – the girl or the friend? Most people will have to reread the sentence in order to puzzle out exactly what is going on. In (3) and (4) the construction of each sentence leads to an ambiguity: what the writer intended to say is not clearly stated. This does not necessarily imply that the reader cannot work out the intended meaning. You are unlikely, for instance, to imagine a lady with an oak case and carved legs in (4). But you arrive at this conclusion **in spite of** the grammar rather than **because of** it. The grammar allows a second meaning which, like an after-image, lurks distractingly in the background. In (5) and (6) the difficulty is that there seems to be a lack of balance, a 'top-heaviness', in the construction of each sentence. To solve this difficulty, one could change the order of the words as follows:

(5a) The problem *arose* of what contribution the public should make to the swimming pool.
(6a) She has given *up* that part-time job in San Francisco.

At this stage we do not attempt to explain exactly what is the matter with (1)–(6); it is enough to note that we see here three types of difficulty in forming and interpreting grammatical sentences: confusing structure (1 and 2), ambiguity (3 and 4), unbalanced structure (5 and 6).

Since using language is a skill, it is not surprising that some people are more skilled at it than others. There is no need to shrink from evaluation of this skill – for example, saying that one writer has a better style of writing than another. But it is helpful, for this purpose, to be aware of the grammatical resources of the language, and the various possibilities open to the user who wants to make effective use of the language. In this way we gain conscious control over the skill of using language. This is one of the main reasons for learning about grammar, and we return to it in Chapters 12 and 13.

1.6 Conclusion

At the other extreme from sentences (1)–(6) are the products of literary masters of prose style. One additional reason for studying grammar is that we can gain an appreciation of how literary writers use language for powerful effects. However, this chapter is already long enough, and the literary topic is one we will have to leave for the next chapter.

Meanwhile, in this chapter we have aimed to provide a backcloth for the study of English grammar. We began with an attempt to 'demythologise' the subject: that is, to dispel some misconceptions about grammar which have been prevalent in the past, and still have influence today.

We showed how the notion of grammar must allow for variation in language, and that we cannot prescribe the form which grammatical rules will take. There is no grammatical analogue of the Ten Commandments. We thus rejected the possibility of evaluating grammar out of context, but went on to begin showing how grammar can be used for more effective or less effective communication. In Part C of this book we will return to some of the points we have raised only briefly and simply so far, and we will also illustrate the practical benefits of studying grammar for understanding our language and using it more effectively.

Part B, which follows the next chapter, aims to make you aware of your knowledge of how standard English is structured. We shall be introducing grammatical terminology and techniques of analysis that will enable you to describe this structure. A large part of understanding grammar is learning how to do it, so we would urge you to work through the exercises in each chapter in order to apply your new knowledge.

––––––––––––––––––––––––– **EXERCISES** –––––––––––––––––––––––––

Exercise 1a   (answers on p. 209)

True/false questionnaire (to test your understanding of the chapter)

Label the following statements either 'true' or 'false':

1. The study of grammar has to include the study of Latin.
2. Grammar can be seen as a set of rules that we follow when we use language.
3. We can follow the grammatical rules of our native language without knowing them consciously.
4. The study of grammar will improve your spelling.
5. Grammar only deals with the study of writing, because it originally meant 'to write' in Greek.
6. Children have to be properly tutored in their language if they are to learn to speak grammatically.
7. Studying grammar involves learning how people should speak.
8. It is incorrect to end a sentence with a preposition.
9. American English is less grammatical than British English.
10. The way we speak depends, among other things, on our personal characteristics.

11. The way we speak to friends is identical to the way we speak to strangers.
12. Dialect is inferior to the standard language.
13. Manual workers in the north and south of Britain differ more in their speech than do doctors.
14. The term *tenor* refers to the pitch of your voice in a given situation.
15. Whatever you can convey in speech, you can equally well convey in writing.
16. The English language as used in medicine could be considered a language domain.
17. All languages follow the same grammatical rules.
18. A sentence which is difficult to understand must be ungrammatical.

Exercise 1b   (answers on pp. 209–10)

Classification of sentences

All of the following sentences appear to have something 'wrong' with them. Try to work out whether each is:

A   ungrammatical in the sense that it does not follow a rule observable in the language behaviour of competent speakers of English;
B   'incorrect' – i.e. 'bad etiquette' from the point of view of prescriptive grammar (see 1.2); or
C   'bad style' in the sense that it does not communicate effectively (see 1.5).

In the case of C, decide whether the 'bad style' is due to confusing structure, ambiguity or unbalanced structure.

1. I can recommend this candidate for the post for which he applies with complete confidence.
2. I ain't going nowhere tonight.
3. We need more experienced teachers.
4. To was or not to was, that be the ask.
5. Me and Jasmin are going to the beach today.
6. How are you, it has a long time that we don't have heared from you again.
7. The principal of the college gave a timely piece of advice to me once.
8. They will tomorrow arrive.
9. Eggs should be stamped with the date when they are laid by the farmer.
10. Where's those books you told me about?

Exercise 1c (answers and sources on p. 210)

Identifying categories of language use (see 1.3.3)

Identify the categories of language use in these samples of language, as follows:

Tenor: relatively formal or informal
Mode: spoken or written
Domain: advertising, journalism, politics or religion

Example: After reading this, other central heating systems won't look so hot.
         Tenor: informal   *Mode* written   *Domain:* advertising.

1. STUNNING Rachel Hunter has dumped pop superstar Robbie Williams because she can no longer cope with his 'paranoia', The Sun can reveal.
2. Praise and glory and wisdom, thanksgiving and honour, power and might, be to our God for ever and ever! Amen.
3. America has entered a great struggle that tests our strength, and even more our resolve. Our nation is patient and steadfast.
4. MSN Messenger: the most popular, fun and personal way to chat online.
5. So what's likely to happen now? Well the report has been sent to the Director of Public Prosecutions, in view of er certain evidence.

Getting Started with Grammar

2

In the last chapter we introduced some ideas about why grammar is useful. In this chapter we approach grammar more directly, but from two different points of view. The first half of the chapter is concerned to show you how grammar can help us to delve into the form and meaning of a text, and thus gain insight into things which would otherwise escape our attention. The second half begins the more formal study of grammar in the most approachable way, by looking at the **grammatical forms of words**: this is the probably the easiest part of English grammar, and is known as MORPHOLOGY.

2.1 Grammar in prose literature

First, to illustrate the value of grammar in more depth, we choose two examples of literary texts – one a prose text and the other a poem. In literature, it can be argued, grammar is shown at its highest level of achievement. In a poem, a play or a prose work, the resources of the language, including grammar, are used not only for **efficient** communication of ideas, but for **effective** communication in a broader sense: communicating and interpreting people's experience of life, individual and collective. This means using language in especially 'foregrounded' or marked ways, as can be illustrated, on a small scale, by even a short sentence like the following:

(1) To live is like to love – all reason is against it, and all healthy instinct for it.
     (Samuel Butler, *Notebooks*)

The difficulty of making sense of (1) is quite different from that of making sense of (1) and (2) on page 13. Here an unusual perspective on life is expressed in a striking and unusual way. This is typical of literary expression, and means that a lot of meaning or effect is condensed into a few words. Let's briefly consider how grammar contributes to the effect. This is done particularly through PARALLELISM: the matching of one pattern of words with another, similar pattern. Figure 2.1 is a visual representation of this parallelism.

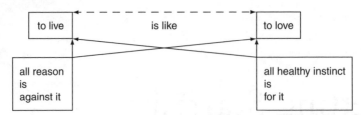

Figure 2.1

As the diagram shows, sentence (1) is cleverly constructed so as to bring out two parallelisms. The first is one of similarity (*to live* ... *to love*) and the second is one of contrast (*all reason* ... *all healthy instinct*). The parallelisms are expressed by symmetry and similarity in the actual choice and combination of words, so that almost every word in the sentence is balanced significantly against another word. Even the sound of words helps to underline these relationships: the analogy between *live* and *love* is emphasised by similar pronunciation /l_v/, and the word *like*, which 'mediates' between the two, resembles *live* in appearance and *love* in meaning: *live* ← *like* → *love*.

Sentences exist primarily in time rather than in space, and so the order in which words occur is important for literary effect. Suppose (1) had read like this, with the sections in italics in reverse order:

(1a) To live is like to love – *all healthy instinct is for it*, and *all reason against it*.

The result would have been to stress the 'reason' for not living at the expense of the 'instinct' to live – almost as if the writer were thinking that life is not worth living, so let's commit suicide. This is because there is a general principle (see 13.2.3) that the most newsworthy and important information in a sentence tends to be saved to the end. Actually sentence (1), as Butler writes it, is optimistic rather than pessimistic: he places *instinct* in a triumphant position at the end, adding the word *healthy* for further optimistic emphasis.

The first part of (1) can provide a further example of the significance of ordering. Let's now imagine that Butler had written *To love is like to live* ... In that case he would be comparing loving with living rather than vice versa. As it stands, (1) seems to say: 'You know about love being the triumph of healthy instinct over reason, don't you? Now I'm telling you that life itself is like that.' That is, the sentence begins with familiar ground (or shared general knowledge) – the traditional idea of love defying reason – and extends this well-known idea to a new sphere – or rather, generalises it to the whole of life. So if Butler had written *To love is like to live*, the whole effect would have been undermined, to the bafflement of the reader.

This simple example shows how much the way we construct a sentence – the way we put the parts together – can contribute to the effect it has on a reader or listener. If we want to understand the know-how of good writing, whether as students of literature or as writers ourselves, we need to understand something of the grammatical resources of the language, and the ways in which they can be exploited. This is not the place to go into the exact grammatical analysis that would be needed to make these relationships of similarity and contrast clear: the idea is that you will be able to undertake this kind of analysis yourself when we reach Chapter 11.

2.2 Grammar in poetry

Grammar is also important in poetry. Poetry and grammar might seem to be poles apart – the one suggestive of 'the spark o' Nature's fire', the other of the cold eye of analysis. But a poet would be foolish to proclaim, 'I am above grammar', as it is by grammatical choice that many of the special meanings of poetry are achieved. Often these effects show 'poetic licence' – the poet's well-known habit of deviation from the rules or conventions of everyday language. If those rules did not exist, of course, the poet's deviation from the rules would lose its communicative force. The following short poem on a nun's taking the veil shows some of the characteristics (in addition to those of metre and rhyme) that we may expect to find in the language of poetry:

(2)   *Heaven–Haven*

  I have desired to go
    Where springs not fail,
 To fields where flies no sharp and sided hail
    And a few lilies blow.

  And I have asked to be
    Where no storms come,
Where the green swell is in the havens dumb,
    And out of the swing of the sea.
             (Gerard Manley Hopkins)

As in (1), but more obviously here, words strike up special relationships with one another because of similarities of sound and meaning, and also because of similarities of grammatical structure. The first tendency is best illustrated by the play on words in the title, where the similar sounds of the words *heaven* and *haven* suggest they have similar meanings. The second tendency is evident in the marked parallelism between the two stanzas, as shown in this 'skeleton' version of their structure:

(2a) I have ____ed to _____   And I have ____ed to_____
     Where_____   Where _____
     To fields where_____   Where _____
     And_____   And_____

We could note, further, the unEnglish grammar of the second line (*Where springs not fail*, rather than *Where springs do not fail*). Also, Hopkins reverses the normal order of words in the third line (*To fields where flies no sharp and sided hail*), and postpones the adjective *dumb* to the end of the seventh line (*The green swell is in the havens dumb*). Such unusual patterns of grammar contribute to a strange dissociation of words from their expected context, so that simple and ordinary words like *springs, flies, blow, swell* and *swing* seem to attain abnormal force. What makes such simple words special here is that they are not confined to their normal grammatical use: *swing* (referring to a rounded to-and-fro movement) is usually a verb, but here occurs as a noun; *side* is normally a noun, but here is used in an adjective form *sided*. All these words have a role to play in a grand metaphor that the whole poem expresses: the likening of a spiritual life to an earthly refuge.

It is enough here to point out that poetic empowerment through language involves both extra freedom (including freedom to depart from the rules of grammar) and extra discipline (the discipline which comes by superimposing special structures on language – in a broad sense, parallelism, including rhyme and metre). We later (Chapter 11) explore further the application of grammar to the study of literature, through analysis of some examples of prose writing.

2.3 A taste of morphology: the structure of words

Now we move to something more down-to-earth and matter-of-fact. Morphology (literally meaning 'the study of form') is the part of grammar dealing with how words are structured. The smallest units of grammar are known as morphemes, but in more everyday language they are called STEMS and AFFIXES. Here is a sentence where the stems and affixes are separated by hyphens:

(3)   Un-know-n to the govern-or-s, there were terr-ible mis-under-stand-ing-s, and the Board utter-ly fail-ed to reach agree-ment.

In this sentence, there are 16 words, but they can be split into many more morphemes (28 actually, separated by hyphens or spaces). Some of the morphemes are STEMS – they are the major parts of words, and can usually stand alone as separate words: *know, govern, there, stand.*

Other morphemes are AFFIXES: they are added before or after a stem, to make a longer and more complicated word: *un-, -n, -or, -s, -ible, mis-.* The affixes added before the stem are called PREFIXES: *un-, mis-,* etc. The affixes added after the stem are called SUFFIXES: *-n, -or, -s, -ible, -ing, -ly, -ed, -ment.*

What about ...*under*... and *terr*...? Are they stems? At the moment, it looks as if ...*under*... is a stem, because it can stand alone as a word. But *terr*... seems not to be a stem, because it cannot stand alone – it has to be followed by a suffix. We will not answer these questions now, but will return to them shortly – in 2.4.1.

2.4 Simple and complex words

Notice in (3) that some words, like *the, there, were* and *reach,* have a stem, but no affixes. These are SIMPLE words, words with just one morpheme.

Other words are COMPLEX words, containing two or more morphemes. *Fortun-ate* has two morphemes, *un-fortun-ate* has three morphemes, and *un-fortun-ate-ly* has four. (Notice we are using hyphens here to show the boundary between morphemes. The hyphen, for the purposes of our notation, will be added to affixes, but not to stems. So *fortunate* consists of the stem *fortun(e)* and the affix *-ate*.)

NOTE

English spelling can be misleading when we try to identify stems and affixes. For example, the stem *fortune* when it occurs as a separate word ends in -e, but when it occurs in a bigger word like *fortunate* it loses its -e, because of the following vowel *a*. There is no need to worry about this kind of thing – it is a feature of the irregular spelling (i.e. the writing system) of English, and not of the grammar. Other changes like this are doubling of consonants (*win – winn-er*) and substituting *i* and *y* for one another (*hurry – hurri-ed, tie – ty-ing*).

2.4.1 The structure of complex words

Complex words have a structure we can show by using bracketing *(...)*, or else by using a TREE DIAGRAM. The easiest way of showing their structure would be to use an 'upside-down tree' as in Figure 2.2, with a vertical branch for each morpheme (the whole word is signalled by the 'tree trunk' at the top).

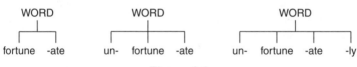

Figure 2.2

This structure can also be shown by bracketing: *(fortun)(-ate), (un-)(fortun) (-ate), (un-) (fortun)(-ate)(-ly)*. However, this one-level bracketing is not the best way to show the structure of the second and third words, because *un-* is actually added to the adjective *fortun-ate*, which we therefore place in brackets as follows: *(un-)((fortun)(-ate))*. Then *unfortunate* as a whole can be shown as bracketed, when *-ly* is added to it, so that the longest word's structure looks like this: *((un-)((fortun)(-ate)))(-ly)*. Each pair of brackets *(....)* contains a morpheme. So some morphemes, like *fortunate*, are complex, in the sense of containing two or more other morphemes. This can alternatively be shown by placing numbers over the morphemes in the order in which they are added, beginning with the root: *un-fortun-ate-ly*. Or, better still, in Figure 2.3 we repeat the same structure in a tree diagram.

What is the point of picturing structure like this? One reason is that the diagram shows why we have no word *un-fortune* in English. This word

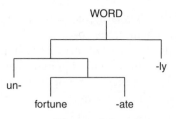

Figure 2.3

makes no sense, because the negative prefix *un-* should link with the adjective *fortunate*, not the noun *fortune*. Consider another example: *un-bear-able*. Here we should not want to bracket *un-bear* together like this: *((un-) (bear))*, because *un-bear* makes no sense as a word: the negative prefix *un-* does not go with the verb *bear*, but with the adjective *bearable*. Hence this bracketing is the right analysis: *(un-)((bear)(-able))*.

SPECIAL NOTE ON STEMS

Stems can be defined as the main elements of words, to which affixes may be added. Going back to *terrible* and *misunderstandings* in (3), we have to note that some English stems cannot stand alone as separate words in today's English. This is because of the history of the language. For example, in *ruth-less* and *un-couth*, *ruth* and *couth* used to mean something in English. But the words passed into disuse, and we are left with a 'fossil' stem. Similarly, in *terr-ible*, the form *terr* used to have a meaning ('fright(en)') in Latin, the language from which many words were formed in past centuries. Now it is a kind of fossil, like *couth*. A stem which cannot stand alone, like these, we will call a bound stem, because it can occur only in combination with some other morpheme.

The situation with *under-* in *understand* (or *misunderstandings*) is the opposite: it looks like a stem, but in fact is best considered an affix. *Under* can occur as a separate word, and therefore seems to be a stem. But when *under* does occur as a separate word, it has a different role – it normally refers to position, as in *under the table*, and is grammatically speaking a preposition (see 4.3.4). But here *under* has no such prepositional meaning, and we can reasonably consider it a prefix. *Under-* as a prefix often has a special meaning particularly when preceding a verb: in *underestimate*, *underdone*, *underpaid* it means 'less than enough'.

To complete this brief sketch of the role of stems in word-structure, we have to consider a common phenomenon of English, where a word contains two stems, one added after the other. Words of this kind are called compounds, and the most frequent examples are nouns: *football, newspaper, weekend*. These nouns actually consist of two nouns placed alongside one another, with the meaning focused on the second noun, such that a *foot+ball* is a kind of *ball*, and a *news+paper* a kind of *paper*. But because both nouns are separate stems, we do not use hyphens here in showing their structure: *(foot)(ball), (news)(paper), (week)(end)*.

2.4.2 The grammatical role of final suffixes

As we have just seen with examples like *football*, not every complex word ends with a suffix. Yet grammatically speaking, the most important part of a complex English word is in general the suffix it ends with: e.g. *-ing*, *-able*, *-ful*, *-ation*, *-ed*. Before we proceed, look at the following words, and note how they contain a stem (underlined) with a following suffix (in bold type). Notice whether the stem is capable of standing as a separate word, or whether it is a bound stem like *terr-*:

found-**ation**   vari-**able**   re-turn-**ing**   dis-turb-**ed**   un-reason-**able**   loc-**ation**
re-spect-**able**

Remember that the spelling of stems can vary slightly, for example through final *y* becoming *i* or through the loss of final *e*. So the stem *vari* in *vari-able* is not a bound stem, but just a slightly different spelling of the verb *vary*. The stems *loc* and *spect* in the last two words above are, on the other hand, bound stems because they do not correspond to any word in English. They come from Latin words meaning 'place' and 'look'. Like many bound stems, though, they occur with the same or a similar meaning in a number of different words: *local*, *locate*, *relocate*, *allocate*, etc.; *respect*, *inspect*, *inspection*, *spectacular*, etc.

TASK

Write out the following list of words in six groups, based on their suffixes. When you write out each word, insert a hyphen before the suffix. Apart from the suffix, what do the members of each group have in common?

1. national	*6. computer*	*11. extremely*	*16. suitable*
2. organize	*7. criticize*	*12. dirty*	*17. lucky*
3. frontal	*8. specialize*	*13. really*	*18. readable*
4. valuable	*9. personal*	*14. funny*	
5. usually	*10. teacher*	*15. manager*	

Assuming you have ordered these words in six lists according to whether they end in the suffix *-al*, *-able*, *-ize* (which has an alternative 'British' spelling *-ise*), *-er* or *-ly*, you may go in two directions in giving the answer to the question 'What do the members of each group have in common?' One kind of answer looks for a common meaning. This is easier with some suffixes than others: for example, the word ending *-er* usually identifies the **doer** of the action: a *teacher* is someone who teaches, a *manager* is someone who manages, and so on. But the meaning, if any, associated with an ending like *-al* (in *national*) is more difficult to pin down.

A different kind of answer looks for the grammatical function of each kind of word. If you are familiar with the terms for word classes such as noun, verb, adjective and adverb, you will recognize the words ending in *-al* and

-able, for example, as adjectives. (If you are unclear about the meaning of these terms, they will be clarified in the next chapter.) Yet a third way to look for a common factor in these groups is to remove the suffix, and find what other kind of word remains. For example, if we remove the *-ly* from the words with this suffix, we end up with adjectives: *real, usual, extreme*. If we remove the *-y* from words with this suffix, we end up with nouns: *fun, dirt, luck*.

NOTE

In some cases, we do not end up with a single word class: if we strip the *-ism* from *organism, criticism* and *specialism*, we are left with *organ* and *critic*, which are nouns, and *special*, which is an adjective.

2.5 Derivational and inflectional suffixes

There are two major kinds of suffixes: DERIVATIONAL and INFLEC-TIONAL SUFFIXES.

As its name implies, a derivational suffix is used to derive one word from another: for example, if we add the derivational suffix *-er* to *sprint*, we change the word *sprint* into a fresh word *sprinter*. This often tells us something about a word's history (the word *sprint* existed in English before the word *sprinter*). More important for the present purpose, it tells us about the word's role in grammar today. Returning to the six suffixes in 2.4.2 above:

- By adding *-al* to *nature*, we change a noun (*nature*) into an adjective (*natural*).
- By adding *-able* to *wash*, we change a verb (*wash*) into an adjective (*washable*).
- By adding *-ize* to *vandal*, we change a noun (*vandal*) into a verb (*vandalize*).
- By adding *-ly* to *hideous*, we change an adjective (*hideous*) into an adverb (*hideously*).
- By adding *-er* to *mow*, we change a verb (*mow*) into a noun (*mower*).
- By adding *-y* to *fluff*, we change a noun (*fluff*) into an adjective (*fluffy*).

INFLECTIONAL SUFFIXES can also more simply be called INFLEC-TIONS. Unlike derivational affixes, they do not derive one word from another; instead, they represent a different form of the same word. For example, *catamaran* and *catamaran-s* are different forms of the same word: they are both nouns, and in a dictionary they would both be looked up under the same headword *catamaran*. The only difference between them is that one of them is singular (referring to one) and the other is plural (referring to more than one). In fact, the number of inflectional suffixes in English is quite small, compared with most other European languages. They are all (apart from some exceptional 'irregular' forms like the *-en* of *oxen*) included in Table 2.1.

If this table looks slightly complex at first glance, just remember all that it contains in a nutshell: it tells you all you need to know about the regular

Table 2.1

Regular verbs in English have four forms:	look	look-ed	look-s	look-ing
	move	mov-ed	move-s	mov-ing
Regular nouns in English have an -s (or -es) in the plural:	pet	pet-s		
	copy	copi-es		
Regular short adjectives (and a few adverbs) have forms ending in -er and -est:	kind	kind-er	kind-est	
	white	whit-er	whit-est	

inflectional morphology of English! Additional to this, there are only exceptional cases – irregular forms of one kind or another – notably those of irregular verbs like *eat* ~ *ate* ~ *eaten*.

In case the distinction between derivational and inflectional affixes is not yet clear, the following tests will help to expand and clarify what has been said about them:

- Inflections have irregular forms (e.g. irregular nouns like *crisis* ~ *crises*; irregular verbs like *know* ~ *knew* ~ *known*; irregular adjectives like *good* ~ *better* ~ *best*; irregular adverbs like *far* ~ *further* ~ *furthest*). But for most words they apply to, inflectional suffixes are regular (e.g. *-s* for the plural of a noun, *-ed* for the past tense of a verb).
- Inflections apply (allowing for irregular forms) to a whole class of words without exception, whereas derivational suffixes are of variable acceptability. Every full verb, for example, has an inflectional form in *-ing*: *teaching, working, hoping, enjoying, liking, choosing, standing*, etc. On the other hand, consider the derivational suffix *-er* changing verbs into 'doer' nouns: *teacher* and *worker* are examples of established and perfectly acceptable nouns in *-er*, but other nouns in *-er* derived from verbs are somewhat or entirely unacceptable: *hoper, enjoyer, liker, chooser, stander*.
- If a word has both a derivational suffix and an inflectional suffix, it is the inflectional suffix that comes last: e.g. in *comput-er-s, wid-en-ed, luck-i-est*, it is the last suffix (in bold type) that is the inflectional one.
- Prefixes are always derivational; there are no inflectional prefixes in English.
- Usually a derivational suffix causes a change in the grammatical word class of a word: e.g. *-ful* is added to a **noun** (e.g. *wonder*) to form an **adjective** (e.g. *wonderful*); *-ness* is added to an **adjective** (e.g. *happy*) to form a **noun** (e.g. *happiness*). However, an inflectional suffix does not change the word class of the word it is added to: e.g. *chair* is a noun, and *chairs* (with the plural inflection added) is still a noun.

2.6 Summary: the main points of English morphology

- MORPHOLOGY is a part of grammar telling how words are structured.
- The units that morphology deals with – MORPHEMES – can be stems or affixes.

- Affixes coming before the stem are PREFIXES; those following the stem are suffixes.
- Suffixes can be either DERIVATIONAL (showing how the word is derived from another, smaller word) or INFLECTIONAL (showing the word is a variant form of the same word without the suffix).
- The (last) suffix of a word is important for showing the word's grammatical class, e.g. noun, verb, adjective or adverb.

A final point is that, unlike most European languages, English has a rather simple, if not impoverished, morphology. Most of the commonest English words are simple – that is, they contain no affixes at all, but just a stem. Examples are *the, can, love, well, big, time*. The shape (i.e. spelling or pronunciation) of these words tells us nothing about their grammatical class; instead we have to look at the context in which they occur – a topic to which we return early in the next chapter.

─────────────────────── **EXERCISES** ───────────────────────

Exercise 2a (answers on p. 210)

1. In the following sentences, which words are (morphologically) simple, and which words are complex? To help you find out, write out the sentences, placing hyphens wherever an affix adjoins a stem:

   a. If half the stories of deception, fraud, terrorist associations, bribery, embarrassed or compromised executives, and Government buckpassing are true, this is a scandal of unprecedented proportions.
   b. Realistically this will have to be the roughest, toughest inquiry ever undertaken by a British Government.

NOTE

There can be legitimate disagreement on the way complex words are broken down into morphemes, especially where Latin stems are in question. For example, it can be argued that *portion* in the word *proportions* is two morphemes, not one: *port-ion*. A similar argument can be made about *decept* and *preced*.

---

2. Now, instead of using hyphens, use the bracketing notation of 2.4.1 to show the structure of any five complex words in sentences a and b. Here are two, to help you: *((terr)(-or))(-ist), (buck)((pass)(-ing))*.

Exercise 2b (answers on p. 210)

1. Write out each of the words below, putting a hyphen between its morphemes and underlining the stem (e.g. *dis-<u>agree</u>-d*).

   reviewed, blackens, kindnesses, unthinkable, overturning, proactively, magnetizing, destabilizes, healthiest, interviewees.

2. Now distinguish between derivational and inflectional suffixes (ignoring prefixes). Put a box around derivational suffixes and put a double line underneath inflectional suffixes. (Ignore spelling variations, e.g. the replacement of *y* by *i* in *healthy* ~ *healthiest*, or the loss of the final *-e* in *magnetize* ~ *magnetizing*.)

   Here is an example to give you the idea: mis-<u>spell-</u>|ing|<u>-s</u>

3. (OPTIONAL) Mark the words in the list above as N (for noun), V (for verb), Aj (for adjective) and Av (for adverb). You can try this if you already know something about grammatical word classes – a topic we return to in Chapter 3.

Exercise 2c

1. Below are some examples of derivational suffixes in English. Add two more examples of English words, to illustrate each suffix.

a.	-or:	*actor, doctor, editor*	j. -ify:	*justify, qualify, clarify*
b.	-ee:	*employee, refugee, trustee*	k. -en:	*threaten, strengthen, weaken*
c.	-ess:	*princess, actress, lioness*	l. -ent:	*different, current, confident*
d.	-ness:	*business, illness, darkness*	m. -ive:	*effective, active, massive*
e.	-ity:	*reality, activity, sanity*	n. -ous:	*various, famous, dangerous*
f.	-ion:	*action, production, region*	o. -ful:	*successful, careful, beautiful*
g.	-ment:	*government, treatment, argument*	p. -less:	*careless, hopeless, aimless*
h.	-hood:	*childhood, neighbourhood, likelihood*	q. -an, -ian:	*human, American, Christian*
i.	-ize, -ise:	*realize, recognize, emphasize*	r. -ist:	*communist, feminist, Marxist*

NOTE

You can recognize a suffix in part by its spelling, and in part by its meaning or semantic function. However, neither of these is a totally reliable guide. English words reflect earlier history of language (including languages like Latin and French), and this can affect both spelling and meaning over the centuries. Often we have to say that the suffix has been added to a bound stem. E.g. *pre-sid-ent* originally meant 'someone who sits before or in front'. Here *pre-* originally means 'before', the bound stem *sid* means 'sit' (from Latin), and *-ent* adds the meaning of doing an action.

2. Some of the words in a–r above contain bound stems as their stems, instead of stems capable of standing alone as words (give or take the odd adjustment of spelling). Which words have bound stems? Write out the words, inserting hyphens between morphemes, and underlining the bound stem.

    To help you, we give you the first example of a bound stem: *doct-or*. Note that *doct* is not a word in English – it comes from the Latin word meaning 'teach', which is also reflected in words like *docile, doctrine*, and *document*.

Exercise 2d (answers on p. 211)

Some derivational suffixes, such as *-ly* and *-al*, are ambiguous; they can do two different 'jobs' according to the kind of stem they are added to. Divide the following list of words ending in *-ly* into two lists (A and B), showing the two different functions that *-ly* can perform in different words:

> *love-ly, real-ly, probab-ly, certain-ly, queen-ly, friend-ly, usual-ly, cost-ly, clear-ly, quick-ly*

Now here is a similar list of words ending in *-al*. Divide it into two lists (C and D), separating the two different functions:

> *natur-al, tri-al, approv-al, with-draw-al, roy-al, norm-al, re-mov-al, music-al, region-al, arriv-al*

FOR DISCUSSION

How did you decide whether to place a word in one list or the other? It could just be intuition, or the decision could be based on meaning, or it could be based on the kind of word that results from adding *–ly* or *–al*. For those of you who are familiar with word classes like noun, verb, adjective and adverb, the decision is not so difficult. Hints: even if you are unfamiliar with word classes, you can try various tests, e.g. to which words can be added an *-er* or *-est* suffix? Which words could follow the word *very*?

Exercise 2e

Prefixes are less important in the grammatical structure of English words than suffixes, so here we just give two examples of a number of common prefixes in English. Add **two** other examples of each prefix from your knowledge of English vocabulary (or you can look in a dictionary):

dis-:	*discover, dismiss*	over-:	*overdone, overseas*
co-:	*co-operate, co-driver*	pre-:	*preview, prepared*
ex-:	*export, exclude*	re-:	*return, rediscover*
in-:	*include, involved*	sub-:	*subject, submit*
inter:	*international, interview*	trans-:	*transport, transaction*
ob:	*object, observe*	un-:	*unlikely, unfair*

Exercise 2f (answers on p. 211)

The words in the following list are all complex words containing two morphemes.

> disappear, straighten, bathroom, mismatch, intermarry, acquittal, realism, lifelong, broadcast, brightest.

Divide them into three lists:

1. Words containing prefix + stem, e.g. *mis+take*
2. Words containing stem + suffix, e.g. *stat+ed*
3. Words containing stem + stem, i.e. compound words, e.g. *day+light*.

Insert a '+' between the two morphemes.

Part B

Analysis

Sentences and Their Parts

Grammar can be briefly described as a set of rules for constructing and for analysing sentences. The process of analysing sentences into their parts, or CONSTITUENTS, is known as PARSING. In this and the next five chapters we will gradually build up a simple technique for parsing English sentences. If parsing seems at first a negative process of taking things to pieces, remember that by taking something to pieces we learn how it works. Analysis and synthesis are two aspects of the same process of understanding. This chapter gives an overview, introducing most of the main concepts of grammar, with examples. It should help you to know that all the topics of Chapter 3 will be dealt with in more detail later on.

3.1 Prologue: parts of speech

3.1.1 A test

First, here is a short test, which can be seen as an easy general-knowledge test about English grammar. Its purpose is simply to start you thinking on the right lines. For some of you, no doubt, this will be too easy; for others, it will mean remembering what you learned some years ago. For others of you, thinking about grammar will be a new experience – so you may find it helpful first to look back to the preliminary way nouns, verbs, adjectives and adverbs were introduced in Chapter 2.

(a) In sentences (1)–(4) make a list, in four columns, of the italicized words which are (i) **nouns,** (ii) **verbs,** (iii) **adjectives,** and (iv) **adverbs** (ignore the other words):

(1) *New cars are very expensive nowadays.*
(2) I *understand* that even *Dracula hates werewolves.*
(3) I have *won* more *rounds* of *golf* than you have *had hot dinners.*
(4) *Mother Hubbard went* to the cupboard, *looking vainly* for *food* to *give* her *dog.*

(b)   Assuming you have made the list, say **why** you classified the words as you did. This will require some kind of definition of what a noun, a verb, an adjective or an adverb is.

If you remember about traditional WORD CLASSES, or PARTS OF SPEECH as they are called, your lists will be something like the following:

> *Cars, Dracula, werewolves, rounds, golf, dinners, food* and *dog* are nouns;
> *Are, understand, hates, won, had, went, looking* and *give* are verbs;
> *New, expensive* and *hot* are adjectives;
> *Very, nowadays* and *vainly* are adverbs.

In order to explain your lists, you may have used familiar definitions like these:

1. 'A **noun** is a naming word: it refers to a thing, person, substance, etc.'
2. 'A **verb** is a doing word: it refers to an action.'
3. 'An **adjective** is a word that describes something about a noun.'
4. 'An **adverb** is a word that says something about other types of words, such as verbs, adjectives and adverbs.'

These are largely **semantic** definitions, i.e. definitions in terms of **meaning**. Such definitions are a useful starting-point, especially in the early days of learning about grammar, but they have two drawbacks: they are often vague and they are sometimes wrong.

For example, *golf* and *dinners* in sentence (3) are nouns, but do not fit the definition given: *golf* names a type of game, and *dinners* a type of meal. This defect could be mended if we included games and meals under the 'etc.' of 1. But having extended the definition of nouns in this way, we would have to extend it in other ways, to include other words such as *rounds*. The plain fact is that it is difficult to see anything in common between all the 'things' to which nouns can refer, except the fact that nouns can refer to them. On the other hand, it is true that the most typical or central members of the class of nouns refer to people, things and substances. These are often called CONCRETE NOUNS.

Similarly with verbs, the definition of a 'doing word' applies naturally to *went, looked, won* and *give,* but does not so easily apply to *are, hates* and *understand.* We could improve the definition by saying that a verb can denote 'states' as well as 'actions', but the difficulty is partly that words like *state* and *action* are themselves vague in meaning. When we say *The girls seem hungry,* for example, does *seem* refer to a state? The adjective *hungry* fits the definition of 'state word' more easily than *seem.* And what about *Two twos are four?* Saying that *are* refers to a 'state' here seems to be pushing the meaning of 'state' a bit too far.

An additional problem is that such definitions fail to keep the parts of speech apart. Compare *hates* in *Dracula hates werewolves* with *hatred* in *Dracula's hatred of werewolves.* It is generally accepted that *hates* here is a verb, whereas *hatred* is a noun; but this cannot be due to the meaning of these words, for they both refer to the same 'thing' – that is, an emotion which

Dracula feels, and which is the opposite of love. We could make the same point about hundreds of ABSTRACT NOUNS which, like *hatred,* are related in form to a verb or an adjective:

| Abstract noun: | *reduction* | *love* | *increase* | *kindness* | *difference* | *cold* |
| Verb or adjective: | *reduce* | *love* | *increase* | *kind* | *different* | *cold* |

3.1.2 An example: 'Jabberwocky'

So we cannot always rely on meaning in defining word classes. This point is put beyond doubt when we notice (as many have noticed before) that in nonsense poems such as Lewis Carroll's well-known poem *Jabberwocky*, we can tell the word class of the nonsense words even though we do not know their meaning. Here is the first verse:

'Twas brillig, and the slithy toves
Did gyre and gimble in the wabe:
All mimsy were the borogoves,
And the mome raths outgrabe.

It is clear, for instance, that *toves* and *borogoves* are nouns, that *gyre, gimble,* and *outgrabe* are verbs, and that *slithy* and *mimsy* are adjectives. But how do we know? Certainly not on account of meaning! Rather, we classify each word on the basis of its form and its **position**. *Borogoves* is a noun because it ends in *-s* (the regular plural ending of nouns), and because it follows *the*. *Slithy* is an adjective because it comes between *the* and the plural noun *toves*, as well as ending in *-y*. *Outgrabe* is a verb because it has a common verb prefix *out-* (as in *outwit, outdo*), and also because if it were not a verb, the sentence would not be complete. These are only part of the explanation, but they show the kind of intuitive skill in grammatical analysis which all of us possess, and which a book on grammar has to explain. They also show that this intuitive skill is not primarily dependent on meaning.

3.1.3 The fuzzy boundaries of grammatical classes: prototypes

We learn, then, that semantic definitions are fallible and are also dispensable. But this does not mean that they are useless. Defining grammatical terms like *noun* and *verb* is like defining many other words of the language, such as *cup, chair, bird, dog, mountain*. We can easily identify the features of the most typical members of the class: for example, a 'prototype' chair – the typical chair we might see in our mind's eye when asked to imagine a chair – has four legs, a back and a seat, is made with wood, and is used for sitting on. But there are other objects which we would be less inclined to call chairs, though they are marginally so: for example, a sofa, a settle, a pew, a garden seat, a bench. In such cases, we cannot easily give a yes-or-no answer to the question 'Is this a chair?' Similarly with birds: the typical bird has two legs, two wings, feathers, a beak and a tail; it flies, perches on branches, lays eggs in a nest, and sings. In this, sparrows and robins are typical, whereas eagles, ducks and penguins are to varying degrees less 'birdy'. The same idea of prototype categories with fuzzy edges applies to grammar. Just as some chairs are less 'chairy' than others, and just as some birds are less 'birdy' than others, so some nouns are less 'nouny' than others, and some verbs less 'verby' than others. The typical, or prototype, nouns are those which refer to people, animals and things – and among these, incidentally, are the nouns which children learn first, when they start to use language to identify the phenomena around them. Similarly, the prototype verb is a 'doing word' such as *help* or *carry* – even though the most common verb of all, to *be*, is far from typical in this respect.

In what follows, then, we shall often, when defining grammatical terms, use words such as 'typical' or 'generally', rather than 'every' and 'always'. This is not a weakness – it is a reflection of the fuzzy boundaries of grammatical classes, especially in the area of meaning.

This concept of a 'fuzzy' category applies not just to meaning, but also to formal aspects of definition. For example, a **typical** noun has a plural in -*s* and a **typical** verb has a past tense in -*ed*; but there are less typical nouns that have no plural (e.g. *sunshine*), and way-out nouns that have a weird plural like -*en* (e.g. *oxen*). There are also less typical verbs which have an irregular past tense, such as *win/won* or *eat/ate*.

Grammar is not a precise logical or mathematical system, but has much in common with systems of organisms in the natural world, in that it involves overlapping criteria, and has fuzzy edges. There are plenty of linguistic parallels to the duck-billed platypus. This means, incidentally, that there may not be a single, uniquely correct parsing of a sentence; there is scope for legitimate disagreement about what is the best analysis. (Now try Exercise 3a.)

3.2 The hierarchy of units

The SENTENCE is the largest unit of language that we are concerned with in grammar. A sentence is composed of smaller units, CLAUSES, PHRASES and WORDS (see Table 3.1).

For convenience in parsing, we give each grammatical category we introduce a shorthand symbol. The symbols and abbreviations used in this book are listed on pp. xiv–xvi.

The units SENTENCE and WORD need little introduction, as they are fairly clearly represented in our writing system. In general we shall identify

Table 3.1

Grammatical units of English	Symbol
Sentence	Se
Clause	Cl
Phrase	Ph
Word	Wo
(Morpheme)	(Mo)

them according to the usual conventions: that is, a sentence will be recognized by an initial capital letter and a final full stop (or question mark or exclamation mark), and a word will be recognized, for most purposes, by a space (or punctuation mark other than a hyphen or apostrophe) on each side.[1]

CLAUSES are the major units of which sentences are composed. A sentence may consist of one or more clauses. For example:

(5) Jack Sprat could eat no fat.

This, standing on its own, is a sentence. But (5) can also occur as part of a larger unit:

(6) [*Jack Sprat could eat no fat*] and his wife could eat no lean.
(7) Every child knows [*that Jack Sprat could eat no fat*].

Here (6) and (7) are sentences, but the parts of them in square brackets are clauses.

PHRASES are units intermediate between **clause** and **word**. Thus (8) consists of nine words, but these words are grouped into four phrases:

(8) (My Uncle Olaf) (was munching) (his peach) (with relish).

Like words, phrases belong to a number of different classes. *My Uncle Olaf* is a NOUN PHRASE, *was munching* is a VERB PHRASE, *his peach* is another noun phrase, and *with relish* is a PREPOSITIONAL PHRASE.

In Chapter 2 we met the smallest unit in the hierarchy: the MORPHEME. In themselves, morphemes are not important for parsing, so we have placed them in brackets in the hierarchy table above. For parsing, morphemes (especially suffixes) are mainly useful because of what they tell us about the grammatical status of words.

The units of grammar can be ordered in terms of RANK (see Figure 3.1).

It is **very important** to notice that we are using 'high' and 'low' in a special way here: what we mean is that a unit of the higher rank consists of **one or more** of the units of the next lower rank. So a sentence can consist of **only one clause** (such sentences are called SIMPLE SENTENCES) and a phrase can consist of **only one word**. Compare sentence (8) with the following:

(8a) [(Olaf) (munched) (peaches) (contentedly)].

The whole of this sentence is a single clause (as signalled by the square brackets), and each word also constitutes a phrase (in round brackets). For that matter, a whole sentence can consist of a single word: *Shoot!* is a

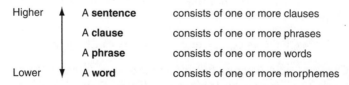

Higher	A **sentence**	consists of one or more clauses
	A **clause**	consists of one or more phrases
	A **phrase**	consists of one or more words
Lower	A **word**	consists of one or more morphemes

Figure 3.1

sentence consisting of just **one clause** consisting of just **one phrase** consisting of just **one word** (consisting of just **one morpheme**).

At first glance this idea of rank may seem strange, but the following analogy may help to clarify it. For another human activity – not talking, but eating – we could set up a rank scale of four units: meal, course, helping, mouthful. A meal may consist of one or more than one course; a course may consist of one or more than one helping; and a helping may consist of one or more than one mouthful (see Figure 3.2).

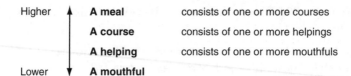

Higher	**A meal**	consists of one or more courses
	A course	consists of one or more helpings
	A helping	consists of one or more mouthfuls
Lower	**A mouthful**	

Figure 3.2

Such a rank scale is adaptable enough to account for a wide variety of human eating behaviour – ranging from a seven-course banquet at which everyone has second helpings, to a brief snack when, literally, someone has a 'bite to eat'. Similarly, the rank scale of grammar accounts for a wide range of language behaviour. Notice that the rank of a unit is not necessarily related to its size, in terms of the number of words. For instance, the sentence in (8a) consists of only four words, whereas the clause in square brackets in (7), which is of lower rank, consists of as many as seven words.

3.3 Grammatical notations

For both clarity and brevity, we need a way of representing grammatical structure on paper. In fact, we will find it useful to have two different graphic notations: BRACKETING, and TREE DIAGRAMS.

3.3.1 Bracketing

We have already used a simple set of BRACKETING conventions:

- Sentences are marked with an initial capital letter and a final full stop.
- Clauses are enclosed in square brackets: [ ].
- Phrases are enclosed in round brackets: ( ).
- Words are separated by spaces.
- If we need to separate the morphemes (i.e. stems and affixes) in words, we use a hyphen.

So in (9)–(11) we have as complete a parsing as can be managed at present:

(9) [(Our land-lady) (keep-s) (a stuff-ed moose) (in her attic)].
(10) [(Uncle Olaf) (savage-ly) (devour-ed) (his six-th peach)].
(11) [(They) ('re play-ing) (Arsenal) (at home) (next week)].

(Notice that *'re* in *They're playing* (11) belongs with *playing* rather than with *They*. To see this, we expand *'re* to *are*, which clearly belongs to the verb phrase *are playing*.)

3.3.2 Tree diagrams

It is very useful, as in (9)–(11), to use [ ] (square brackets) for **clauses** and ( ) (round brackets) for **phrases**, and we will do this when needed throughout the book. These bracketings are easy to use, but they do not give a very clear visual picture of the relation between constituents. For this, when we want to, we can replace the brackets by a tree diagram (see Figure 3.3), which we can think of as an upside-down tree with its branches pointing downward rather than upward.

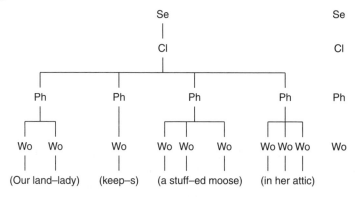

Figure 3.3

The symbols Cl, etc., which we introduced earlier, are here used as LABELS for nodes on the tree, so that all units of the same rank (as shown on the right-hand side) appear at the same level of the tree. Each 'branch' of the tree represents a relation of 'containing'; for example, the left-hand part of the diagram means 'The phrase *Our landlady* contains two words, i.e. *Our* and *landlady*.'

The conventions of bracketing and tree-diagramming should be our slaves and not our masters; we should use them only to show what is needed for our purpose. For example, if a sentence contains a single clause, it is often unnecessary to show the clause level, and it is often unnecessary to label the words. The tree shown in Figure 3.4, which may be called an ABBRE-VIATED tree diagram, shows some simplifications, by omitting the labels Cl and Wo, and simply joining up the lines where those labels would have been.

We may even want to simplify things even further, and produce an unlabelled tree diagram (see Figure 3.5).

Thus we can use the notations flexibly, to show whatever information we consider important. But it is also important to be able to do a complete parsing when necessary, and for this we need to be able to draw a FULLY LABELLED tree diagram, such as Figure 3.3, where every constituent is labelled. (Now try Exercise 3b.)

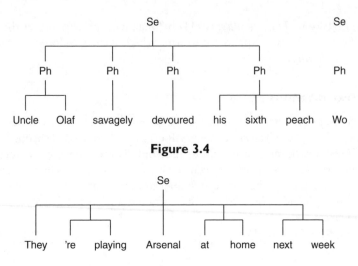

Figure 3.4

Figure 3.5

3.4 Using tests

We already have handy tools for parsing a sentence. But, as will become more and more clear, we often cannot tell the structure of a sentence simply by passively observing it; we need to investigate actively the relations between its parts by using various grammatical tests.

3.4.1 Expansion tests

In *They're playing* (11) we expanded *'re* into *are,* and so made it clear that *'re* is a separate verb, belonging to the phrase *'re playing,* rather than with *They.* We can also expand a word by adding other words to it, to show that the word is acting as a phrase. For example, each of the words of (8a) can be expanded into a word group:

(8a) [(Olaf)   (munched)   (peaches)   (contentedly)].
(8b) [(*Uncle* Olaf) (*has* munched) (*his* peaches) (*very* contentedly)].

Such additions, although they add something to the meaning, do not change the relations between the parts of the sentence. Hence the round brackets in (8a) correctly show (*Olaf*), (*munched*), etc., as phrases, capable of expansion into multi-word phrases like the phrases of (8b).

3.4.2 Substitution tests

Sometimes, even though we cannot use an expansion test, by substituting a word sequence for a word we can see that the word is actually behaving as a phrase. For instance, in (11) we marked *They* and *Arsenal* as one-word phrases:

(11a) [(They) (are playing) (Arsenal) (at home) (next week)].

And to help show that this analysis is correct, we can replace each of these constituents by a word group having the same function, and a similar meaning:

(11b) (Their team) (are playing) (the best team in the world) (at home) (next week).

On the use of the plural *are* following *team*, see 4.2.1 (collective nouns).

3.4.3 Subtraction tests

The opposite of an expansion test is a subtraction test, i.e. omitting some part of a construction. In *Jabberwocky* in 3.1.2, in *the slithy toves* we recognised *toves* as a noun, and this in part was because intuition tells us that *tove* (without the -*s*) would also be grammatical. Equally, in (10), we marked the -*ed* as a separate grammatical suffix of *devour-ed*, and this is partly justified by the fact that the remaining part of the word, *devour*, is itself capable of standing alone as a separate word.

Returning to sentence (8), suppose we modified the wording as follows:

(8c) [(Dear old Uncle Olaf) (devoured) (the peach) (with relish)].

We would recognize *Dear old Uncle Olaf* as a noun phrase, because we could subtract the initial three words and end up with a noun, *Olaf*, which has a similar function to the whole. The usefulness of this test will become clearer later on.

3.4.4 Movement tests

In (10) on page 38, *Uncle Olaf savagely devoured his sixth peach,* we treated *savagely* as a separate phrase rather than as part of a phrase *savagely devoured,* and this was because *savagely* can be moved elsewhere in the clause, without noticeably changing its meaning or function in the clause, and without dragging *devoured* with it:

(10a) [(Savagely) (Uncle Olaf) (devoured) (his sixth peach)].

These tests will be refined as we go, and at the moment must be used with caution. Also bear in mind that, because grammatical categories have fuzzy edges, one test is rarely enough; we often have to rely on a number of different tests in deciding which analysis is the correct or best one. Nevertheless, the tests are already useful, and this is particularly evident in recognising types of phrase. Each phrase class has a 'keyword' which is essential to it, and which provides it with a name. For example, in (12) the 'keywords' of the phrases are as follows:

(12)

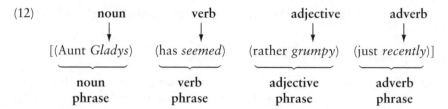

And we can see that these words – noun, verb, adjective, adverb – are essential to the structure, so that if we reduce the sentence to a minimum by subtraction or substitution, we end up with them alone:

(12a) [(Gladys) (seemed) (grumpy) (recently)].

If we want to indicate which constituents are optional, we can place them in {} (curly brackets), as in (12b). Here is another useful piece of notation:

(12b) [({Aunt} Gladys) ({has} seemed) ({rather} grumpy) ({just} recently)].

(Now try Exercise 3c.)

3.5 Form and function

This brings us to the general question of how to classify grammatical units. To explain how sentences are constructed, it is not enough to identify constituents such as clauses, phrases and words; we also need to identify these as belonging to various classes.

3.5.1 Form classes

As we have seen, words are divided into word classes such as NOUN (N), VERB (V), ADJECTIVE (Aj) and ADVERB (Av). Similarly, phrases are subdivided into phrase classes such as NOUN PHRASE (NP), VERB PHRASE (VP), ADJECTIVE PHRASE (AjP), ADVERB PHRASE (AvP) and PREPOSITIONAL PHRASE (PP). We will look at these word classes and phrase classes later (see 4.2, 5.3–5.5). For the moment, notice that one reason why we need to identify such classes is to explain the order in which elements of the sentence occur. It would not do to put the phrases of (9) into any order (an asterisk (*) before a sentence marks it as being ungrammatical):

(9a) [(Our landlady) (keeps) (a stuffed moose) (in her attic)].
(9b) *[(Keeps) (a stuffed moose) (our landlady) (in her attic)].
(9c) *[(A stuffed moose) (keeps) (in her attic) (our landlady)].

Nor would it do to put the words in any other order within the phrases:

(9d) *[(Landlady our) (keeps) (stuffed a moose) (in attic her)].

The tree diagram shown in Figure 3.6, adapted from sentence (12), shows how the extra information about phrase and word classes can be included, by using CLASS LABELS.

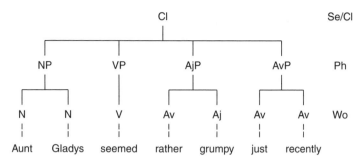

Figure 3.6

Alternatively, we can show the same detail by LABELLED BRACKETING, placing the class label as a subscript before each word and opening bracket:

(12c) Cl[NP(NAunt NGladys) VP(Vseemed) AjP(Avrather Ajgrumpy) AvP(Avjust Avrecently)].

Grammar has to state which orders are permitted. For example, the order VP NP NP AvP in (9b) above is ungrammatical in English (although not necessarily in other languages).

3.5.2 Function classes: elements of the clause

Classes such as NP, VP and AjP are called FORM CLASSES because the classification of phrases in this way depends on how the unit is composed of smaller units, or on how its form can vary. But it is also necessary to classify units into FUNCTION CLASSES: that is, to classify them according to how they are used to form larger units. A unit's function class determines such things as what positions it can fill, and whether it is optional.

The need for function classes is illustrated by another version of (9):

(9a) [(Our landlady) (keeps) (a stuffed moose) (in her attic)].
(9e) [(A stuffed moose) (keeps) (our landlady) (in her attic)].

The sequence of phrase types is the same in both (9a) and (9e): NP VP NP PP. But the relationship between phrases in the clause is quite different, and this is reflected in the very different meaning of (9e). In traditional terms, *our landlady* in (9a) is the SUBJECT (*S*) of the clause, and *a stuffed moose* is the OBJECT (*O*). In (9e) these functions are reversed, so that *a stuffed moose* is the subject, and *our landlady* is the object. We will use these traditional terms, but we will also combine them with a less traditional, but useful, term for the verbal element: we will call *keeps* in both sentences the PREDICATOR (*P*). To exemplify the idea of function, we limit our attention at this point to these three elements, *S*, *O* and *P*, leaving till 6.1 the fuller treatment of CLAUSE functions, including those of units such as *in the attic*. We use the term ELEMENT for members of function classes such as *S*, *O* and *P*. We can also think of them as 'slots' in the clause pattern, capable of being filled by various phrase types. These three elements can be distinguished as follows:

1. *P* is the only element of a clause which is a verb phrase, and so there is little difficulty in identifying it.
2. In English *S* typically comes before *P*, whereas *O* typically comes after *P*.
3. *S* typically denotes the doer ('actor') of the action represented by *P*, whereas *O* typically denotes the doee ('sufferer') of the action.
4. *S* must normally be present (in main declarative clauses such as we have seen in example sentences so far), whereas *O* is often not needed.

Using this starting-point, we can identify the functions of the phrases in (13)–(17). Notice, by the way, another piece of notation – we mark the function class of a unit by a raised italic letter immediately in front of it (when writing function labels, use underlining: e.g. for *P* write P.):

(13) [*S*(Her heart) *P*(sank)].

(14) [*S*(A big red apple) *P*(might have fallen)].

(15) [*S*(Many gentlemen) *P*(prefer) *O*(blondes)].

(16) [*S*(Empty vessels) *P*(make) *O*(the most sound)].

(17) [*S*(Everyone) *P*(will enjoy) *O*(Uncle Olaf's funeral)].

3.5.3 Function classes: elements of the phrase

To finish this brief sketch of grammatical classes, let's take a look at the functions of words in phrases. We will identify two function classes: HEAD (*H*) and MODIFIER (*M*). In the examples shown in Table 3.2 (though this is not always the case) modifiers come before the head.

In general, the head is the word which cannot be omitted from the phrase, whereas modifiers are optional. This applies to AjP, AvP and a lot of the

Table 3.2

	Modifiers (*M*)	Head (*H*)
Noun phrase (NP)		Boris
	my	bicycle
	that strange	feeling
	both his rich elderly spinster	great-aunts
	Britain's only known surviving Victorian cast-iron outside public	convenience
Adjective phrase (AjP)		pleasant
	more	careful
	much much	happier
	extremely	narrow
Adverb phrase (AvP)		now
	too	slowly
	very very	often

words in NP. In verb phrases, however, the relation between the constituents is different from this, and instead of the terms modifier and head, we use the terms AUXILIARY verb and MAIN verb (see Table 3.3).

Table 3.3

	Auxiliaries (*Aux*)	Main verb (*Mv*)
Verb phrase (VP)		is
	had	received
	must be	working
	may have been	broken

Prepositional phrases, on the other hand, are essentially noun phrases (NPs) with an initial preposition (p) such as *of, in, on, under* (see Table 3.4).

Table 3.4

	p	Modifiers (*M*)	Head (*H*)
Prepositional phrase (PP)	in		luck
	of	strong	convictions
	under	the squeaky old oak	floorboards

We can now represent sentence (12) as a tree diagram, this time using FUNCTION LABELS instead of FORM LABELS for each node (see Figure 3.7). (Here two further function classes, *C* = complement and *A* = adverbial, are used – see 4.2.3 and 4.2.4.)

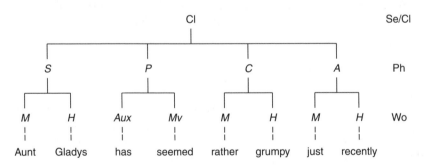

Figure 3.7

Alternatively, we can represent the same sentence as a bracketing with function labels:

(12d) [^{S}(^{M}Aunt ^{H}Gladys) ^{P}(^{Aux}has ^{Mv}seemed) ^{C}(^{M}rather ^{H}grumpy) ^{A} (^{M}just ^{H}recently)].

(Now try Exercises 3d and 3e.)

3.6 Summary

In this chapter we have mentioned in a preliminary way:

- A **rank scale** consisting of four units: sentence (Se), clause (Cl), phrase (Ph) and word (Wo).
- **Form** classes of word: noun (N), verb (V), adjective (Aj), adverb (Av) and preposition (p).
- **Form** classes of phrase: noun phrase (NP), verb phrase (VP), adjective phrase (AjP), adverb phrase (AvP) and prepositional phrase (PP).
- **Function** classes within the phrase: modifier (*M*) and head (*H*); auxiliary verb (*Aux*) and main verb (*Mv*).
- **Function** classes within the clause: subject (*S*), object (*O*), predicator (*P*) (two further elements, complement (*C*) and adverbial (*A*), will be considered later).
- The following are conventions for brackets:

  ( ): round brackets enclose a phrase
  [ ]: square brackets enclose a clause
  { }: curly brackets enclose an optional constituent (one that can be omitted).

─────────────── **EXERCISES** ───────────────

Exercise 3a

It is a significant point about nonsense words, such as those in *Jabberwocky*, that we can put these words to work in new sentences which we know to be grammatical. For example:

1. A tove is mimsier than a rath, but a borogove is mimsiest of all.
2. Did you see that slithy tove gimbling and outgribing?

But the following, for example, are not grammatical:

3. *I momed a rath mimsy.
4. *Our brilligs have toved slithy.

Think up five new examples of (a) sentences which are grammatical, and of (b) sentences which are ungrammatical, using Carroll's nonsense words. Discuss the reasons for the differences between (a) and (b). Also, see how many grammatical forms of the same word (e.g. *mimsy/mimsier/mimsiest*) you can find.

Exercise 3b (answers on pp. 211–12)

Draw tree diagrams like Figure 3.1 for the following sentences:

1. [(Those students) (have made) (an interesting discovery)].
2. [(Without doubt) (the play) (has been) (tremendously successful)].

Now reduce these diagrams to (a) abbreviated tree diagrams, and (b) unlabelled tree diagrams. Lastly, translate the tree diagrams shown in Figures 3.8a and 3.8b into bracketed sentences like 1 and 2.

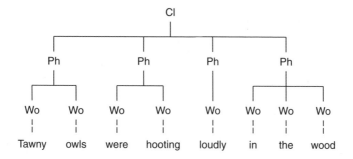

Figure 3.8a

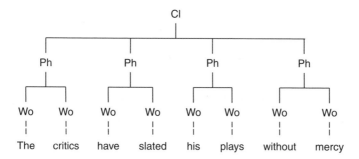

Figure 3.8b

Exercise 3c

Using expansion and substitution (3.4.1–3.4.2), convert the one-word phrases in the following sentences into units of two or more words (choose your own vocabulary, and make minimal changes to each sentence as it stands):

1. [(Tonight) (we) (leave) (London)].
2. [(Sometimes) (she) (looks) (tired)].

Now, using subtraction and substitution (3.4.2–3.4.3), reduce the phrases of the following sentences to one-word phrases, so that each sentence consists of just four words (you can use pronouns such as *he, she, it* and *they* as substitutes):

3. [(The paintings in the Ducal Palace) (are considered) (without doubt) (his greatest masterpieces)].
4. [(Her first novel) (had made) (Emily Brontë) (almost as famous as her sister)].

Exercise 3d (answers on p. 212)

1. Translate the tree diagram shown in Figure 3.9 into a sentence with bracketing labelled with form labels, like (12c), p. 43.

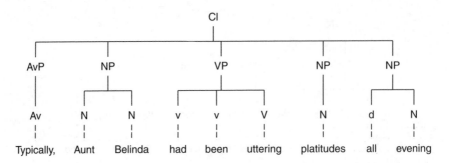

Figure 3.9

2. Translate the following sentence into a labelled tree diagram, like Figure 3.9:

CI [NP(N Jane) VP(V is V finding) NP(Aj modern Aj French N literature) AjP(Aj fascinating)].

3. Translate the tree diagram shown in Figure 3.10 into a sentence with bracketing labelled with function labels like (12d), p. 45.

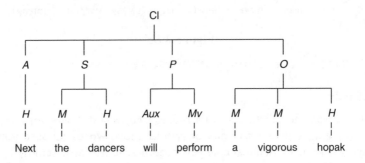

Figure 3.10

4. Translate the following sentence into a labelled tree diagram like Figure 3.10:

[S(H Computers) P(Aux can Mv search) O(M vast H databases) A(M very H rapidly)].

Exercise 3e (answers on p. 212)

Insert the function labels S (subject), P (predicator), and O (object) as appropriate in front of the phrase brackets in the following sentences. (Hint: first identify the predicator, then the subject and then the object (if any)):

1. [(M Little H Joanna) (Aux was Mv sleeping)].
2. [(M This H job) (Aux must Aux be Mv finished)].
3. [(M The M poor H girl) (Aux has Mv seen) (M seven H ghosts)].
4. [(H You) (Aux must Mv meet) (M my H sister)].
5. [(M My H teeth) (Aux were Mv chattering)].

Words

In the next three chapters we extend and explain in greater detail the concepts of grammar introduced in Chapter 3. It is simplest for us to start at the bottom of the rank scale, focusing on **words** in this chapter, then ascending the scale to **phrases** in Chapter 5, and to **clauses** in Chapter 6. It will become clearer, though, that we cannot fully understand one unit of grammar without taking account of the others. This is true for words: to see how words work in grammatical structure, we need to understand something about the morphemes they contain (particularly suffixes) and how the words themselves function in phrases and clauses.

4.1 Open and closed word classes

Our first task is to elaborate on the form classes, or parts of speech, already introduced in 3.1. There are two major kinds of word classes in English: OPEN CLASSES and CLOSED CLASSES. We have already met the open classes, which are the ones shown in Table 4.1.

These classes are known as open classes because we can readily invent new words to add to them (either real words, or nonsense words such as *slithy* and

Table 4.1

Open class	Symbol	Examples
Noun	N	girl, chair, water, thing, beauty, thought
Verb (= full-verb)	V	sing, walk, go, become, seem, water
Adjective	Aj	good, watery, calm, unlimited, friendly, able
Adverb	Av	now, there, calmly, actually, past, away, today

tove – see 3.1.2). Their membership is fairly open-ended; for instance, the word *blackbox* is a noun which was coined fairly recently (referring to an electronic device). But in our library there was a notice on a book-rack: *Books to be blackboxed.* Here *blackbox* has become a verb, and refers to the action of putting books through a black box! This is a small illustration of how English vocabulary is continually being extended to meet new demands. Note also here that a member of one class may be identical in spelling and pronunciation with a member of another class – for example, *water* can be a noun or a verb: *We water*(verb) *our plants with rain water*(noun).

The closed classes, on the other hand, have a fairly fixed membership. We rarely invent new words like *the, she, which, must* and *in*, and it is possible to give a reasonably full listing of each closed class. In the lists shown in Table 4.2 we give some common members of each. (You will see that we use small letters for the closed class symbols, whereas we used initial capitals for the open class symbols. This is another feature of notation to remember.)

Table 4.2

Closed class	Symbol	Examples
Determiner	d	the, a, this, that, some, any, all, many
Pronoun	pn	I, me, you, he, she, it, her, them, one, some, someone
Preposition	p	of, in, on, at, before, under, past, from, to, by, for
Conjunction	cj	and, or, but, if, when, because, that, so
Operator-verb	v	can, may, will, shall, have, be, do
Interjection[†]	ij	oh, ah, ooh, gee, ugh, hell, shoo, hey
Enumerator[†]	e	one, two, three, first, second, eighteenth

[†] In some ways interjections and enumerators are like open classes, but for our present purpose they are more happily placed here among the closed classes.

The closed classes are straightforward enough, but they are not quite so simple as they seem. First, like open classes, and grammatical classes in general, they have 'fuzzy edges': for example, on the outskirts of the preposition class are combinations like *instead of, away from, with reference to*, which behave in some ways like a single preposition, and in other respects like a sequence of words. Secondly, again like the open classes, they have members which are identical in form to members of other classes: for example, *this* can be either a determiner or a pronoun (see 4.3.1–2); *since* may be either a preposition or a conjunction. We can distinguish these words, when we like, by using separate labels: $_d$*this* and $_{pn}$*this*. There are even cases where the same form is shared by an open class word and a closed class word: for example, *about* can be either an adverb or a preposition; *round* can be either an adjective or a preposition – it can also belong to three other word classes, including noun and verb.

There is another little complication about open and closed classes. Although this distinction is generally very useful and important, it cuts right across one traditional word class, that of verbs. In functional terms, there is a distinction between a main verb, and a 'helping' verb, or auxiliary verb (see 3.5.4). This usually corresponds to a distinction of form between a large open class of FULL-VERBS, and a very small closed class of OPERATOR-VERBS, these being verbs which can act as operator (see 4.3.6, 6.4.1) in the formation of questions, negation, etc. We distinguish these, in our labelling system, simply by the capital V and lower case v. (When we wish to refer to verbs in general, we use the capital V.)

4.2 The open classes

In defining the open classes of N, V, Aj and Av, we will use three types of test, or criterion:

1. FORM: We can tell the class of a word partly from its form, made up of morphemes:

    ■ We have seen that DERIVATIONAL SUFFIXES (2.5) are characteristic of certain word classes, e.g. *electric-ity* (noun); *electr-ify* (verb); *electr-ic, electric-al* (adjectives).
    ■ We have also seen that INFLECTIONAL SUFFIXES (2.5) can be added to change the form of a word: *box, box-es* (noun); *work, work-ed* (verb); *tall, tall-er* (adjective). These purely grammatical endings can be simply called inflections and, compared to some other well-known European languages (e.g. Latin, German, Russian, French), English has only a few of them (see 2.3.2).
    ■ In some less regular cases, English words have inflections which involve some other change in the form of a word, e.g. a change of vowel (*man* ∼ *men, sing* ∼ *sang*), or in a few extreme cases a complete change in the word (*go* ∼ *went, good* ∼ *better* ∼ *best*).

2. FUNCTION: We can tell the class of a word by the way it occurs in certain positions or structural contexts. Another way to put this is to say that a word has certain function(s) in phrases, and therefore indirectly in clauses. For example, in *The cook does not actually cook the meal* we can recognise the first *cook* as a noun and the second as a verb because of their function. Obviously there is no overt difference of form to help us, so it must be the position of the word in relation to other words that tells us the word class.

3. MEANING: This is a less reliable criterion, as pointed out in Chapter 3. But if you learn to recognise certain semantic types of word (i.e. word types classified according to meaning), such as action verbs, state verbs, abstract nouns, etc., this will help you to check the purely structural criteria, those of form and function.

These three tests can be placed in the following order of importance:

Function is most important
Form is next most important
Meaning is least important.

Why this order? First, we have already seen (3.1) that **meaning** is not a reliable guide to word class, for example:

(1) I *love*(verb) my country, but my *love*(noun) of humanity is greater.

In (1), *love* and *love* have the same meaning: they both refer to a particular emotion. But they differ in word class. Second, we cannot always rely on a word's **form**, because many words contain no suffix (*help, water, male, much, rather*), and many words (*the, of, too, quite*) are invariable – i.e. they do not change their form by inflection at all. Also, just as with word-forms, we must also allow for ambiguous use of suffixes, e.g. *-ing* marks three different word classes in:

(2) It is very *amusing*(adjective) to watch Mungo *trying*(verb) to paint the *guttering*(noun).

Similar cases are:

-ed can end an adjective (e.g. *tired*) as well as a verb (e.g. *looked*)
-ic can end a noun (e.g. *a comic*) as well as an adjective (e.g. *basic*)
-ly can end an adjective (e.g. *friendly*) as well as an adverb (e.g. *happily*).

Even suffixes which seem to be thoroughly safe indicators of a word class can sometimes be deceptive, e.g. *-ion* usually indicates a noun, but forms like *mention* (as in *Don't mention it*) can also be verbs.

But let's not be too hasty in downgrading the criterion of form. Where we can use a test of **inflection**, it is often conclusive. For example, *question* as a verb has inflected forms *questions, questioned* and *questioning*. As a noun, however, *question* has only the plural inflected form *questions*. If we meet the word *question*, we can decide whether it is a verb by thinking up similar sentences with the inflected forms:

(3)   We (always) *question* the usual suspects.
(3a) We *questioned* the usual suspects.
(3b) We are *questioning* the usual suspects.

In (3) *question* is a verb because we can say (3a) and (3b), which are similar to (3) in structure and meaning. But English has few inflections, so this inflectional test applies mainly only to nouns and verbs.

Because of the limitations of form and meaning as criteria, we chiefly rely on a word's **function** as a criterion of its class. In what follows, we look at the four open word classes in turn, each from the viewpoints of function, form and meaning.

4.2.1 Nouns (N)

The class of nouns (N) is by far the most numerous word class.

(a) FUNCTION

Nouns can function as the **head** (**H**) of a noun phrase (NP) – see 3.5.3:

$_{NP}(^H$**donkeys**)
$_{NP}(^M$our ^{H}**town**)
$_{NP}(^M$the ^{M}worst ^{H}**journey** ^{M}ever)
$_{NP}(^M$Stanley's ^{M}historic ^{H}**meeting** $^M_{PP}$(with Livingstone)).

(Notice that now, for the first time, we are combining function labels (**M, H**) with form labels (NP, PP). As these examples show, the head may be preceded or followed by modifiers.)

A good way to recognise an NP is to see whether it will fit into a frame such as *Have you heard about ...?* or *Did you know about ...?* It is also generally possible for an NP to begin with *the*, and so a good test for a noun (which does not apply, however, to proper nouns – see (ii) below) is whether it can fit the frame '*the* —'. (*The*, the most common word in English, has a special name: the DEFINITE ARTICLE.) Try these tests on the four examples above: for example, we can say *Did you know about donkeys?* and *Did you know about the donkeys?*

(b) FORM

(i) As we saw in 2.3.2, many nouns have characteristic suffixes: e.g. *-er* (*singer*), *-ist* (*hypnotist*), *-ism* (*fascism*), *-ion* or *-ation* (*station, caution*) *-ity* (*university*), *-hood* (*falsehood*), *-ence* (*preference*), *-ness* (*goodness*). There are many exceptions, however, where these endings do not signal a noun: e.g. *longer* is an Aj, *linger* is a V.

(ii) Most nouns can change their form from singular to plural by adding *-s* or *-es* (*goal* ∼ *goals*; *dress* ∼ *dresses*) or by some other change of form (*woman* ∼ *women*; *foot* ∼ *feet*; *bacillus* ∼ *bacilli*). These nouns are count nouns, as opposed to mass nouns (see (i) below).

(c) MEANING

Nouns typically refer to physical things: people (*student*), objects (*book*), places (*city*), substances (*gold*), etc. These nouns are called concrete nouns; but there are also abstract nouns referring to events, states, activities, processes, times, occasions, etc.: *birth, happiness, refinement, revival, birthday, meeting.*

Members of such a large class of words as nouns will obviously not all behave in the same way. We distinguish these subclasses in terms of form, function and meaning:

1. COUNT/MASS NOUNS: Count nouns (e.g. *table, dog, idea, mile*) refer to things that can be counted, and so can have a plural form (*tables*, etc.). Mass nouns, on the other hand, refer to substances, qualities, etc. that we do not think of as coming in countable 'lumps'; such nouns normally have no plural (**golds, *goodnesses*). Notice, however, that the same noun may belong to both categories: in *Her hair is brown, hair* is a mass noun, but in *I found a hair in my soup*, it is a count noun. *A/an* is termed the INDEFINITE ARTICLE, and, like the numbers *one, two, three* etc., is a good indicator of count nouns: *a hair* and *two hairs* make good sense, but not **a sunshine, *two sunshines*.

2. PROPER/COMMON NOUNS: Proper nouns denote an individual person, place, etc., whereas common nouns classify things into types. A proper noun normally begins with a capital letter: *John, Goldilocks, London, Africa*, etc. It generally has no plural form (**Johns, *Africas*), and cannot generally occur after *the* or *a/an*: (**a John, *an Africa*) Common nouns, on the other hand, can occur after *the*. So all the count

and mass nouns discussed in 1 are common nouns. (Sometimes, however, proper nouns are treated like common nouns: *There's a London in Ontario*; *I know several Johns*; etc.)

3.   COLLECTIVE NOUNS: These are generally count nouns, but even in the singular they refer to groups of people, animals or things: *family, government, committee, team*. Grammatically, the thing to notice about collective nouns is their ability, sometimes, to go with a plural verb even when they themselves are singular: *Her family live/lives in Bangalore. The crowd was/were chanting* (see 3.4.2, 12.5).

(Now try Exercise 4a.)

4.2.2 Verbs (V)

(a) FUNCTION

Verbs as we discuss them now are full verbs; that is, they always function as the main element of a verb phrase. They can stand on their own as a predicator, or they can follow other (operator) verbs: [^{S}(Most wombats) ^{P}($_V$bite)], [^{S}(One peach) ^{P}(had been $_V$eaten)], [^{S}(The cat) ^{P}(was $_V$purring)], [^{S}(I) ^{P}(must have been $_V$dreaming)].

Because the predicator is the central or pivotal element of a clause, and because every predicator contains a main verb, it is always a good idea to begin an analysis by **looking for the verb** (or verbs) first.

(b) FORM

(i)   Some verbs, as we saw in 2.3.2, have derivational suffixes like *-ise, -ize* (*realise/realize*) and *-ify* (*clarify*), but these are not very important.

(ii) Much more important are inflections: each verb has up to five different inflectional forms, which we can label Vo, Vs, Ved, Ving and Ven, as shown in Table 4.3. Notice that most verbs are REGULAR, and have forms like those of *ask*. For these verbs, the Ved and Ven forms are identical. For IRREGULAR VERBS (there are about two hundred of them in English) the Ved and Ven forms can vary in a number of different ways: for example, we call the Ven forms 'Ven' because they sometimes have the distinctive suffix *-en* (as in *eaten, written*), instead of *-ed*.

Table 4.3

	Vo	Vs	Ved	Ving	Ven
Regular	ask	asks	asked	asking	asked
	wash	washes	washed	washing	washed
Irregular	show	shows	showed	showing	shown
	write	writes	wrote	writing	written
	put	puts	put	putting	put
	give	gives	gave	giving	given

Notice that the Vo form of a verb is the form without any suffix. We will call this form the plain form, as distinct from the s-form, the ed-form, the ing-form and the en-form.

(c) MEANING

Verbs can express actions, events, processes, activities, states, etc. Such 'happenings' can be physical (*eat*), mental (*think*), perceptual (*see*), social (*buy*), and so on.

An easy test for a verb is: Can the word vary its form from present tense to past tense? The plain form and the s-form are used for the present tense, while the ed-form is used for the past tense. (Now try Exercise 4b.)

4.2.3 Adjectives (Aj)

(a) FUNCTION

Adjectives in general have two functions:

(i)   as head of an adjective phrase (AjP):

   (4)   [Dukes can be $_{AjP}(^M_{Av}$ very $^H_{Aj}$rich)].

(ii) as modifier in a noun phrase (NP): $_{NP}(^Ma \, ^M_{Aj}rich \, ^Hduke)$.

If a word can fill both these positions we can feel confident that it is an adjective.

(b) FORM

Most common adjectives are gradable (see below), and can vary for comparative and superlative: *rich, richer, richest*. Thus we can often tell an adjective by its ability to take *-er* and *-est* as suffixes.

(c) MEANING

Adjectives typically describe some quality or property attributed to nouns. Most commonly they are used to narrow down, or specify more precisely, the reference of nouns, as *sympathetic* specifies what kind of *face* in:

(5a) $_{NP}$(her $_{Aj}$sympathetic $_N$face).

(5b) [(Her $_N$face) ($_v$was) ($_{Aj}$sympathetic)].

Adjectives have various types of meanings, for instance:

■ physical qualities of colour, size, shape, etc.: *green, large, heavy, tall, round*;
■ psychological qualities of emotion, etc.: *funny, brave, sad, amazing, interested*;
■ evaluative qualities: *good, wrong, foolish, beautiful, clever*;
■ qualities relating to time: *new, old, young, early, late*.

In the clause of (5b), *(sympathetic)* is called the COMPLEMENT (*C*) – more precisely, the SUBJECT COMPLEMENT (see 6.6) – because it follows the predicator, and attributes some quality to the subject. It is a good test of adjectives that they can follow the so-called COPULA verb *to be*, acting as the head of an AjP in the frame 'NP *be* ——', as in:

(6a) [^S(Her eyes) ^P(were)^C(brown/blue/wary/intelligent)].

It is also a good test of adjectives that they can occur between *the* and the head of an NP, in the frame '*the* —— N'. This is because as modifiers they come before the noun, but after articles and other determiners:

(6b) _{NP}(^Mher ^Mbrown/blue/wary/intelligent ^Heyes).

A further test is the insertion of the adverb *very* before the adjective, as a modifier in an adjective phrase:

(6c) [^S(Her eyes) ^P(were) ^C(^Mvery ^Hbrown/blue/wary/intelligent)].

This test, however, applies to GRADABLE but not to NON-GRADABLE adjectives. Gradable adjectives describe qualities that vary along a scale of degree or extent, such as size, age, weight, etc.: *large/small*; *old/young*; *heavy/light*. Non-gradable adjectives refer to 'all-or-nothing' qualities, like sex/gender and nationality: *male, Austrian, chemical, wooden*. But adjectives move rather easily from one of these subclasses to another, often with a subtle change of meaning. *Wooden* meaning 'made of wood' is non-gradable, but when we say *His performance of Hamlet was very wooden*, we refer to a gradable quality ('behaving as if made of wood'). As Table 4.4 shows, gradable adjectives can be modified by DEGREE adverbs like *very, extremely, utterly, rather*. They can also have comparative and superlative forms. The shorter and more common gradable adjectives take *-er* and *-est* suffixes, while the longer and less common ones are modified by a separate comparative or superlative adverb: *more* or *most*. There are also a few irregular adjectives which have special comparative and superlative forms, like *good/better/best*.

Table 4.4

	Plain	**Comparative**	**Superlative**	**Degree adverbs**
Gradable	*funny*	*funnier*	*funniest*	*very funny*
	beautiful	*more beautiful*	*most beautiful*	*rather beautiful*
	good	*better*	*best*	*quite good*
Non-gradable	*male*	**maler*	**malest*	**somewhat male*

Because of their meaning, non-gradable adjectives can only occur in the plain construction. Although we can talk of *a male wombat*, it is non-English to say **a maler wombat, *the malest wombat*, or **a very male wombat*. To be more precise, we **could** say *He was really a very male wombat*, but then *male* would take on a subtly different meaning, presumably referring to his macho qualities. (Now try Exercises 4c and 4d.)

4.2.4 Adverbs (Av)

We can distinguish three major types of adverb (Av), but there is considerable overlap between them:

▪ CIRCUMSTANCE ADVERBS add some kind of circumstantial information (of time, place, manner, etc.) to the state of affairs expressed in the core of the clause:

(7) [^{S}(He) ^{P}(sold) ^{O}(the car) $^A(_{Av}$*hurriedly*) $^A(_{Av}$*yesterday*)].

(On the symbol **A**, see below.)

▪ DEGREE ADVERBS modify adjectives and other words in terms of gradability ($_{Av}$*fairly new*, etc. – see Table 4.4).

▪ SENTENCE ADVERBS, which apply semantically to the whole clause or sentence, express an attitude to it, or a connection between it and another clause or sentence:

(8) [$^A(_{Av}$**So**) ^{S}(the whole thing) ^{P}(was) $^A(_{Av}$*frankly*) $^C(_{Av}$too awful for words)].

(a) FUNCTION

The primary function of an adverb is to be head of an adverb phrase. It can typically be preceded and/or followed by a modifier, which is often itself a degree adverb:

(9) [She spoke $^A_{AvP}(^H_{Av}$***frankly***)].

(10) [She spoke $^A_{AvP}(^M_{Av}$very $^H_{Av}$***frankly*** $^M_{Av}$indeed)].

(11) [She spoke $^A_{AvP}(^M_{Av}$too $^H_{Av}$***frankly*** $^M_{PP}$(for comfort))].

These examples show us a second function, especially of degree adverbs: an adverb can act as modifier in an adjective phrase (e.g. *too* in (8)) or in an adverb phrase (e.g. *very*, *indeed* and *too* in (10) and (11)).

As head of an AvP, an adverb very often stands on its own as an adverbial element (**A**) in clause structure (see 6.1.3). In this function, it is typical of adverbs that they can be omitted from the clause, or moved to a different position in the clause, without making it ungrammatical. This can be illustrated by (7) and (8). Both of these sentences can be simplified by omission of adverbs: *He sold the car. The whole thing was too awful for words.* Also, both sentences can be rearranged by moving the adverbs to different positions: **Yesterday** *he* **hurriedly** *sold the car.* **So frankly,** *the whole thing was too awful for words.* Note there is some overlap between adverbs of different classes. For example, in *She answered the question sensibly*, *sensibly* is the manner adverb, but in *She sensibly answered the question*, *sensibly* is an adverb of attitude. Again, looking back to an earlier illustration, in (9)–(11) *frankly* was a manner adverb, but in (8) *frankly* was an attitude adverb.

(b) FORM

(i) The examples we have given illustrate that many adverbs are formed by the addition of *-ly* to an adjective.
(ii) In addition, a few adverbs resemble adjectives, in having comparative and superlative forms: *fast, faster, fastest; well, better, best;* etc.

(Now try Exercise 4e.)

(c) MEANING

Adverbs can express many different types of meaning, especially as adverbials in the clause. We can only give the most important categories, and to distinguish them, it is useful to use a **question test**: for example, *home* answers the question *Where ... to?* in the following exchange (see also Table 4.5 below):

(12)   *Where* did he go *to*? He went *home*.

Table 4.5

Adverb type	Eliciting question	Examples
Manner adverb	How?	well, nicely, cleverly
Place adverb	Where?	here, there, everywhere
Direction adverb	Where to? Where from?	up, back, forward, home
Time-*when* adverb	When?	then, once, tonight, soon
Duration adverb	How long?	long, briefly, always
Frequency adverb	How often?	always, weekly, often, usually
Degree adverb	To what degree? How much?	rather, quite, much, pretty

Unlike these, sentence adverbs, like *fortunately, probably, actually* and *however*, do not answer questions. But they can be divided into two main categories:

■ ATTITUDE ADVERBS: *fortunately, actually, oddly, perhaps, surely*
■ CONNECTIVE ADVERBS: *so, yet, however, therefore, secondly, though.*

For example, in (13) *fortunately* is an attitude adverb, while in (14) *however* is a connective adverb:

(13)   (^{A}($_{Av}$*Fortunately*) ^{S}(elephants) ^{P}(cannot fly)].

(14)   [^{S}(Some of them) ^{P}(can run) ^{A}(pretty fast), ^{A}($_{Av}$*however*)].

(Now try Exercises 4f and 4g.)

4.3 Closed word classes

We turn now to the seven CLOSED WORD CLASSES. Luckily these do not need so much individual attention as the open classes. They have relatively few members, so we can, if we want to, identify each of them by listing their members. A thorough treatment of each class in terms of function, form and meaning would be possible. A more practical way to deal with them, however, is to focus on their function within the higher units. In this way, you will gradually grow familiar with these small but important word classes in the next two chapters, as we deal with phrases and clauses. All closed class words tend to occur at or towards the beginning of the larger units of which they are part; in this respect they are useful identifying MARKERS of the units they introduce.

Now here are brief definitions of the closed classes, and a fairly full listing of their members.

4.3.1 Determiners (d)

DETERMINERS introduce noun phrases, and function as modifiers. Unlike adjective modifiers, however, they are sometimes obligatory. If the head of an NP is a singular count noun, then some determiner has to be added. So (15a) is not acceptable in English grammar, but (15b) is:

(15a) *[($_N^H$Dog) ($_V^{Mv}$bit)($_N^H$ man)].

(15b) [($_d^M$The $_N^H$dog) ($_V^{Mv}$bit) ($_d^M$a $_N^H$man)].

The ARTICLES *the* and *a* are the most common determiners.

Determiners

the, a/an; this, that, these, those; all, some, any, no, every, each, either, neither, one, several, enough, such; many, much, more, most; (a) few, fewer, fewest; (a) little, less, least; what, which, whatever, whichever, half, my, our, your, his, her, its, their.

4.3.2 Pronouns (pn)

PRONOUNS are words which are in a sense 'dummy' Ns or NPs, because they have a generalised or unspecific meaning. Because they are normally obligatory elements of noun phrases, we consider them to be the head of such phrases, though they are limited in terms of what modifiers can be added to them. For example, we cannot say *a strange it* or *the old everybody*.

> ### Pronouns
>
> *I, me, mine, myself; we, us, ourselves, ours; you, yourself, yourselves, yours; he, him, himself, his; she, her, herself, hers; it, itself; they, them, themselves, theirs; this, that, these, those; all, some, any, none, each, either, neither, one, oneself, several, enough; everybody, everyone, everything; somebody, someone, something; anybody, anyone, anything; nobody, no one, nothing; many, much, more, most; (a) few, fewer, fewest; (a) little, less, least; who, whom, whose; what, which; whoever, whichever, whatever; each other, one another.*

You can see that there is a large overlap between determiners and pronouns: *this, that, all, some, which*, for instance, can belong to either category. Take *this* as an example:

(16a) [^{S}(*This wine*) ^{P}(*is*) ^{C}(*very sweet*)].   (*This* is a determiner)

(16b) [^{S}(*This*) ^{P}(*is*) ^{C}(*a very sweet wine*)].   (*This* is a pronoun)

Similarly, in ^{M}*some* ^{H}*girls*, *some* is a determiner, whereas in ^{H}*some* ^{M}(*of the girls*) (where *some* is followed by a prepositional phrase), *some* is a pronoun.

4.3.3 Enumerators (e)

ENUMERATORS include CARDINAL NUMBERS (*one, two, three, … ten …*); ORDINAL NUMBERS (*first, second, third, … tenth …*), and a few GENERAL ORDINALS (*next, last, other, further*, etc.).

4.3.4 Prepositions (p)

PREPOSITIONS introduce prepositional phrases, and express relations of possession, place, time, and many other meanings: $_{PP}(_p$*of the world*), $_{PP}(_p$*by it*), $_{PP}(_p$*on the coldest night of the year*). What follows the preposition in the PP has the structure of an NP.

> ### Prepositions
>
> *about[‡], above[‡], across[‡], after[‡], against, along[‡], alongside[‡], amid, among, around[‡], as, at, before[‡], behind[‡], below[‡], beneath, beside, besides[‡], between[‡], beyond, by[‡], despite, down[‡], during, for, from, in[‡], inside[‡], into, of, off[‡], on[‡], opposite[‡], outside[‡], over[‡], past[‡], round[‡], since[‡], than, through[‡], throughout[‡], till, to, toward{s}, under[‡], underneath[‡], until, up[‡], via, with, within[‡], without[‡].*
>
> [‡] These prepositions can also be adverbs (sometimes called prepositional adverbs or particles).

There is large overlap between prepositions and adverbs, particularly adverbs of place or direction:

(17) [^{S}(I) ^{P}(looked) ^{A}($_p$up the chimney)].

(18) [^{S}(I) ^{P}(looked) ^{A}($_{Av}$up)].

(19) [^{S}(I) ^{P}(looked) ^{A}($_{Av}$up) ^{O}(the word)].

In (17) *up* is a preposition, while in (18) and (19) *up* is an adverb.

4.3.5 Conjunctions (cj)

CONJUNCTIONS like prepositions, are introductory linking words, but they often introduce clauses rather than phrases. In fact they subdivide into two main classes: SUBORDINATING conjunctions and COORDINATING conjunctions.

Subordinating conjunctions

after, although, as, because, before, but, if, how, however, like, once, since, than, that, till, unless, until, when, whenever, wherever, whereas, whereby, whereupon, while; in that, so that, in order that, except that; as far as, as soon as; rather than, as if, as though, in case.

Coordinating conjunctions

and, or, but, nor, neither.

As the list shows, some of the subordinating conjunctions are written as more than one word. In addition, in both categories, there are a number of CORRELATIVE CONJUNCTIONS: that is, two conjunctions occurring together, one preceding one construction, and another preceding the other.

Subordinating correlative conjunctions

if ... then, although ... yet, etc.

Coordinating correlative conjunctions

both ... and, either ... or, neither ... nor.

4.3.6 Operator-verbs (v)

As already explained, these constitute a closed class of verbs which can function as auxiliaries in the verb phrase (see 3.5.3), or more precisely, as operators (see 5.5.2, 6.4.1). They fall into two main categories: MODAL VERBS and PRIMARY VERBS.

Modal verbs

can, will, may, shall; could, would, might, should; must, ought to.

Primary verbs

Vo	Vs	Ved	Ving	Ven
be, *am, are*	*is*	*was, were*	*being*	*been*
have	*has*	*had*	*having*	*had*
do	*does*	*did*	*doing*	*done*

The modal verbs are best considered invariable words, though for some purposes *could, would, might* and *should* can be regarded as Ved forms of *can, will, may* and *shall*. The primary verbs are the three most important verbs in English, and we shall refer to them by their Vo form: *be, have* and *do*. They are very irregular, and are in fact the only English verbs that have an irregular Vs form. Another important thing about them is that they can each function **either** as auxiliaries **or** as main verbs (see 5.5).

4.3.7 Interjections (ij)

INTERJECTIONS are rather peripheral to language: 'words' like *ugh, phew, oh, ah* and *ouch* are (linguistically) somewhat primitive expressions of feeling, only loosely integrated into the language system. We can include here, too, swear words (*damn*, etc.), greetings (*hello*) and other signalling words like *goodbye, yes, no, okay, shoo*, etc.

4.3.8 Particles

There is a distinction, among closed class words, between words which have a function in phrases (e.g. determiners are modifiers in noun phrases) and words which are simply 'markers' (as prepositions are introductory markers in prepositional phrases). For these 'marker words', which include prepositions, conjunctions and interjections, we are using the time-honoured grammatical term particle, which literally means 'little part'. We can say that prepositions and conjunctions are 'little parts' of sentences in that they do not enter into the structure of phrases; they are rather like arithmetical signs +, −, ×, etc. – which is not to say, of course, that they are lacking in meaning or importance.

To illustrate the use of particles, we represent the structure of the clause *But gee, am I hungry* as follows:

(20)   [$_{cj}$But $_{ij}$gee, $_{VP}^P$($_v^{Mv}$am) $_{NP}^S$($_{pn}^H$I) $_{AjP}^C$($_{Aj}^H$hungry)].

Or in tree diagram form (see Figure 4.1).

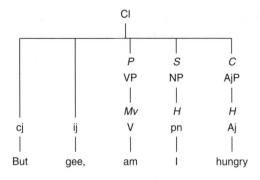

Figure 4.1

4.4 Summary

We have now said something about all the word classes used in this grammar. One last thing: some words are unique in function, and cannot be readily classed with any other words – for example, the *to* which precedes a verb (*to work, to have*) and the negative word *not*. For these words we do not need any special label; we can simply make use of these words in their normal written form: to, not.

The word classes we have now distinguished are:

Open classes

noun (N), verb (i.e. full-verb) (V), adjective (Aj) and adverb (Av).

Closed classes

determiner (d), pronoun (pn), enumerator (e), preposition (p), conjunction (cj), operator-verb (v) and interjection (ij).

(Now try Exercise 4h.)

========================= **EXERCISES** =========================

Exercise 4a (answers on p. 213)

1. Which of the following nouns are count nouns (having a plural), and which are mass nouns?

   weed, gold, rigidity, laugh, rubbish, employer, music, steam, week.

2. Many nouns (like *hair*) are capable of acting as both count nouns and mass nouns, but with some difference of meaning.
   a. Explain such differences of meaning in the following:

      paper, grass, cake, coffee, room, business, success, kindness, rope.

   b. Alternatively, illustrate the differences with simple sentences of your own.

3. Some English nouns have irregular plural forms (e.g. the plural of *man* is *men*, not the regular *mans*). Find two examples of each of the following kinds of irregular plural:

    a. plurals involving a change of vowel in the stem;
    b. plurals ending in *-i*;
    c. plurals ending in *-a*;
    d. plurals which have the same form as the singular.

Exercise 4b (answers on p. 213)

1. Make a table like Table 4.3, showing the Vo, Vs, Ved, Ving and Ven forms for the following verbs: *take, receive, begin, run, sleep, meet.* Which of these verbs is regular?
2. Find ten irregular verbs (apart from the verbs already listed or discussed), and list their five forms. (We talk of 'five forms', but two or more of these forms may of course have the same spelling and pronunciation: e.g. the Vo, Ved and Ved forms of *put* are all *put*.)

Exercise 4c (answers on p. 213)

Which of the following adjectives are gradable? Explain how you arrived at the answers.

a *kind* thought	a *male* pig
dirty water	a *chauvinist* pig
a *major* success	an *absolute* pig
criminal law	*careful* speech
a *Japanese* wrestler	a *whole* pizza

Exercise 4d (suggested answers on p. 213)

Some adjectives are capable of being gradable or non-gradable with some difference of meaning: for example, in *odd behaviour, odd* is gradable; while in *an odd number, odd* is non-gradable. Find pairs of phrases, like these, which exemplify the gradable and non-gradable use of these adjectives: *human, guilty, musical, economic, original, modern, common, royal, free.*

FOR DISCUSSION

How do the two uses of each adjective differ in meaning?

Exercise 4e (answers on p. 214)

Many adverbs are derived from adjectives by the addition of *-ly*. Some adverbs, however, do not add the *-ly*, but have exactly the same form as adjectives. Which is the adjective and which is the adverb in the following sentences? A further question for discussion is why.

1. The *early*[1] train arrived *early*[2].
2. I have *long*[1] hated *long*[2] skirts.
3. She's not just a *pretty*[1] face, she's also *pretty*[2] good at grammar.
4. A *daily*[1] newspaper is one that's printed *daily*[2].
5. That's *right*[1], turn *right*[2] at the next crossroads.
6. The arrow fell a *short*[1] distance *short*[2] of the target.
7. When your health is *better*[1], you'll play *better*[2].
8. I tried *hard*[1], but the exercise was too *hard*[2].

Exercise 4f (answers on p. 214)
Here are some further examples of word forms which can belong to more than one word class. Identify the word classes of the repeated words in the following:

1. Her fur *coat*[1] was *coated*[2] with ice.
2. Herman is more *German*[1] than any of the *Germans*[2] I've met.
3. He *left*[1] her alone on the *left*[2] bank of the Seine.
4. There's no point in *drying*[1] your clothes if they're already *dry*[2].
5. Arabella *pointed*[1] at me, and made a very *pointed*[2] remark.
6. She drew the curtains to make the room *lighter*[1], then *lighted*[2] her cigarette with a *lighter*[3].
7. After he had *drunk*[1] the whisky, the *drunk*[2] was very *drunk*[3] indeed.
8. The *referee*[1] who *referees*[2] the *match*[1] has to *match*[2] the toughness of the players.

Exercise 4g (answers on p. 214)
Now that you have studied the open word classes, we can take another look at nonsense words such as those which occur in *Jabberwocky*. Identify the nouns, verbs, adjectives and adverbs in the following:

> And then, whozing huffily, with cruppets in his spod, podulously priddling across the vomity, yipped Podshaw, that gleerful glup, brandling bindily a groon and flupless whampet. Magistly, mimsiness and manity gumbled on Podshaw's blunk gooves.

Exercise 4h (answers on p. 214)
1. Here is a sentence which contains just one instance of each of the eleven word classes introduced in this chapter. Match each word to its word class:

   But alas, the two ugly sisters had gone home without her.

2. Find another example (preferably a better one!) of a sentence which, like the one above, contains just one member of each of the eleven word classes.

Phrases

5

Now that we have investigated word classes in English, it is not too difficult to explain phrase classes. This will mean taking a further look at the closed classes of words (such as determiners) which play an important role in phrases, and becoming familiar with the classes of phrase already introduced in 3.5.3.

5.1 Classes of phrase

We will recognise six classes of phrase. Of these, NOUN PHRASES (NP), ADJECTIVE PHRASES (AjP) and ADVERB PHRASES (AvP) all have the same basic structure:

$$(\{M^*\} \ H \ \{M^*\})$$

The asterisk (*) means that there can be one or more than one modifier (*M*). These phrases must have a head (*H*), but the modifiers are optional ({ }). Thus some of the possible structures of phrases are:

H, M H, H M, M H M, M M H, H M M, M M H M.

In 3.5.3 we showed modifiers only in front of the head, but now we will have two kinds of modifiers: PREMODIFIERS precede the head, while POST-MODIFIERS follow the head:

(1) $_{NP}(^M awful \ ^H weather)$: (*awful* is a premodifier)

(2) $_{NP}(^H something \ ^M awful)$: (*awful* is a postmodifier).

Of the remaining three types of phrase, both PREPOSITIONAL PHRASES (PPs) and GENITIVE PHRASES (GPs) can be thought of as NPs with an extra particle or marker added to them:[2]

(3) the bride $_{PP}(_p of \ ^M_d the \ ^H_N heir \ ^M_{Aj} apparent)$.

The part of (3) in round brackets is a **prepositional phrase**.

(4) $_{GP}(^M_d the \ ^H_N heir \ ^M_{Aj} apparent-'s)$ bride.

The part of (4) in round brackets is a **genitive phrase.** The difference between them is that the preposition is added to the front of the PP, whereas the genitive marker (*'s*) is added to the end of the GP. Also the genitive marker, spelt *'s* or *'*, behaves more like a suffix than a separate word. Although the genitive phrase is one of the oddest constructions in English, the point we draw attention to in (3) and (4) is that PPs and GPs are very similar – the one being a kind of mirror image version of the other.

Finally the VERB PHRASE (VP) is peculiar to itself, having a rather different structure from those of other phrases, and having a special pivotal role in the clause. We will discuss it last, as this will lead us on to the treatment of clauses in Chapter 6.

5.2 Main and subordinate phrases

The distinction between main and subordinate **clauses** is probably familiar to many of you: Chapter 7 of this book is devoted to subordinate clauses. But here we introduce the same distinction for phrases. A MAIN PHRASE is one which is a direct constituent of a clause, i.e. which is not part of another phrase, while a SUBORDINATE PHRASE is one that **is** part of another phrase. Now this idea must be explored.

5.2.1 Subordinate phrases

In 3.2 we presented the rank hierarchy of units, and said that a unit (e.g. a clause) higher in the scale consists of one or more examples of the next lower unit (e.g. a phrase). This statement was correct, but could have misled by what it did not say. Now we have to add to it: we have to allow the possibility that units are not merely divisible into units of the next lower rank, but can contain as their elements units of the same, or even of a higher rank. This is the phenomenon of SUBORDINATION – and it is important because it allows us to make sentences as complex as we like.

So, returning to (3) above, note that *the bride of the heir apparent* is a phrase (actually an NP), and that it contains another phrase (a PP) as a postmodifier within it: *of the heir apparent*. Similarly, in (4) *the heir apparent's bride* is an NP containing another phrase, the GP *the heir apparent's*, as a premodifier. We can represent these cases of subordination as brackets within brackets as follows:

(3a) $_{NP}$(the bride $_{PP}^{M}$(of the heir apparent))

(4a) $_{NP}$($_{GP}^{M}$(the heir apparent's) bride).

Wherever we have two sets of round brackets like these, one within the other, the inner brackets enclose a subordinate phrase. Consider now:

(5)   [$_{NP}^{S}$(The heir apparent) $_{AvP}^{A}$(nearly) $_{VP}^{P}$(became) $_{NP}^{A}$(an Olympic champion)].

Here *The heir apparent* is functioning as an element of clause structure, i.e. as subject. It is therefore a main phrase. We can tell this at a glance, because the round brackets are immediately within the square brackets of the clause. In simple bracketing notation, then, the following are indicators of main and subordinate phrases:

Main phrase   **Subordinate phrase**
[... (Ph) ...]   (... (Ph) ...)

In terms of tree diagrams, the following configurations indicate main and subordinate phrases respectively:

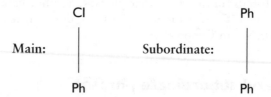

Where there is a subordinate phrase, it will always be directly or indirectly a part of a main phrase:

(6)   [$_{NP}^{S}$(The bride $_{PP}^{M}$(of the heir apparent)) (nearly) (had) (a fit)].

Here, *of the heir apparent* is a subordinate phrase and *the bride of the heir apparent* is the main phrase which includes it.

   Once we have allowed the possibility of phrases within phrases, there is nothing to stop subordinate phrases themselves containing further subordinate phrases, and so on indefinitely:

(7)   (his book (on gastronomy (in the Dark Ages)))
(8)   (my review (of his book (on gastronomy (in the Dark Ages))))
(9)   (his reply (to my review (of his book (on gastronomy (in the Dark Ages))))).

Subordination of phrases is one of the chief sources of complexity in grammar, particularly in NPs (see pp. 70–2, 115). In the form of a tree diagram, (7) looks as in Figure 5.1 and (8) looks like Figure 5.2.
   (Now do Exercise 5a.)

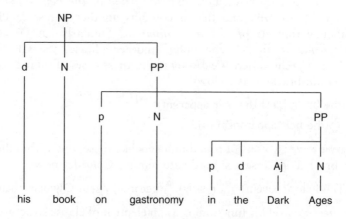

Figure 5.1

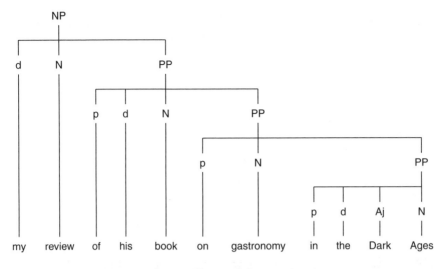

Figure 5.2

5.2.2 Subordinate clauses

While on the subject of subordination, we should mention that subordinate **clauses** work on the same principle, as we will see more fully in Chapter 7. This time subordination is indicated by a nesting of square brackets:

(10) [Joel thinks [that Anna loves him]].
(11) [Ann thinks [that Joel thinks [that she loves him]]].
(12) [Joel thinks [that Anna thinks [that he thinks [that she loves him]]]].

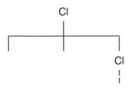

Figure 5.3

Taking the matter just one stage further, we have to allow for the possibility of the subordination of one unit (say a clause) within a unit of **lower** rank (say a phrase) – see further 7.5. In such a case the bracketing will show square brackets inside round brackets:

(13) (the house [that Jack built])
(14) (the malt [that lay (in the house [that Jack built])])
(15) (the rat [that ate (the malt [that lay (in the house [that Jack built])])])

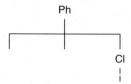

Figure 5.4

The clause *that Jack built* here is called a relative clause (7.2.3), and is part of an NP. Again there is the possibility of repeated subordination in the same structure. Example (14) shows us one relative clause indirectly inside another relative clause. These points will be taken up later in 7.2. If you find the notion of subordination puzzling at this stage, there will be plenty of opportunity later to become more familiar with it. (Now try Exercise 5b.)

5.3 Noun phrases and related phrase classes

Like words, phrases can be classified partly by their external function and partly by their internal form. By 'form', with phrases as with words, we mean the way the structure of the unit is made up of other, smaller constituents. Typically, in a phrase composed of head and modifiers, premodifiers tend to be single words and postmodifiers tend to be phrases or clauses. Although the genitive phrase (as we saw in 5.1) is an important exception, this tendency is illustrated by the structure of the NP, shown in 5.3.1.

5.3.1 The noun phrase (NP)

(a) FUNCTION

In the clause, NPs are important and versatile elements: they can act as subject (*S*), as object (*O*), or as complement (*C*):

(16) [$_{NP}^S$(*The house*) ^{P}(*was*) ^{C}(*quite empty*)].   NP = S

(17) [^{S}(*We*) ^{P}(*have bought*) $_{NP}^O$(*the house*)).   NP = O

(18) [^{S}(*This*) ^{P}(*must be*) $_{NP}^C$(*the house*)].   NP = C   (see 4.2.3)

Some kinds of NPs (e.g. some NPs of time) can even act as adverbials (*A*):

(19) [^{S}(*We*) ^{P}(*walked*) $_{NP}^A$(*five miles*) $_{NP}^A$(*last week*)].   NP = A

(On adverbials, see 4.2.4 and 6.1.3.)
   Subordinate NPs act as modifiers in other NPs:

(20) ($_d^H$*my* $_N^H$*friend* $_{NP}^M$(*the professional diver*))

(21) ($_N^H$*Buffy* $_{NP}^M$(*the Vampire Slayer*))   NP = M

This construction, in which one NP is 'defined' by another, is called APPOSITION.

(b) STRUCTURE

The structures of NPs are very diverse, but the chief elements are these:

■ The head of an NP can be:

1. a **noun**: (the ^{H}doll), (dear ^{H}Margaret), etc.
2. a **pronoun**: (^{H}it), (^{H}herself), (^{H}everyone (in the street)), etc.
3. (less usually) an **adjective** (the ^{H}absurd), an **enumerator** (all ^{H}fifteen), or a **genitive phrase** (^{H}(John's)).

Two of the less usual possibilities in 3 are illustrated in:

(22) [[If you offer them three types of ice cream,] $_{NP}^S$(the $_{Aj}^H$greedy) (will take) $_{NP}^O$(all $_e^H$three)].

But in such cases there is usually a noun which semantically is understood to be the head: e.g. the last part of (22) means: [(The greedy people) (will take) (all three types of ice cream)].

■ The PREMODIFIERS of an NP can be:

1. Determiners: (^{M}this morning), (^{M}what ^{M}a girl), (^{M}some water)
2. Enumerators: (^{M}two eggs), (the ^{M}third man), (my ^{M}last throw)
3. Adjectives: (^{M}red shoes), (^{M}older children), (the ^{M}strangest coincidence)
4. Nouns: (a ^{M}garden fence), (a ^{M}gold ring), (^{M}London pubs)
5. Genitive phrases: (^{M}(Gina's) pet marmoset), (^{M}(someone else's) problems)
6. Adverbs (in initial position): (^{M}quite a noise).
7. An assortment of other categories, such as adjective phrases ($_{AjP}^M$(awfully bad) weather); other phrases ($_{PP}^M$(round-the-clock) service); compound words of various kinds (the kind-hearted vampire); Ven and Ving forms of verbs (grated cheese), (a working mother).

This last set of premodifiers is so miscellaneous that we cannot hope to deal with it thoroughly. There is often doubt as to whether, for example, a modifier is a phrase or compound word, and whether a word ending in -ed or -ing is a verb or an adjective derived from a verb. For parsing purposes, we may have to take some rather arbitrary decisions. For example, we can let hyphenation or lack of a space in writing determine whether something is to be treated as a single word, and we can make some semantic distinctions determine bracketing, to resolve ambiguities such as:

(23) $_{NP}$(a (steel cutting) blade) – 'a blade for cutting steel'
(23a) $_{NP}$(a steel (cutting blade)). – 'a cutting-blade made of steel'

■ The POSTMODIFIERS of an NP can be:

1. Prepositional phrases: (the best day $_{PP}^M$(of my life)).
2. Relative clauses: (a quality ^{M}[that I admire]).

3. Various other types of modifier, including **adverbs** (the girl $^M_{Av}$*upstairs*) **adjectives** (something $^M_{Aj}$*nasty* (in the woodshed)), **noun phrases** in apposition (the bandicoot, $^M_{NP}$(*a tiny marsupial*)), and other types of clause (see 7.3).

Because of these various kinds of modifier, it is possible for an NP to reach considerable complexity. With premodification alone, such phrases as (24) are possible, though rare:

(24) ($^M_{Av}$absolutely $^M_d$the ^M_elast ^M_etwo $^M_{Aj}$unsold $^M_{Aj}$ripe $^M_{Aj}$juicy $_H$peaches).

In postmodification there is in principle no limit to the length of NPs. The occurrence of subordinate PPs as postmodifiers is very common, and it is important to distinguish cases like:

(25) (the girl $_{PP}$(by the table $_{PP}$(with the carved legs)))

(26) (the girl $_{PP}$(by the table) $_{PP}$(with the sunburnt legs)).

In (25) one PP postmodifies *girl*, and the other PP is subordinate to it, postmodifying *table*. In (26), however, both PPs postmodify *girl* – it is the legs of the girl, not the legs of the table, that we are discussing. (Now try Exercises 5c and 5d.)

5.3.2 Pronouns (pn) and determiners (d)

Pronouns and determiners are two closed word classes in the NP which have similar subdivisions:

1. **PRONOUNS** function as *H*
   Personal pronouns: *I, you, he, she, it, we, they, me, us, him, her, them, myself, yourself, himself, herself, itself, ourselves, yourselves, themselves, one, oneself.*
   Possessive pronouns: *mine, ours, yours, his, hers, theirs.*
   Demonstrative pronouns: *this, that, these, those.*
   Quantifier pronouns:
   - General: *all, some, any, none, one, another, each, both, several, either, neither,* etc.
   - Compound: *everybody, somebody, anybody, nobody, everyone, someone, anyone, no one, everything, something, anything, nothing.*
   - Gradable: *many, much, more, most; few, fewer, fewest; little, less, least.*

   Wh- pronouns: *who, whom, whose, what, which, whatever,* etc.
2. **DETERMINERS** function as *M*
   Articles: *the, a/an.*
   Possessive determiners: *my, our, your, his, her, its, their.*
   Demonstrative determiners: *this, that, these, those* (**the same as pronouns**).

Quantifier determiners:

- General: *all, some, any, no, every, another, each, both, several, either, neither*, etc.
- Gradable: *many, much, more, most, few*, etc. (**the same as pronouns**).

Wh- determiners: *what, which, whose, whatever, whichever*.

Notice that, for example, the demonstratives and the gradable quantifiers are the same for both pronouns and determiners. The other classes are also very similar, except that personal pronouns are always pronouns, and articles are always determiners. Nevertheless, we treat these as separate word classes, the simple rule being that words from these classes which function as **heads** are **pronouns**, and those which function as **modifiers** are **determiners**. This rule applies even to POSSESSIVE words (see Table 5.1).

Table 5.1

Possessive pronouns	Possessive determiners
mine, ours, yours, his, hers, theirs	my, our, your, his, her, its, their

Possessive pronouns can stand alone as the head of an NP: (This) (is) (^{H}mine). Possessive determiners are modifiers, which need a head to follow them: (This) (is) (^{M}my ^{H}mouse); similarly *your sister, her book*, etc. In meaning, words like *my* and *your* are equivalent to genitive phrases (as in *Gina's mouse*), but as they are single words filling the determiner 'slot', it is simpler to treat them as determiners like *the, a, every*, etc.[3] Compare the d and pn labels in these examples:

(27) $[^S(^H_{pn}$Those) $^P_{VP}$(are) $^C_{NP}$ (^M_dyour ^H_Nbooks)].

(28) $[^S(^M_d$Those ^H_Nbooks) $^P_{VP}$(are) $^C_{NP}(^H_{pn}$yours)].

Or, equivalently, in the tree diagrams shown in Figure 5.5 and 5.6.

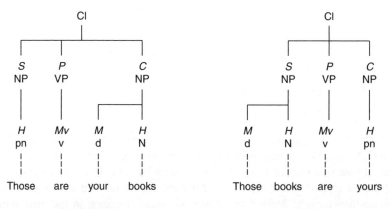

Figure 5.5   **Figure 5.6**

These sentences also show the difference between *those* as a pronoun and *those* as a determiner. (Now try Exercises 5e and 5f.)

5.3.3 Prepositional phrases (PP)

(a) FUNCTION

In the clause, PPs act as adverbials (**A**):

(29) [$_{PP}^{A}$(*On Monday*) (*we*) (*arrived*) $_{PP}^{A}$(*by train*) $_{PP}^{A}$(*in Omsk*)].

The adverbial PPs have various meanings (see 6.1.3). Thus in (29) the three PPs are adverbials of time-*when*, of means, and of place, answering the questions *When?*, *How?* and *Where?* PPs are also common as subordinate phrases: in NPs, AjPs, AvPs and PPs they act as postmodifiers (see 5.3.1, 5.4).

(b) STRUCTURE

We have already noted in 3.5.3 that PPs have exactly the same structures as NPs, except that they are introduced by a preposition; i.e. PP = p + NP. Normally prepositions are inseparable from the head (and modifiers) that follow them. There are, however, various circumstances in which a preposition can be separated from its following NP.

Compare:

(30)   (problems [$_{PP}^{A}$(*with which*) $_{NP}^{S}$(*everyone*) $_{VP}^{P}$(*must live*)])

(31)   (problems [$_{NP}$(*which*) $_{NP}^{S}$(*everyone*) $_{VP}^{P}$(*must live*) $_{p}$(*with*)]).

In (30) *with which* is a PP, but in (31) the preposition has been left 'stranded' at the end of the clause, and the pronoun *which* which follows it in (30) has turned itself into a separate NP.

SPECIAL NOTE ON PREPOSITIONAL VERBS AND PHRASAL VERBS

Another way in which prepositions can separate themselves from the following NP is in idioms like *look at, look for, approve of, deal with,* etc. We can compare two apparently similar sentences:

(32) Most monkeys live in trees.

(33) The gangs indulge in wild gunplay.

In (32) the PP clearly has an adverbial function (*Where do most monkey live? In trees*). But in (33) *in* seems more closely connected with *indulge*, so that *indulge in* can almost be regarded as an idiomatic compound verb. Thus while the clause structure of (32) is S P A, that of (33) might be transcribed as S P p O, the preposition being a 'floating' constituent of clause structure, in the manner of particles discussed in 4.3.8.

Idioms like *look at, care for, indulge in*, etc., are often called prepositional verbs, and the NPs which follow them prepositional objects. Mention should also be made of another type of verb idiom very common in English: that of phrasal verbs like *make up, take off, hang about.* But in these cases, the second word *up, off, about,* etc., is an **adverb** rather than a **preposition** (see 4.3.4).

Phrasal verbs and prepositional verbs constitute an important but rather problematic area of English grammar (for details, see Quirk et al. 1985: 1150–68). This discussion illustrates the principle that in grammar we are often trying to weigh up the merits of alternative solutions. There is no such thing as a 'correct' analysis of sentences like (33), but we may be able to argue for one analysis being better than another.

In this book we treat phrasal verbs like *hang on* and *sum up* as combinations of two words (verb + adverb), even though semantically they may behave as a single unit. For parsing, however, we treat the adverb as part of the VP, rather than as a separate adverb phrase.

5.3.4 The genitive phrase (GP)

We have already given some attention to this construction, and need to do little more than summarise what has already been said.

(a) FUNCTION

GPs function either as premodifiers (*M*) or as heads (*H*) in NPs. Compare:

(34) $[^S(^H_{pn}$ These) $^P_{VP}$(are) $^C_{NP}(^M_{GP}(the\ technician's)\ ^H_N tools)]$.

(35) $[^S(^M_d$ These $^H_N tools)\ ^P_{VP}$(are) $^C_{NP}(^H_{GP}(the\ technician's))]$.

(b) STRUCTURE

GPs are just like NPs except that they end with the particle 's (i.e. GP = NP + 's, as in *the boy's*). In the plural, after a noun with -*s*, the particle is not separately pronounced, and is simply written as an apostrophe ('): *the boys'*.

5.4 The adjective phrase and the adverb phrase

Compared with NPs, AjPs and AvPs tend to have a simple structure. Although potentially they consist of the same elements ($\{M^*\}\ H\ \{M^*\}$), in practice they often consist of only a head, and it is unusual for them to have more than one premodifier and one postmodifier.

5.4.1 The adjective phrase (AjP)

(a) FUNCTION

In a clause, AjPs function as complement (*C*):

(36) [The weather has turned $_{AjP}^{C}$(*milder*)].
(37) [Adolphus likes his coffee $_{AjP}^{C}$(*very milky*)].

As subordinate phrases, AjPs can function as premodifiers in NPs:

(38) [The Mad Hatter took $_{NP}$($_{d}^{M}$*a* $_{AjP}^{M}$(*very large*) $_{N}^{H}$*slice*)].

But we only analyse the modifier as an AjP if the adjective has one or more modifiers. A single adjective without modifiers in front of a noun (e.g. *a large slice*) does not count as an AjP.

(b) STRUCTURE

The head of an adjective phrase is an adjective, which can be plain (*big*), comparative (*bigger*), or superlative (*biggest*) (see 4.2.3).
 Premodifiers are mostly adverbs: typically, adverbs of degree (*extremely*, *rather*, *too*, *very*). Some, especially *very* and *too*, can be repeated (*very very very tall*). Postmodifiers can be either adverbs (*indeed*, *enough*) or PPs:

(39) ($_{Av}^{M}$*very* $_{Aj}^{H}$*tall* $_{Av}^{M}$*indeed*)

(40) ($_{Aj}^{H}$*nice* $_{Av}^{M}$*enough*)

(41) ($_{Av}^{M}$*rather* $_{Av}^{M}$*too* $_{Aj}^{H}$*hot* $_{PP}^{M}$(*for comfort*)).

We also find certain kinds of clauses as postmodifiers: *younger* [*than I thought*], *too hot* [*for me to drink*], etc. We deal with these later, in Chapter 7.

5.4.2 The adverb phrase (AvP)

(a) FUNCTION

AvPs function in the clause as adverbials (*A*). (See 6.1.3.)

(b) STRUCTURE

The head of an adverb phrase is an adverb (Av). Otherwise, the structure of AvPs is the same as that of AjPs:

(42) ($_{Av}^{H}$*often*)   ($_{Av}^{M}$*rather* $_{Av}^{M}$*too* $_{Av}^{H}$*quickly* $_{PP}^{M}$(*for comfort*))

(43) ($_{Av}^{M}$*quite* $_{Av}^{H}$*often*)   ($_{Av}^{M}$*more* $_{Av}^{H}$*quickly* $_{PP}^{M}$(*than last year*)).

5.5 The verb phrase (VP)

(a) FUNCTION

The VP is the pivotal element of the clause, and always acts as predicator (*P*). Although we will need to distinguish in 6.3 between **tensed** and **tenseless** clauses,[4] at present we limit ourselves to tensed clauses, which means that we concentrate on the fullest kind of VP, the tensed verb phrase (the kind of VP that has present or past tense).

(b) STRUCTURE

We have already outlined (in 3.5.3) the structure of the VP in terms of two kinds of element: the **main verb** (*Mv*) and **auxiliaries** (*Aux*). The auxiliaries are optional, and precede the main verb. At the most general level the structure of the VP is:

{Aux} {Aux} {Aux} {Aux} Mv

with any number of auxiliaries from zero up to four. But this is not by any means the whole story. In practice we can distinguish four different functions performed by the auxiliaries themselves (see Table 5.2), and these can combine to create sixteen different kinds of VP.

Table 5.2

S NP	P VP					A AvP	
	Modal	**Perfect aspect**	**Progressive aspect**	**Passive voice**	**Main verb**		
M *H* *d* N	*Mod* m	*Perf* hv	*Prog* be	*Pass* be	*Mv* V	*H* Av	
the branch					shook	violently	1
the branch	might				shake	violently	2
the branch		had			shaken	violently	3
the branch			was		shaking	violently	4
the branch				was	shaken	violently	5
the branch	might	have			shaken	violently	6
the branch	might		be		shaking	violently	7
the branch	might			be	shaken	violently	8
the branch		had	been		shaking	violently	9
the branch		had		been	shaken	violently	10
the branch			was	being	shaken	violently	11
the branch	might	have	been		shaking	violently	12
the branch	might	have		been	shaken	violently	13
the branch	might		be	being	shaken	violently	14
the branch		had	been	being	shaken	violently	15
the branch	might	have	been	being	shaken	violently	16

Note: Where there is no passive voice auxiliary, the verb phrase is in the ACTIVE VOICE.

In Table 5.2, we have replaced the general label *Aux* by some more specific 'slots' or function labels: *Mod*, *Perf*, *Prog* and *Pass*. *Mod* is always filled by one of the modal verbs (m) (4.3.6). *Perf* is always filled by the primary verb *have* (hv), and *Prog* is always filled by the primary verb *be* (be); similarly, the *Pass* position is always filled by *be*, and the main verb position (*Mv*) can be filled either by any full verb (V), or by one of the primary verbs (be, hv, do). We can now explain the structure of the VP in more detail as: ({*Mod*} {*Perf*} {*Prog*} {*Pass*} *Mv*). The terms 'modal', 'perfect', 'progressive' and 'passive' relate to the kinds of meaning expressed by the elements they label. (Remember that { } means optional!)

The formula just given explains that the elements of the VP can only occur in a fixed order. For example, *could have worked* and *had been waiting* are good grammatical combinations, but **have could worked* and **been had waiting* are not. However, there is still something to be explained: namely, that each auxiliary determines the form of the verb which follows it, e.g. *has worked* occurs, but **has working* does not. To explore this further, we have to return to the description of verb forms.

5.5.1 Verb forms

In Table 5.3, the tables of verb forms given in 4.2.2 and 4.3.6 are expanded, so as to apply not only to full-verbs but also to operator-verbs (i.e. to modals and primary verbs). We also make a distinction here between TENSED and TENSELESS forms. In the TENSED VERB PHRASE, the first word is always a TENSED VERB FORM.

Table 5.3

			Tensed forms			Tenseless forms		
			Tense			Infinitive	Participles	
			Present		Past		Past	Present
			3rd person singular	Other				
			Vs:	Vo:	Ved:	Vi:	Ven:	Ving:
Full-verbs	Regular		reaches	reach	reached	reach	reached	reaching
	Irregular		writes sinks puts	write sink put	wrote sank put	write sink put	written sunk put	writing sinking putting
Operator-verbs	Primary verbs	(do) (hv) (be)	does has is	do have am/are	did had was/were	do have be	done had been	doing having being
	Modals	(m)	may etc.		might etc.			

In Table 5.3 we have also labelled an extra verb form, in addition to Vo, Vs, Ved, Ving and Ven. This new form is the INFINITIVE form (Vi) of the verb, but it differs from Vo only in the verb *be*. To all intents and purposes, then, the infinitive is the form of the verb which has no ending, the **plain** form, just like Vo. The rules for combining verbs in the verb phrase can now be expressed as in Table 5.4.

Table 5.4

	Function	**Class of verb**	**Form of following verb**
Optional elements	Modal (*Mod*)	Modal verb (m)	Infinitive (Vi)
	Perfect aspect (*Perf*)	Have (hv)	-en participle (Ven)
	Progessive element (*Prog*)	Be (be)	-ing participle (Ving)
	Passive voice (*Pass*)	Be (be)	-en participle (Ven)
Obligatory	Main verb (*Mv*)	Verb (V)	(There is none)

Thus if we want to construct a VP with the structure *Perf Mv*, the rules of Table 5.4 say that the *Mv* must be a Ven: e.g. *has taken*. If we want to construct more complex phrases such as *Mod Prog Mv* or *Mod Pass Mv*, the rule will work as shown in Figure 5.7 (see below).

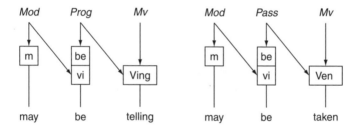

Figure 5.7

The initial parts of tensed VPs are tensed, whereas non-initial parts of *any* VP are always tenseless (Vi, Ving, or Ven). This means that there could be a quite different way of describing the structure of the VP, this time not in terms of *Aux* and *Mv*, but in terms of tensed and tenseless verbs:

$$+T \{-T\} \{-T\} \{-T\} \{-T\}$$

where $+T$ = tensed, and $-T$ = tenseless.

The English VP, in fact, cannot all be described by means of one set of labels: it is a structure of interlocking patterns. However, these matters do not have to bother us when we are parsing a sentence. For most purposes, it will be enough to label phrases with the function slots *Aux* and *Mv*, and the form labels m (for modal), be, hv, do and V. For example:

VP($^{Mv}_V$eats)   VP($^{Aux}_{be}$is $^{Mv}_V$playing)   VP($^{Aux}_m$must $^{Mv}_V$go)

VP($^{Aux}_m$should $^{Aux}_{be}$be $^{Mv}_V$working)   VP($^{Aux}_m$must $^{Aux}_{be}$be $^{Aux}_{be}$being $^{Mv}_V$done).

Here we have used the more detailed form labels m, be, hv and do for operator-verbs, but a simpler way of labelling would be just to use the single label v in place of all these four labels.

5.5.2 The 'dummy operator' do

One important facet of the VP has still to be dealt with: the special role of the auxiliary *do*.

Earlier we identified the small closed class of verb (4.1) as **operator-verbs** (v). This name is especially appropriate, because these verbs in their tensed form (normally as first word in the VP) are used in various 'operations' such as making a clause negative or interrogative.[5]

Consider **negation:**

(44) She *can sing.*   ⟶ (44a) She *cannot sing.*   (or: She *can't sing*)

(45) She *is singing.* ⟶ (45a) She *is not singing.* (or: She *isn't singing*)

(46) It *has been sung.* ⟶ (46a) It *has not been sung.* (or: It *hasn't been sung*)

To form the negative, we simply add the particle *not* (or its reduced version *n't*) after the first word of the VP, which is a tensed operator. But what about this case:

(47) She *sang.*   ⟶ (47a) *She *sang not.*   (or: *She *sangn't*)

       ⟶ (47b) She *did not sing.*   (or: She *didn't sing*)

In (47a) we cannot add *not* after the tensed operator, because there is no operator-verb in the VP: there is only the full-verb *sang*. So the negative rule just stated cannot work, unless we can find an operator-verb. The DUMMY OPERATOR *do* comes to the rescue: it is the verb we introduce to take the role of operator where there is no other verb to do so, as in (47b). Notice, though, that the verb *be* acts as an operator even when it functions as a *Mv*:

(48) Bunter *is* my friend ⟶ Bunter *is* not my friend.

The same sometimes applies, in some varieties of English, to *have* as main verb: *He hasn't any ideas.* But nowadays most people prefer the operator *do* before *have*: *He doesn't have any ideas.* (Now try Exercise 5g.)

5.6 Summary

The following, then, are the **formal structures** of our six types of phrase:

1. **Noun phrases** (NP): {M*} H {M*}
    where H (head) can be: N, pn, (or sometimes Aj, e, or GP)
    M before H (premodifiers) can be: d, e, Aj, N, GP, etc.
    M after H (postmodifiers) can be : PP, NP, Av, Aj, relative clause, etc.
2. **Prepositional phrases** (PP): p {M*} H {M*}
    where p is a preposition, and
    M, H, and M are exactly as in noun phrases.

3. **Genitive phrases** (GP): {*M**} *H* {*M**} 's
   where 's is the genitive particle, and
   M, H, and M are as in noun phrases (although postmodifiers are rare in GPs).
4. **Adjective phrases** (AjP): {*M**} *H* {*M**}
   where *H* (head) is an Aj
   M before *H* (premodifiers) are normally Av
   M after *H* (postmodifiers) are PP, Av, and some clauses.
5. **Adverb phrases** (AvP): {*M**} *H* {*M**}
   where *H* (head) is an Av, and
   M is as in AjPs.
6. **Verb phrases** (VP): {*Aux*} {*Aux*} {*Aux*} {*Aux*} *Mv*
   where any *Aux* is a v (operator-verb), and
   the *Mv* is either a v (operator-verb) or V (full-verb).

The **functions** of these phrase classes in the clause can be summarised as shown in Figure 5.8. The arrow X → Y is to be interpreted: 'X can be a Y'. We move on in Chapter 6 to a more detailed description of how phrases behave in clauses.

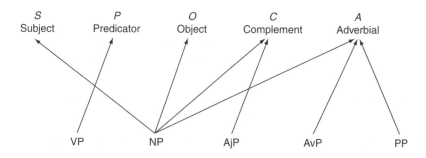

Figure 5.8

Exercise 5a (answer on p. 214)
Draw a tree diagram corresponding to example (9) (p. 68). Use form labels, as in Fig. 5.2.

Exercise 5b (answers on pp. 214–15)
Which phrases, in the following, are main and which are subordinate?

1. [(Mary) (had) (a little lamb)].
2. [(The fleece (of the little lamb)) (was) (as white (as snow))].
3. [(Everyone (in town)) (admires) (the whiteness (of the fleece (of (Mary's) little lamb)))].

Exercise 5c (answers on p. 215)

Examples (25) and (26) on p. 72 illustrate a possible ambiguity of prepositional phrases. To which of the examples below do these descriptions apply:

a. Two PPs postmodify the same head: (...H (PP) (PP)):
    e.g. (the largest bird (of prey) (in Africa)).
b. One PP is subordinate to another PP: (...H (p...H (PP))):
    e.g. (lectures (by the leading poets (of the day)).
c. The interpretation is ambiguous between (a) and (b):
    e.g. (a book (on games) (for children)) OR (a book (on games (for children))).

 1. (her interest in the coins of Roman Britain)
 2. (the outbreak of the revolution in Camelot)
 3. (the courage of a stag at bay)
 4. (a battle of words in Parliament)
 5. (the fall of Rome in 1527)
 6. (the highest rate of inflation in Europe)
 7. (a father of ten kids with a criminal record).
 8. (a conference on wild life in Canada)
 9. (rap for people over sixty)

FOR DISCUSSION

What differences of meaning are implied in the different analyses?

Exercise 5d (answers on pp. 215–16)

The following are NPs in which the order of premodifiers is scrambled:

 1. sisters, two, Cinderella's, ugly
 2. jade, idol, carved, green, a, small
 3. designs, interlocking, Chinese, intricate, old, those, all
 4. old, disgusting, Victorian, a, drawings, few, quite
 5. brilliant, new, Moldwarp's, hypothesis, geological
 6. cylindrical, second, Morgan's, steam, condenser, revolutionary
 7. an, tower, church, Gothic, grey, ancient
 8. first, hundred, tourists, the, foreign, all, almost
 9. responsibilities, moral, new, her, heavy
10. life, hectic, my, social, London

A. Unscramble the words into their correct grammatical order. (Occasionally there may be more than one possible order.)
B. In doing A, you have used your ability, as a speaker of English, to apply rules for ordering premodifiers in an NP. What are these rules? First, work out the order in which these classes normally occur if they are combined before the head noun: N, e, GP, Aj, d, Av. Secondly, if there is more than one member of the same class in the same NP, are there any principles for deciding in which order to put them?

Exercise 5e (answers on p. 216)

In the following examples, give function labels and form labels for each of the words and phrases that are heads or modifiers of each NP. For example, the NP *the new factory here in Chennai* can be analysed:

($^M_d$the $^M_{Aj}$new ^H_Nfactory $^M_{Av}$here $^M_{PP}$(in Chennai)).

1. she
2. the skeleton in the cupboard
3. that strange feeling
4. half the people present
5. Stanley's historic meeting with Livingstone at Ujiji
6. all those utterly fruitless afternoon meetings of the committee last year

Exercise 5f (answers on p. 216)

The most important category of pronouns is that of the **personal pronouns.** In Table 5.5 the personal pronouns are arranged according to distinctions traditionally known as **person** (first, second, third), **number** (singular, plural), **case** (subject, object, genitive, etc.)[†] and **gender** (masculine, feminine, neuter). Often these distinctions are **neutralised**, which means that the same form has to go in two different boxes (e.g. this is true of boxes 3 and 11). Complete the table by filling in the numbered gaps.

[†] The object form of the pronoun is not limited to pronouns functioning as object. In what other functions is the object form used? (See further section 12.4.)

Table 5.5

Person	Function	First		Second		Third			
Number →		Sing.	Plur.	Sing.	Plur.	Sing.			Plur.
Gender →						Masc.	Fem.	Neut.	
Case ↓									
Subject	H	I	2	3	4	5	she	7	8
Object	H	9	us	11	12	him	14	15	16
Reflexive	H	17	18	yourself	yourselves	21	22	23	themselves
Possessive determiner[†]	M	my	26	27	28	29	30	its	32
Possessive pronoun	H	mine	34	35	36	37	38	–	40

[†] We have included the possessive determiners *my*, etc. in the pronoun table, because they are closely related to personal pronouns in form, and in the way they vary for person, number and gender.

Exercise 5g (answers on p. 217)

(This is a preliminary look at constructions to be re-examined later.)

Look at these sets of sentences in which the VPs are italicized, and then describe a rule, as well as you can, for: (i) how to form the constructions 2, 3, 4, 5, 6 below, and (ii) when to use the dummy auxiliary *do* in English. Do your best to state (i) and (ii) as general rules.

1. **Ordinary declaratives**
   She *is working*.
   They *had eaten* them.
   She *works* hard.
   They *made* a mistake.

2. **Negative sentences with *NOT***
   She *is not working*.
   They *had not eaten* them.
   She *does not work* hard.
   They *did not make* a mistake.

3. **Questions**
   Is she *working*?
   Had they *eaten* them?
   Does she *work* hard?
   Did they *make* a mistake?

4. **Emphatic sentences**
   Yes, she *is working*.
   Yes, they *hàd eaten* them.
   Yes, she *dòes work* hard.
   Yes, they *dìd make* a mistake.

5. **Tag questions**
   She's *working, isn't* she?
   They'd *eaten* them, *hadn't* they?
   She *works* hard, *doesn't* she?
   They *made* a mistake, *didn't* they?

6. **Comparative clauses**
   She's *working* harder than Bill *is*.
   They'd *eaten* more than we *had*.
   She *works* harder than I *do*.
   They *made* more mistakes than we *did*.

6 Clauses

6.1 Elements of the clause

We have identified five main elements of the clause, and it is now time to explain them more carefully. They are listed in Table 6.1 in order of the degree to which they are 'peripheral' to clause structure, starting with *P* as the most 'central' element.

Table 6.1

Clause elements	Label
Predicator	*P*
Subject	*S*
Object	*O*
Complement	*C*
Adverbial	*A*

These five clause elements are illustrated in (1):

(1)   [^{S}(Many people) ^{P}(are painting) ^{O}(their houses) ^{C}(white) ^{A}(these days)].

This example also gives the typical ordering of these elements.

6.1.1 Predicator (*P*) and subject (*S*)

The PREDICATOR is the only element which is a verb phrase. The SUBJECT normally precedes the predicator, and there is CONCORD between the subject and predicator as regards NUMBER and PERSON (see Exercise 6e, p. 102). That means, for example, that if the subject is singular (referring to just one person, thing, etc.), the verb also has to be singular (ending in *-s*). Number concord (also called 'agreement') is illustrated in:

(2)   [^{S}(His sister) ^{P}(cooks) excellent Chinese dinners].
      (**singular** *S*, **singular** *P*)

(3)   [^{S}(His sisters) ^{P}(cook) excellent Chinese dinners].
      (**plural** *S*, **plural** *P*)

It is often possible to use a **substitution test**, substituting one of the **subject pronouns** *I, we, he, she, they* (see pp. 59–60) for the phrase in subject position. This is a very useful test, since apart from *you* and *it* personal pronouns have distinctive forms when they act as subject: compare *He prefers her, She prefers him.*

We should emphasise the need to use several tests for identifying clause elements. Consider the sentences in (4) and (5):

(4) [^{A}(In the box) ^{P}(are) ^{S}(six skulls)].

(5) [^{S}(The box) ^{P}(contains) ^{O}(six skulls)].

The criteria of position and meaning (3.5.2) do not help to identify *S* in (4), but we can still rely on tests of concord and pronoun substitution – thus we can say: *They are in the box*; and in (5) the verb *contains* ends in *-s*, because the subject *The box* is singular. In these examples, the subject does not refer to the 'doer' of an action, so we have to rely on form and function, not meaning, to see that the subject is *six skulls* in (4) and *The box* in (5).

6.1.2 Object (O) and complement (C)

The OBJECT is very closely tied to the predicator in terms of meaning, and typically denotes the person or thing most intimately affected by the action or state, etc., denoted by the *P*. The COMPLEMENT can look superficially like an object (both can be NPs), but in terms of meaning it **describes** or **characterizes** the *S* or *O*. Objects and complements normally follow the *P*:

(6) [^{S}(They) ^{P}('ve elected) ^{O}(Harry)].

(7) [^{S}(Harry) ^{P}(will be) ^{C}(the next leader of the school)].

If there are both an *O* and a *C* in the clause, then normally the *C* follows the *O*:

(8) [^{S}(They) ^{P}('ve elected) ^{O}(Harry) ^{C}(the next leader of the school)].

In (8) as in (7), *the next leader of the school* characterizes *Harry*.

6.1.3 Adverbials (A)

ADVERBIALS fill out the clause by adding extra circumstantial information of various kinds, ranging from time and location to the speaker's attitude. Of the clause elements that we have examined, adverbials are the least closely integrated into clause structure – and this goes especially for sentence adverbials.

The first point about adverbials is that there is no fixed number of them in a clause; in this they are rather like modifiers in the NP. The more common adverbial types are listed in Table 6.2, together with typical questions which elicit them.

The clause in (9) has four adverbials:

(9) [^{A}(Actually), ^{S}(she) ^{P}(works) ^{A}(at home) ^{A}(very rarely) ^{A}(these days)].

Table 6.2

Adverbial type	Eliciting question	Example
Place	*Where?*	(there), (on a box)
Direction	*Where to/from?*	(home), (to/from Paris)
Time–*when*	*When?*	(tomorrow), (on Sunday)
Duration	*How long?*	(for a month), (since 1990)
Frequency	*How often?*	(once a week), (every day)
Manner	*How? In what manner?*	(quickly), (with confidence)
Agency	*By whom?*	(by a tall dark stranger)
Goal	*To/For whom?*	(to Mary), (for himself)
Reason	*Why?*	(because of her mother)
Condition	*In what circumstances?*	(if you do the dishes)
Degree	*How much? How far?*	(completely), (to some extent)
Sentence adverbial	*Expresses attitude, connection*	(in fact), (consequently)

Its variants (9a) and (9b) show that adverbials are generally much more mobile in the clause than the other clause elements we have met:

(9a) [^{S}(She) ^{A}(very rarely) ^{P}(works) ^{A}(at home) ^{A}(these days), ^{A}(actually)].

(9b) [^{A}(These days) ^{S}(she) ^{A}(very rarely) ^{A}(actually) ^{P}(works) ^{A}(at home)].

So mobile are certain adverbials that they can be placed in the middle of the P, interrupting its elements, as in (10), where we use a new symbol (⌐—————⌐) to link the interrupted elements of the phrase:

(10) [^{S}(The place) ^{P}(is ^{A}(fast) going) ^{A}(to the dogs)].

(Compare: *The place is going to the dogs fast.*)

Adverbials are also **optional** in most clause types. They can normally be omitted from the clause, as we see in comparing (9) with (11):

(11) [She works *at home very rarely*] ⟶ [She works *at home*] ⟶ [She works].

(Now try Exercises 6a and 6b.)

6.2 Complex sentences

So far we have dealt only with SIMPLE SENTENCES consisting of a single MAIN CLAUSE (MCl), which is precisely a clause that can stand alone as a simple sentence (since this is the only element in the sentence, no function label is necessary):

(12) Se MCl[They'll support you].

But the majority of English sentences that you are likely to meet in texts are COMPLEX SENTENCES, i.e. sentences which contain additional clauses.

There are two ways in which additional clauses can occur in a complex sentence. Two or more clauses can be COORDINATED; that is, they can be linked as units of equal status:

(13) _Se_ MCl[You support your team-mates] and MCl[they'll support you].

Or there may be one or more SUBORDINATE CLAUSES (SCl), i.e. clauses which are grammatically SUBORDINATE (see 5.2) because they are part of another clause. A subordinate clause is either an element in a 'higher-up' clause, e.g. an adverbial (A):

(14) _Se_ MCl[$^A_{SCl}$[If you support your team-mates] $^S_{NP}$(they) $^P_{VP}$('ll support) $^O_{NP}$(you)].

or else a postmodifier (M) in a phrase within a clause:

(15) _Se_ MCl[(^H_NPlayers $^M_{SCl}$[who support their team-mates]) are supported in turn by them].

For clarity, we present (14) and (15) as tree diagrams, in Figures 6.1 and 6.2.
    Complex sentences can also result from a combination of coordination and subordination of clauses, for example:

(16) _Se_ MCl[She looked as cool as a cucumber], and MCl[SCl[if she could fool herself] she could fool anybody].

This is enough to give you a taste of subordinate clauses. We will be dealing with **subordination** and **coordination**, and with classes of subordinate clauses, in the next chapter. The remainder of this chapter, from 6.4, will be concerned primarily with classes of **main clause**.

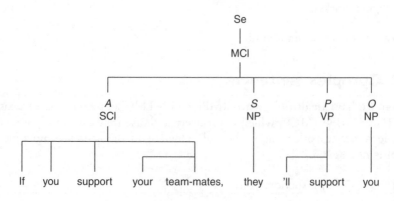

Figure 6.1

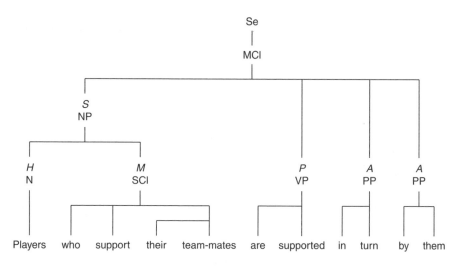

Figure 6.2

6.3 Tensed and tenseless clauses

So far we have dealt only with TENSED VERB PHRASES, containing a tensed verb, which is a verb showing TENSE (past or present) and SUBJECT CONCORD (for person and number). A tensed verb is either the OPERATOR (the first auxiliary verb in the VP) or the MAIN VERB (the only verb in the VP) if there is no operator (see 5.5.1).

But there are also many tenseless verb phrases, containing **no** tensed verb. Table 6.3 shows that in a tenseless VP all the verbs must be Vi, Ving or Ven. (A tenseless verb can be any verb – either an operator-verb or a full-verb – except for modal verbs, which have no tenseless forms.) Examples of tensed and tenseless VPs (see 5.5.1) are shown in Table 6.3. The particle *to* is always followed by Vi, and it can be considered an optional part of the Vi form. In fact, it is the usual practice in English to quote verbs in the to-infinitive form (*to* Vi): *to be, to create, to bludgeon.*

Table 6.3

Tensed VP	Structure	± Tense	Tenseless VP	Structure	± Tense
ate	Ved	+T	eating	Ving	−T
will eat	m Vi	+T −T	to eat	to Vi	−T −T
is eaten	be Ven	+T −T	be eaten	be Ven	−T −T
have been eating	hv be Ving	+T −T −T	having been eaten	hv be Ven	−T −T −T

+T = tensed verb; −T = tenseless verb

The terms 'tensed' and 'tenseless' also apply to clauses. The clauses we have dealt with so far have been TENSED CLAUSES, in which P has been a tensed VP. But there are also many TENSELESS CLAUSES, i.e. clauses in which P is a tenseless VP. Examples of corresponding tensed and tenseless subordinate clauses are (17)/(18); (19)/(20); (21)/(22):

(17) [It would be best $_{\text{SCl}}$[if you $\overset{P}{_{\text{VP}}}(\overset{M}{_{\text{Ved}}}$told) everyone]].
(tensed SCl)

(18) [The best thing would be $_{\text{SCl}}$[for you $\overset{P}{_{\text{VP}}}($to $\overset{Mv}{_{\text{Vi}}}$tell) everyone]].
(tenseless SCl)

(19) [$_{\text{SCl}}$[That Newcastle $\overset{P}{_{\text{VP}}}(\overset{M}{_{\text{Vd}}}$slid) down the table] is hardly attributable to Robson's lack of flair].
(tensed SCl)

(20) [$_{\text{SCl}}$[Newcastle $\overset{P}{_{\text{VP}}}(\overset{M}{_{\text{Ving}}}$sliding) down the table] is hardly attributable to Robson's lack of flair].
(tenseless SCl)

> Note that a third alternative would be *Newcastle's slide down the table is* ...,
> where the subject of the clause is a NP with the abstract noun *slide* as its head.

(21) [$_{\text{SCl}}$[As the job $\overset{P}{_{\text{VP}}}(\overset{Aux}{_{\text{Ved}}}$was $\overset{Mv}{_{\text{Ven}}}$done), we went home early].
(tensed SCl)

(22) [$_{\text{SCl}}$[The job $\overset{P}{_{\text{VP}}}(\overset{M}{_{\text{Ven}}}$done)] , we went home early].
(tenseless SCl).

The tensed subordinate clauses have tensed verbs (Vo, Vs and Ved) as well as tenseless ones, while the tenseless subordinate clauses have only tenseless verbs (Vi, Ving and Ven). A large majority of tenseless clauses are subordinate clauses. (Exceptions are imperatives like *Sit down!* (see 6.4.2 below) and headlines like *Princess to marry*.)

6.4 Declarative, interrogative and imperative clauses

Now we turn to main clauses, of which there are three major types in English. The DECLARATIVE type is generally used to make statements. It is the most usual form of the clause, and the clauses we have been using as examples up to now have almost all been declaratives:

(23) Jim will post these letters.

There is no need to describe them any further here. The interrogative type is mostly used to ask questions:

(24) Will Jim post these letters?

(25) Who will post these letters?

Finally, the IMPERATIVE type is most commonly used to give orders or make requests:

(26) Post these letters.

6.4.1 The interrogative

There are two kinds of interrogatives. The YES–NO INTERROGATIVE, e.g. (24) above, asks for a yes/no answer. It is always the (tensed) **operator** that carries this contrast between yes and no – not only negation (see 5.5.2), but also strong, positive affirmation:

(27) Jim *won't* post these letters.
(28) Jim *will* post these letters.   (*will* carries the emphasis)

In forming yes–no interrogatives we place the **operator** in the prominent position before *S* in the clause:

(29) *Have* ^{S}(you) *seen* the latest blockbuster?   (P = v ... V)
(30) *Haven't* ^{S}(you) *seen* the latest blockbuster?   (P = v ... V)

As with negation (5.5.2), if there is no operator in the declarative, then the corresponding interrogative needs dummy auxiliary *do*, followed by an infinitive.

(31) [^{S}(He) ^P_v*squeezed* her hand].   (P = V)
(32) [$_v$*Did* ^{S}(he) $_v$*squeeze* her hand]?   (P = v ... V)

It is *do* (Ved = *did*) that is the tensed verb, and thus expresses present and past tense. Also notice that in the interrogative, the verb phrase is **split** into two parts, rather as the verb phrase is split when an adverbial is shifted into it (see p. 87):

(33) [^{S}(He) ^{S}(is ^{A}(always) making) ^{O}(things) ^{C}(difficult)].

(34) [$_v$Is ^{S}(he) ^{A}(really) ($_v$making) ^{O}(things) ^{C}(so difficult)]?

A second kind of interrogative is the WH- INTERROGATIVE, e.g. (25) above, an interrogative that asks about one of the clause elements *S, O, C* or *A* (or sometimes about a part of a phrase) using a WH- WORD:

WH- DETERMINERS:	*what, which, whose*
WH- PRONOUNS:	*who, who(m), whose, which, what*
WH- ADVERBS:	*where, when, why, how*

Note that *how* counts as a *wh-* word in spite of its spelling. Imagine it is spelt *whow*!

Because a *wh-* interrogative is an interrogative, the operator is normally placed before S, and then, because the *wh-* word is the focus of attention, it is placed before the operator:

(35) [^{O}(What) $_v$did ^{S}(she) ^{P}(say)]?

(36) [^{A}(Where) $_v$has ^{S}(she) ^{P}(hidden) ^{O}(it)]?

(37) [^{O}(^{M}Whose ^{H}book) $_v$was ^{S}(she) ^{P}(reading)]?

(38) [^{A}(^{M}How ^{H}long) $_v$will ^{S}(she) ^{P}(be staying)]?

In those cases where the *wh-* word is in the S element, however, the rule that places the *wh-* word first is obeyed without changing the normal, declarative, order. There is no need for special use of the operator, and the use of the dummy operator *do* is also unnecessary:

(39) [^{S}(Who) ^{P}(ate) ^{O}(that sandwich)]?

(39a) [^{S}(^{M}Which ^{H}window) ^{P}(was broken)]?

6.4.2 The imperative

While the declarative and interrogative both have a tensed P and an S (which for the interrogative **may** be an interrogative pronoun like *who*), the imperative has a tenseless P and no S.

We can think of the imperative as being derived from a declarative by omission of ^{S}(*you*) and of the VP operator *will* or *must*:

(40) [^{S}You) ^{P}(will listen) to me].

(40a) [^{P}Listen) to me].

(41) [^{S}You) ^{P}(must come) ^{A}(into my cubbyhole).

(41a) [^{P}Come) ^{A}(into my cubbyhole).

In the imperative, the first verb in the VP is thus a Vi. How do we know that it is not Vo, which is identical to Vi for all verbs except *be*? There are two reasons. First, when we have the verb *be* in an imperative, it takes the Vi form, not the Vo form:

(42) Be quiet! NOT: *Are quiet!

Secondly, if it were Vo, P would be tensed, and therefore a contrast in tense between present (Vo) and past (Ved) would be possible. But there is no such contrast:

(43) Run to the shop. NOT: *Ran to the shop.

So the verb must be Vi. In fact, this is always a good TEST FOR TENSEDNESS of a VP. If the VP is tensed, it can show subject concord and an alternation in tense between Vo/Vs and Ved, while if it is tenseless it does not. Since Vo = Vi for all but one verb, and Ved = Ven for very many verbs, it can be a good idea to test P for finiteness.

6.5 Active and passive clauses

We have already met the active and passive voice in the verb phrase (5.5); now we need to consider them in the clause. The ACTIVE VOICE is the basic, unmarked, most frequent form of the clause:

(44)   [^{S}(She) ^{P}(has eaten) ^{O}(my porridge)].

(45)   [^{S}(She) ^{P}(told) ^{O}(them) ^{O}(the whole story)].

(46)   [^{S}(She) ^{P}(was sleeping) $^A_{PP}$(in this bed)].

The PASSIVE VOICE is the more marked form of the clause in which the S corresponds in meaning to an O of a corresponding active clause. So parallel to (44)–(46), we have the corresponding passives:

(47)   [^{S}(My porridge) ^{P}(has been eaten)].

(48)   [^{S}(They) ^{P}(were told) ^{O}(the whole story)].

   [^{S}(The whole story) ^{P}(was told) ^{O}({to} them)].

(49)   [$^S_{NP}$(This bed) ^{P}(was being slept) ($_p$in)].

The S of the corresponding active becomes an optional A of AGENCY in the passive, nearly always a PP marked with the preposition *by*:

(50)   [^{S}(This porridge) ^{P}(had been eaten) $^A_{PP}$($_p$by *Goldilocks*)].

6.6 More on clause structure

Having defined the clause elements S, P, O, C, A, we must now look further into the details of clause structure.

There are two kinds of object (O), and two kinds of complement (C). A DIRECT OBJECT (Od) is the most usual kind of object, and an INDIRECT OBJECT (Oi), when it occurs, comes between the predicator and the direct object: S P Oi Od. The Oi is normally optional, and can very often be replaced by an A element, a PP introduced by *to* or *for*, coming after the Od:

(51)   [^{S}(You) ^{P}(can't teach) $^{Oi}_{NP}$(an old dog) ^{Od}(new tricks)].

(51a) [^{S}(You) ^{P}(can't teach) ^{Od}(new tricks) $^A_{PP}$(to an old dog)].

(52)   [^{S}(Milly) ^{S}(built) $^{Oi}_{NP}$(her brother) ^{Od}(a sandcastle)].

(52a) [^{S}(Milly) ^{S}(built) ^{Od}(a sandcastle) $^A_{PP}$(for her brother)].

Semantically, the direct object Od is 'direct' in the sense that it generally refers to something **directly** affected by the action of the verb. The indirect object, on the other hand, refers (generally) to a person who is **indirectly** affected by the action – typically, someone who benefits from the action. Occasionally, the Oi occurs alone after the S, as in the joke:

(53)   Waiter, do you serve ^{Od}(crabs)?

   Sit down, sir. We serve ^{Oi}(anybody).

The ambiguity of *Od* and *Oi* allowed the waiter to misinterpret the customer's question. But unless there is a need to distinguish them, we will use *O* for both *Oi* and *Od*.

There are also two kinds of complement, SUBJECT COMPLEMENT and OBJECT COMPLEMENT. When we wish to distinguish them, we can symbolise them *Cs* and *Co*. The subject complement characterises or describes the subject, whereas the object complement characterises or describes the direct object:

(54)   [^{S}(Joe Walcott) ^{P}(was) ^{Cs}(*a great boxer*)].

(55)   [^{S}(Everyone) ^{P}(considered) ^{O}(Joe Walcott) ^{Co}(*a great boxer*)].

Once again, the difference between the two subclasses can be usually recognised by their position, as well as by their meaning. The *Cs* normally follows *P* (which typically contains the copula verb *to be*), and the *Co* normally follows *O*. A clause normally contains only one complement, either *Cs* or *Co*.

To complete the list of what can occur in a clause, we finally mention some 'peripheral' elements. First, two closed classes of words – **conjunctions** and **interjections** (see 4.3.5, 4.3.7):

(56) $_{ij}$*Ugh*, it's a coffee-cream again!

(57) $_{cj}$*And* so it went on.

We treat these simply as particles (see 4.3.8). Secondly, an NP may occur as a VOCATIVE (*Voc*), a phrase which identifies the person addressed:

(58)   It was pretty fresh, $^{Voc}_{NP}$(dude).

(59) $_{ij}$Hi $^{Voc}_{NP}$(Ben), how are you doing, $^{Voc}_{NP}$(you little monster)?

Vocatives are optional, and mobile, and are therefore more like adverbials than any other type of constituent. Notice the difference in role between the vocative in imperative clauses, and the subject in declarative clauses:

(60a) $^{Voc}_{NP}$(Jock), pay attention.   (imperative)

(60b) $^{S}_{NP}$(Jock) pays attention.   (declarative)

Only the vocative can be omitted or moved to the end of the clause: *Pay attention, Jock*. (Now try Exercise 6c.)

6.7 Clause patterns

Adverbials (*A*) and peripheral elements (cj, ij and *Voc*) tend to be optional parts of the clause. When we have stripped away the optional elements of each clause, we are left with a nucleus which can be called its CLAUSE PATTERN, and which expresses the kernel of its meaning. For example:

(61)   But gee, Alice, *you must be kidding me* now, baby.

The clause has the structure [cj ij *Voc S P O A Voc*]. But once we have thrown away the optional elements, we are left with a nucleus [*S P O*] (*you must be kidding me*), the clause pattern. When illustrating clause patterns, it is convenient to use a **main clause** in the **declarative** form, in the **active voice** (see 6.4, 6.5), and with the **unmarked** (or most neutral) word order. *S* and *P* are always obligatory, but whether *O*, *C* and *A* are obligatory or even possible chiefly depends on the main verb, for example:

(62) *The chef stuffed. *[*S P*] The chef stuffed a chicken. [*S P O*]

The chef talked. [*S P*] *The chef talked a story. *[*S P O*]

*The chef seemed. *[*S P*] The chef seemed hungry. [*S P C*]

The chef served lunch. [*S P O*] The chef served me lunch. [*S P Oi Od*]

We can arrange the principal clause elements in a hierarchy: *S, P, Od, Oi, C, A*. Then, using *S* as a reference point, the further down the hierarchy we move, the more likely the clause element is to be optional, and the more free is its position in the clause. So *S* is generally obligatory in declaratives, but *A* is obligatory with only a small number of verbs such as *put*. The position of *S* is relatively fixed, but the position of *A* is rather free.

The most common clause patterns for English are shown in Table 6.4,

Table 6.4 The major clause patterns for English

[*S P*]: [He walks].	[*S P Od*]: [He caught it].
Verbs: *walk, die, work, come, run, sleep, dream, eat, look, behave,* and many more	**Verbs**: *catch, hit, kiss, find, pull, work, run, buy, take, kill, eat,* and many more
[*S P Oi*]: [She served the customers].	[*S P Oi Od*]: [She sold him the book].
Verbs: *serve, tell,* and a few others; this is in fact an uncommon clause pattern in English	**Verbs**: *sell, give, tell, send, buy, make,* and some others; this is an important but limited clause pattern in English
[*S P C*]: [He is kind/a nurse].	[*S P Od C*]: [He proved her wrong/a liar].
Verbs: *be, become, seem, look, appear,* and a few others; this is a limited but important clause pattern	**Verbs**: *prove, call, make, think,* and some *others*; this is a fairly limited clause pattern
[*S P A*]: [He is there].[†] [She thinks about it].	[*S P Od A*]: [He puts it there].[†] [She tells him about it].
Verbs: *be, stand, lean, live, reside, know, think, talk, grieve, worry,* and a few others	**Verbs**: *put, place, keep, tell, treat, sprinkle,* and a few others

[†] With the *S P A* and *S P O A* patterns, different verbs require different obligatory adverbials.

together with an example of each, and a list of some of the verbs that take that pattern. These clause patterns can always be extended with additional optional clause elements: particularly *A*, and sometimes *C* and *O*. For instance, we could extend the [*S P O A*] and [*S P Oi Od*] patterns, using the examples in Table 6.4:

(63) He always puts it there in the evening. [*S A P O A A*]

(64) Actually, he sold her the book cheap, too, darling. [*A S P Oi Od C A Voc*]

Among the verbs listed in Table 6.4 for each clause pattern there is a great deal of overlap, for many verbs can occur in more than one pattern, often with a noticeable or even extreme change in meaning. For instance, the verb *keep* occurs in all the patterns in (65):

(65) [S P O]:   Gladys keeps a pet python.

 [S P O C]:   Gladys is keeping the children happy.

 [S P O A]:   Gladys keeps her pet python in the bath.

 [S P Oi Od]:   Gladys is keeping Archie a piece of pie.

 [S P C]:   Gladys is keeping very fit.

 [S P A]:   The piece of pie is keeping well.

The verbs of English are, by and large, remarkably flexible in the clause patterns which they govern, and though it often takes some imagination to think of plausible examples, users of the language are constantly putting the verbs to new uses. (Now try Exercises 6d and 6e.)

6.7.1 Passive clause patterns

It is a general rule that a clause pattern with an object can be changed into a passive clause pattern, with the same main verb, in which this object functions as subject. Thus each clause pattern with an *O* on the **right-hand side** of Table 6.4 above can be converted into a passive pattern which fits into the corresponding position on the **left-hand side**:

(66) [S P O] → [S P]

 [(Jim) (caught) (the ball)] → [(The ball) (was caught) {by Jim}].

(67) [S P Oi Od] → [S P Oi]

 [(He) (sold) (me) (the car)] → [(The car) (was sold) (me) {by him}].

(68) [S P O C] → [S P C]

 [(The team) (voted) (her) (captain)] → [(She) (was voted) (captain) {by the team}].

(69) [S P O A] → [S P A]

 [(Sid) (put) (the pepper) (in my soup)] → [(The pepper) (was put) (in my soup) {by Sid}].

For the [S P Oi] and [S P Oi Od] patterns, there is also a more common passive version, in which the Oi becomes the subject: for example, *I was served {by a surly shopkeeper}* [S P {A}], *I was sold a pup* [S P O]. Each passive pattern has an optional PP of agency (*by him*, etc.). The passive allows us to change the semantic focus of the clause, and also to omit reference to the doer of the action – by leaving out the agent phrase – if we want to.

6.8 The structure of tenseless clauses

Corresponding to the three tenseless forms of the verb (Vi, Ving, Ven) mentioned in 5.5.1, there are three types of clause where those forms occur as the first (or only) element of the predicator. We call these types of clause INFINITIVE CLAUSE (Cli), ING-CLAUSE (Cling) and EN-CLAUSE (Clen) respectively. Even though they lack a tensed verb, such constructions are analysed as clauses, because they can be analysed into S, P, O, C, A, etc., just like tensed clauses:

(70) infinitive clause:

We need space [$_{cj}$for $_{NP}^{S}$(the kids) $_{VP}^{P}$(to play) $_{NP}^{O}$(volleyball)]. [S P O]

(71) *ing*-clause:

[^{S}(Her) ^{P}(being fired)] was an act of discrimination. [S P]

(72) *en*-clause:

We had [$_{NP}^{S}$(the brakes) $_{VP}^{P}$(fixed)] last year. [S P]

There are one or two details, apart from the verb, which distinguish tenseless from tensed clauses. For example, in infinitive clauses like (70) a conjunction *for* normally precedes the subject, and the infinitive particle *to* normally precedes the VP. In *ing*-clauses like (71) the subject is sometimes the possessive form, like *her* above (but see 12.4.3). But more importantly, apart from this, these tenseless clauses have almost the same structural possibilities as tensed clauses. They can, for instance, be classified in terms of the clause patterns in Table 6.4. An important point about tenseless clauses, however, is that the S is frequently omitted:

(73) [The best thing would be $_{Cli}$[^{P}(to tell) ^{O}(everyone)]].

(74) [$_{Cling}$[^{P}(Having) ^{O}(pointed ears)] is a characteristic of Vulcans].

(75) [$_{Clen}$[^{P}(Established) ^{A}(in Calcutta) ^{A}(in the 1970s)], the theatre group has had worldwide success].

(The *en*-clauses are passive in meaning, and have passive clause patterns.) Tenseless clauses also have no operator. They are often useful for compressing information, particularly in written language.

6.9 Parsing a simple sentence

We now have all the grammatical resources we need to parse a simple English sentence. For this purpose, we return to our sentence which contains all word classes (p. 65):

(76) But alas, the two ugly sisters had gone home without her.

There is no single right way to parse a sentence, but generally it pays to work down the rank scale (3.2), starting with the sentence and working down to the words of which it is composed. At each rank, we suggest, you:

1. identify the elements of structure (usually units of the next rank down),
2. then identify the grammatical **function** of each element,
3. and finally, identify the **class** of units that fills each of these functions.

Step 3 gives us a new set of units to begin the whole cycle of steps 1, 2 and 3 all over again (see Figure 6.3).

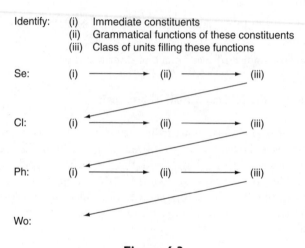

Figure 6.3

Because a tree diagram brings out the nature of grammatical analysis visually, we will build up a tree diagram (or rather, build one down!) for (76) above, step by step.

Se: 1.   here is only one VP, (*had gone*), so there should be only one clause (see Figure 6.4).

Figure 6.4

Se: 2.   Because we have a single clause in a complete sentence, it must be a main clause. We do not use a function label: none is needed (see 6.2).

Se: 3.   This is a main clause (MCl) (see Figure 6.5).

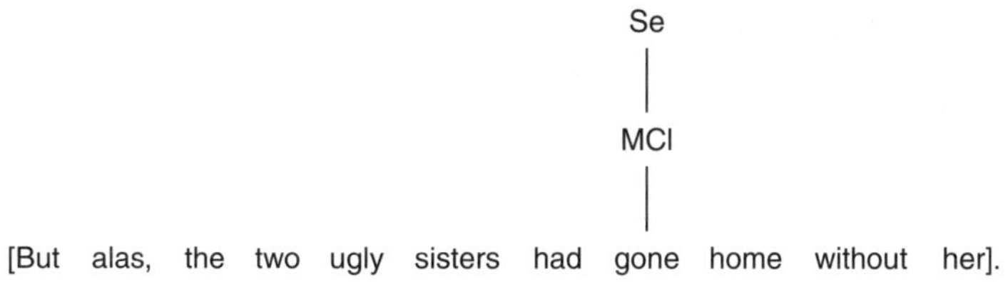

Se

|

MCl

|

[But alas, the two ugly sisters had gone home without her].

Figure 6.5

We now have a clause to parse:

Cl: 1. We bracket the constituent phrases. Note that *but* is a conjunction (cj), and therefore does not count as a phrase (see 4.3.8). The same applies to the interjection (ij) *alas*. (See Figure 6.6.)

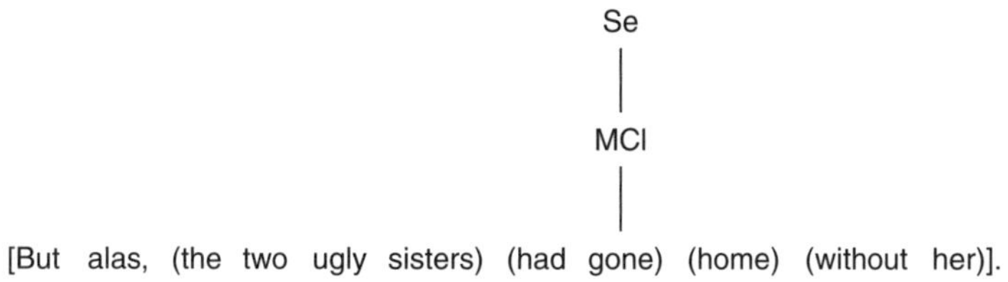

Se

|

MCl

|

[But alas, (the two ugly sisters) (had gone) (home) (without her)].

Figure 6.6

Cl: 2. We identify the clause elements (see 6.1, 6.6 if in doubt). (See Figure 6.7.) Note that *but* and *alas* do not have function labels, because they are grammatical particles (see 4.3.8).

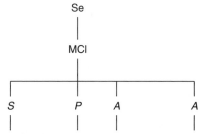

[But alas, (the two ugly sisters) (had gone) (home) (without her)].

Figure 6.7

Cl: 3. Now identify the class of phrase filling each function (see Chapter 5). (See Figure 6.8.) Note that *but* and *alas* are labelled at this stage because, although they are not phrases, they are clause constituents.

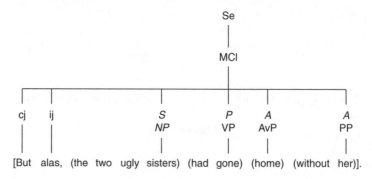

Figure 6.8

We now have four phrases to parse:

Ph: 1. This step is unnecessary in this case, since all the elements of the phrases are words, and these are already identified for us by our writing system. But later, when we parse phrases with subordinated phrases in them, this step will be a necessary one.

Ph: 2. Now identify the phrase elements (see Chapter 5). This is fairly easy, but remember the VP (see 5.5) and prepositions (see 5.3.3). The brackets become superfluous at this stage, so we omit them (see Figure 6.9).

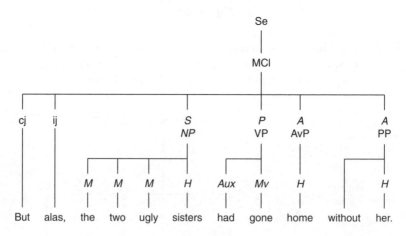

Figure 6.9

Ph: 3. Identify the class of the words filling each phrase function (see Chapter 4). Remember that we have already identified the class of *but* and *alas*, and remember the preposition *without*, which does not receive a function label because it is a particle (see Figure 6.10).

We have now parsed the sentence as fully as we can do without parsing words into their stems and affixes. That last step is not necessary, so this is a good point to end the chapter. (Now try Exercise 6f.)

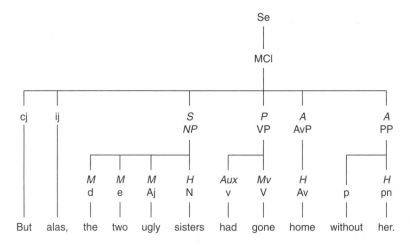

Figure 6.10

6.10 Summary

In this chapter we have distinguished:

1. These components of clauses:

   ■ the clause elements *P* (predicator), *S* (subject), *O* (object), *C* (complement) and *A* (adverbial);
   ■ the **peripheral** elements *Voc* (vocative), cj (conjunction) and ij (interjection);
   ■ *Od* (direct object) and *Oi* (indirect object), *Cs* (subject complement) and *Co* (object complement).

2. Main clauses (MCl) and subordinate clauses (SCl), which are parts of other clauses.
3. Declarative, interrogative and imperative types of MCl.
4. Clause patterns [*S P*], [*S P O*], [*S P Oi*], [*S P Oi Od*], [*S P C*], [*S P O C*], [*S P A*] and [*S P O A*].
5. Three kinds of tenseless clause: infinitive clauses (Cli), *ing*-clauses (Cling), and *en*-clauses (Clen).

━━━━━━━━━━━━━━━ **EXERCISES** ━━━━━━━━━━━━━━━

Exercise 6a (answers on p. 217)

Identify the **clause structures** (in terms of S, P, O, C, A) of the following (the first example is done for you, and phrases are identified by round brackets):

1. [*S*(My wife) *A*(always) *P*(has) *O*(a good cry) *A*(over a wedding)].
2. [(That story about the alligators in the canal) (has been denied)].
3. [(All of them) (were worrying) (about their own problems)].
4. [(The police) (caught) (the thief) (red-handed)].

5. [(We)('ll rehearse) (Reggie's act) (once again)].
6. [(On wages policy), (the leader of the opposition) (is being) (extremely cautious)].
7. [(No doubt) (they) (will tell) (us) (the same old story) (tomorrow)].

Exercise 6b (answers on p. 217)

Now identify the **phrase classes** of the clause elements in the above sentences. For example, sentence 1 is labelled as follows:

1. NP(My wife) AvP(always) VP(has) NP(a good cry) PP(over a wedding)].

You can write this simply: [NP AvP VP NP PP].

Exercise 6c (answers on p. 217)

Distinguish the clause structures of these pairs:

1. (The porter) (called) (me) (a taxi).   [S P Oi Od]
    The porter called me a yob.
2. I once wrote an essay on the beach.
    I once wrote an essay on marsupial courtship rituals.
3. Robert sounds an interesting guy.
    Robert knows an interesting guy.
4. She found her mother a reliable companion.
    She found her mother a reliable companion. (The same example, with a different meaning)
5. Most of us are working this evening.
    Most of us are dreading this evening.
6. We stayed in a camp for teenagers.
    We stayed in a camp for ages.

Exercise 6d (answers on p. 217)

Identify the **clause patterns** (see Table 6.4, p. 95) of the sentences in Exercise 6a, by deleting optional adverbials. For example, sentence 1 has the clause pattern [S P O].

Exercise 6e (answers on p. 217)

Grammatical ambiguities play a part in some (often rather feeble) jokes. Explain how the following jokes exploit ambiguities of clause structure and/or word meaning:

1. 'The police are seeking a man with one eye.'
    'Typical inefficiency! – and the usual lack of resources!'
2. 'How do you get down from an elephant?'
    'You don't – you get down from a duck.'
3. 'You've been working in the garden for hours. What are you growing?'
    'Tired.'
4. 'David cursed the day he was born.'
    'What an amazing baby!'

Exercise 6f (answers on pp. 218–19)

Parse fully the following sentences, by drawing tree diagrams as recommended in 6.9:

1. [(No man) (is) (an island)].
2. [(Shakespearean comedy) (simply) (doesn't travel) (well).
3. [(Dad)('s given) (the carol singers) (a cheque (for a thousand pounds))].

(In labelling constituents of the verb phrase, you need to use only *Aux*, *Mv*, v and V.)

Subordination and Coordination

After three chapters on the grammatical units of word, phrase and clause, you may now be expecting a chapter on the highest unit of all on our grammatical rank scale (3.2), the SENTENCE. We will not entirely disappoint you, but, in fact, the sentence does not have a structure like that of lower units: 'sentence' is simply a name for the largest stretch of language we normally consider in grammar, and which normally consists either of (a) a **single** clause, in which case it is known as a SIMPLE SENTENCE, or of (b) **more than one** clause, in which case it is known as a COMPLEX SENTENCE. In the complex sentence the clauses may be related to one another by SUBORDINATION or by COORDINATION (see 6.2).

Subordination, as we have seen (5.2), is not necessarily a relation between two clauses: it may be a relation between two phrases, or even two words (see 7.5.1). The same applies to coordination (see 7.7). But to begin with, we limit our attention to subordinate and coordinate CLAUSES:

(1) [You buy all the food]. [I'll do the cooking].   (Two simple sentences.)
(2) [You buy all the food] and [I'll do the cooking].   (Two coordinate main clauses in one sentence.)
(3) [[If you buy all the food], I'll do the cooking].   (One subordinate clause and one main clause within one and the same sentence.)

The bracketing of (2) and (3) reveals a crucial difference between the two relations: a subordinate clause is always **part** of another clause, while a

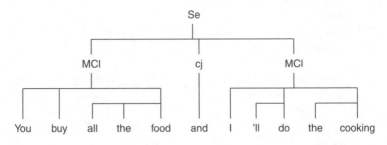

Figure 7.1

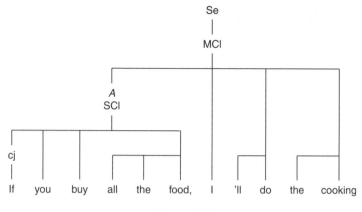

Figure 7.2

coordinate clause is joined with another clause (or clauses) of the **same status**, i.e. at the same level of the tree. This becomes clearer in tree diagrams (see Figures 7.1 and 7.2).

We are going to deal with subordinate clauses first, and return to coordination in 7.7. Thus by the end of the chapter we will have dealt with the various ways in which sentences can be composed of clauses.

7.1 Subordinate clauses (SCl)

Like other kinds of grammatical construction, subordinate clauses are recognised in part by their function, and in part by their internal structure.

7.1.1 Function

We can recognize different kinds of subordinate clauses by their ability to function within larger units, especially within clauses. For example, the subordinate clause *what this country needs* functions as **S**, **O** and **C** in the following:

(4) [[*What this country needs*] is a Minister of Fun].
    (SCl = subject)
(5) [As a politician, you should know [*what this country needs*]].
    (SCl = object)
(6) [A decrease in taxation is exactly [*what this country needs*]].
    (SCl = complement)

In filling the slots of **S**, **O** and **C**, this kind of subordinate clause is comparable to a noun phrase. We can therefore say that *what this country needs* in (4)–(6) is a NOUN CLAUSE (NCl), with a function similar to that of a NOUN PHRASE (NP). The label 'NCl' is more specific than 'SCl', although both labels can be correctly applied to *what this country needs*. On the other hand, in (7) the subordinate clause *while this guy was apologizing* is an

ADVERBIAL CLAUSE (ACl), because it has an ADVERBIAL function in the clause:

(7)   [She just walked away [*while this guy was apologizing*]].

We can tell that the function of the clause is adverbial because it has the characteristics of adverbials as discussed in 6.1.3:

- It is optional; i.e. it can be omitted: *She just walked away.*
- It is mobile; i.e. it can be moved: *While this guy was apologizing, she just walked away.*
- It answers the question *When did she walk away?*, and thus shows itself to be an adverbial (of time) in terms of meaning.

In these respects, *while this guy was apologizing* is like a PP of time, such as *in the middle of his apology*, or like an adverb, such as *meanwhile*:

(8)   She just walked away (*in the middle of his apology*).
      (*Meanwhile*) she just walked away.

7.1.2 Structure

Like main clauses, subordinate clauses are divisible into the clause elements S, P, O, C, A. If they were not, there would be no justification for calling them clauses at all. For instance, *What this country needs*, which is S of the main clause in (4), can itself be broken down into the elements O, S, P:

(4a)   [^{S}[^{O}(*What*) ^{S}(*this country*) ^{P}(*needs*)] ^{P}(is) ^{C}(a Minister of Fun)].

But, in addition, subordinate clauses usually have some marker or badge to help indicate their subordinate status. There are three types of marking:

1. A SUBORDINATING CONJUNCTION (see 4.3.5): e.g. *if, when, that, because, although.*
2. A WH- ELEMENT: e.g. *what, who, whoever, which girl, what time, how.* A *wh*- element is a phrase which contains or consists of a *wh*- word (cf. 5.3.2).
3. A TENSELESS PREDICATOR (see 6.8). As mentioned in the last chapter, tenseless clauses (Cli, Cling, Clen) are those which have Vi, Ving or Ven as the first verb of their predicator. They rarely occur as main clauses.

Examples are:

1.   [Martha will look chic ^{A}[$_{cj}$if ^{S}(she) ^{P}(wears) ^{O}(those clothes)]]].
2.   [Martha will look chic ^{A}[^{O}(whatever) ^{S}(she) ^{P}(wears)]]].
3.   [Martha will look chic ^{A}[^{P}(wearing) ^{O}(those clothes)]]].

Wh- elements, like subordinating conjunctions, generally come at the beginning of the clause. But what distinguishes a *wh*-element from a conjunction is that it is one of the major elements in the subordinate clause, such as S, O or A. In addition, it has a special interrogative or relative function. A conjunction, on the other hand, is simply a particle (or 'little word') that comes at the beginning of the clause.

Remember also that, as with *wearing those clothes* in 3, a tenseless clause often has no subject. So we can usually identify a subordinate clause **by its very first word**, which is likely to be a marker of types 1, 2 or 3 above.

But there are two difficulties. The first is that there is an overlap between conjunctions and *wh-* words. *When* and *where*, for example, belong to both categories. The second is that there are certain types of clause, especially common in informal English, which have no introductory marker at all. We will call these ZERO clauses, because they have no overt sign of their subordination to another clause (see 7.2.1 below). Let's now examine the various classes of subordinate clause, concentrating first on tensed clauses. (Now try Exercise 7a.)

7.2 Tensed subordinate clauses

There are five major kinds of tensed subordinate clause to consider.

7.2.1 Noun clauses (NCl)

The main types of tensed NCl are these:

1. *THAT*-CLAUSES begin with the conjunction *that*:

    (9)   [^{S}[*That ghosts exist*] (is) (hardly controversial)].

    (10) [(Seamus) (believes) ^{O}[*that ghosts vanish at sunrise*]].

2. ZERO *THAT*-CLAUSES are just like *that*-clauses, except that *that* itself is omitted. A test for a zero *that*-clause therefore is whether we can insert the cj *that* at the front of the clause:

    (11) [(I) (might have known) ^{O}[*you couldn't resist a gossip*]].
          (zero *that*-clause)

    (12) [(I) (might have known) ^{O}[***that** you couldn't resist a gossip*]].
          (*that*-clause)

3. *WH-* CLAUSES begin with a *wh-* element which may function within them as S, O, C, A, etc.:

    (13) ^{S}[^{S}(*Who*) (stole) (the teaspoons)] (is) (a mystery)].

    (14) [(The nurse) (just) (asked) (me) ^{Od}[^{C}(*how old*) (the baby) (was)]].

    (15) [(You) (can ask) ^{Od}[^{Od}(*whichever* girl) (you) (like)] (to the party)].

Just as *that* noun clauses often have the role of indirect statements (see p. 178), so *wh-* noun clauses often have the role of indirect questions. We can thus compare (11), an example of an indirect statement, with (16), which is an indirect yes–no question:

(16) [(The burning issue) (was) ^{C}[$_{cj}$*whether* (Marguerite) (had repaid) (the prize money)]].

7.2.2 Adverbial clauses (ACl)

Like adverbs and phrases which act as adverbials, ADVERBIAL CLAUSES can be classified semantically according to what questions they answer.

Table 7.1

Adverbial clause of	Eliciting question	Subordinating conjunctions
Place	*Where?*	where, wherever
Time[†]	*When?*	when, before, after, as, while, until, since, whenever
Manner/comparison	*How?*	as, as if, as though
Reason	*Why?*	because, as, since
Purpose	*Why?*	so that, in order that
Condition	–	if, unless
Contrast	–	although, though

[†] Adverbial clauses have meanings which are not often found in other adverbials, and vice versa. This is why the table of meanings here is somewhat different from those in 4.2.4 and 6.1.3. For example, we have found it convenient to combine the meanings of time-*when*, duration and frequency in one category of adverbial clauses of time.

Table 7.1 shows some major types. Examples of these types are:

(17) [They went ^A[*wherever they could find work*]].   (place)

(18) [I lent her my savings ^A[*because she was short of money*]].   (reason)

(19) [^A[*When the weather improves*], we are going on holiday].   (time)

(20) [I lent him some money ^A[*so that he could buy himself a meal*]]. (purpose)

(21) [^A[*If you follow the instructions carefully*], nobody will be hurt]. (condition)

(22) [^A[*Although no goals were scored*], it was an exciting game].   (contrast).

Again we have to beware of overlapping uses of conjunctions. For example, *as* has a number of different meanings, and *since* can express either time or reason:

(23) [[*Since* I lost my glasses yesterday], I haven't been able to do any work].

This sentence is ambiguous between the two interpretations, although the 'time' interpretation is more likely.

All these ACls are introduced by a conjunction. There are also WH-ADVERBIAL CLAUSES (beginning with a *wh-* element) and ZERO ADVERBIAL CLAUSES (with no introductory marker), but these are less common, and tend to function as sentence adverbials – (24) and (26) illustrate the *wh-* type, and (25) the zero type:

(24) [^A[*However hard I try*], I always fail the test].

(25) [Wombats, ^A[*I understand*], are virtually tailless].

(26) [They breed copiously, ^A[*which is a pity*]].

The ACl in (26) is very similar to a relative clause (see 7.2.3 below), except that it is a comment on the whole of the clause or sentence. Such clauses are sometimes called 'sentence relative clauses'.

7.2.3 Relative clauses (RCl)

RELATIVE CLAUSES function as postmodifiers in a noun phrase or prepositional phrase, and are thus only indirectly part of another clause (see 5.2.2, 7.5.2). Tensed relative clauses typically begin with a RELATIVE PRONOUN, so called because it relates the clause to the word, normally a noun or pronoun, which is the head of the NP:

(27)   [Do you know $_{NP}^{O}(_{pn}^{H}$ anyone $_{RCl}^{M}$[who can lend me a laptop])]?

(28)   [Do you have $_{NP}^{O}$(a $_{N}^{H}$ laptop $_{RCl}^{M}$[which you can lend me])]?

In (27) and (28) the arrow shows the relation between the relative pronoun and the head of the NP.

   Like noun clauses, relative clauses can be introduced by a *wh-* word, as in (27) and (28), or by *that*, or by zero. We may thus distinguish WH-RELATIVE CLAUSES, (27), (28), from *THAT* RELATIVE CLAUSES, (27a), (28a), and ZERO RELATIVE CLAUSES, (28b). The last two types are illustrated by:

(27a)   [Do you know (anyone [*that* can lend me a laptop])]?
(28a)   [Do you have (a *laptop* [*that* you can lend me])]?
(28b)   [Do you have (a *laptop* [you can lend me])]?

But the word *that* in (27a) and (28a) is different from the *that* which introduces noun clauses – as in examples (9) and (10). Here *that* is considered a relative pronoun, like *who* and *which* in (27) and (28), rather than a conjunction. To see this, notice that the words *who, which* and *that* in these sentences have a NP-like function of *S* or *O* in the RCl itself:

   ... $(_{pn}^{H}$ anyone $_{RCl}^{M}[^{S}$(***that/who***) ^{P}(can lend) ^{Oi}(me) ^{Od}(a laptop)])
   ... (a $_{N}^{H}$ laptop $_{RCl}^{M}[^{Od}$(***that/which***) ^{S}(you) ^{P}(can lend) ^{Oi}(me)]).

By the way, in standard English only in the second case can the pronoun be omitted: a zero relative clause cannot normally be formed by deleting a relative pronoun filling the S slot in the relative clause:

(27b)   *[Do you know (anyone [can lend me a laptop])]?

In addition to relative pronouns (*who, whom, which, whose, that*) there are relative adverbs (*where, when, that*), which also introduce relative clauses:

(29)   (the house [^{A}(*where*) ^{S}(I) ^{P}(spent) ^{O}(my childhood)])
(30)   (the year [^{A}(*when*) ^{S}(I) ^{P}(was born]).

Two other possibilities, for a RCl introduced by an adverbial, are a *that* RCl in which *that* functions as an adverb, and a zero RCl in which the relative adverb is omitted:

(30a)   (the year [^{A}(that) ^{S}(I) ^{P}(was born)]).

(30b)   (the year [^{S}(I) ^{P}(was born)])

Yet a further possibility is the use of a prepositional phrase in which the relative pronoun acts as head:

(30c)   (the year [$^A_{PP}$(in *which*) ^{S}(I) ^{P}(was born)])

(31)   (the children [$^A_{PP}$(with *whom*) ^{S}(I) ^{P}(used to play)]).

Even this does not exhaust the number of structural variations on sentences like (30). It is possible to leave the preposition 'stranded' (5.3.3) at the end of the clause, and to place the relative pronoun in its usual front position, or else to omit it:

(30d)   (the year [^{A}(that) ^{S}(I) ^{P}(was born) $_p$in])

(31a)   (the children [^{S}(I) ^{P}(used to play) $^A_p$with]).

(Now try Exercise 7b.)

7.2.4 Comparative clauses (CCl)

COMPARATIVE CLAUSES are like RCls in that they have a postmodifying function. Unlike RCls, however, they may postmodify not only nouns, but also adjectives and adverbs. The most common and most typical comparative clause is easy to recognize, because it follows a comparative form such as *more*, *less*, *bigger*, and is introduced by the conjunction *than*:

(32)   [In this country, we eat $^O_{NP}$(more food $^M_{CCl}$[$_{cj}$*than we can grow*])].

(33)   [He's $^C_{AjP}$(less noisy $^M_{CCl}$[$_{cj}$*than his sister was at that age*])].

(34)   [You must have been working $^A_{AvP}$(harder $^M_{CCl}$[$_{cj}$*than I thought*])].

(35)   [The job took me ^{A}(longer $^M_{CCl}$[*than it took Monica*])].

As we can see from (35), a CCl can be a full clause, with a structure like *S P O*; but more often it has one or more 'missing' elements. We will have more to say about these omissions in 8.3. Under this same heading of 'comparative clause' can be included a range of clauses of degree, introduced by such constructions as *as ... as, so ... as, so ... that*:

(36)   [She went ($_{Av}$as $_{Av}$quickly $_{CCl}$[$_{cj}$*as she could possibly run*])].

(37)   [Ben is not ($_{Av}$so $_{Aj}$stupid $_{CCl}$[$_{cj}$*as some people think*])].

(38)   [It was ($_{Av}$so $_{Aj}$hot $_{CCl}$[$_{cj}$*that the rails buckled*])].

7.2.5 Prepositional clauses (PCl)

PREPOSITIONAL CLAUSES, like prepositional phrases, begin with a preposition. Just as PPs are like NPs with an introductory preposition

(3.5.3, 5.3.3), so PCls are like NCls with an introductory preposition. In symbolic form, we may represent this parallel as follows: p + NP = PP; p + NCl = PCl. In tensed prepositional clauses the preposition is followed by a *wh-* element:

(39)   [The butler was astonished $_{PCl}^{A}$[at what he saw]].

(40)   [We have $_{NP}^{O}$(little ^{H}evidence $_{PCl}^{M}$[of who committed the murder])].

The function of a PCl, as these examples illustrate, is the same as that of a PP: it can be either an adverbial, or a postmodifier.[6]

7.3 The functions of subordinate clauses

Table 7.2

Directly subordinate clauses (i e. clauses which are elements of clauses)			
Noun clauses (see 7.2.1)	function as	S, O, C	Compare: NP
Adverbial clauses (see 7.2.2)	function as	A	Compare: AvP
Prepositional clauses (see 7.2.5)	function as	A	Compare: PP

Indirectly subordinate clauses (i.e clauses which are elements of phrases)			
Relative clauses (7.2.3)	function as	M in NP	Compare: Aj, PP
Comparative clauses (7.2.4)	function as	M in NP, AjP or AvP	Compare: Av, PP
Prepositional clauses (7.2.5)	function as	M in NP, AjP or AvP	Compare: PP

Table 7.2 gives a summary of the functions of the subordinate clauses illustrated in 7.2.1–7.2.5. On the right of this table, we have listed the elements which are closest in their function to the clause classes listed on the left. In the middle of the table are given the most common functions of each class. We should mention, in conclusion, that there are some less common functions of subordinate clauses which have not been illustrated. Consider this example:

(41)   [$_{NP}^{S}$(The report $_{NCl}^{M}$[that elephants were stampeding on the South Downs]) ^{P}(proved) ^{C}(totally incorrect)].

After certain nouns such as *report* in (41) we can have a NCl, as well as a RCl, as postmodifier in an NP. The *that* clause in (41) can be mistaken for a RCl, but one way to distinguish it from a RCl is to note that in it *that* does not have the function of a relative pronoun: *that* cannot, for instance, be replaced by *which*: *the report [which elephants ...] The following sentence, in fact, is ambiguous between the two interpretations:

(42)   [He received (the message [*that* she had left him])].

If [*that she had left him*] in (42) is a relative clause, the NP means 'a message *which* she had left him'; but if it is a NCl, the meaning is: 'a message *to the effect that* she had left him'.

A further type of NCl function, postmodifier in an adjective phrase, is illustrated in (43):

(43) [^{S}(I) ^{P}(am) ^{C}(afraid $_{NCl}^M$[that the Yorkshire pudding has collapsed])].

And the same function may be filled by a PCl:

(44) [^{S}(Our team) ^{P}(is) ^{C}(ready $_{PCl}^M$[for whatever our opponents may do])].

7.4 Tenseless subordinate clauses

In the last chapter (6.8) we introduced tenseless clauses, and divided them into three types according to the form of the predicator: **infinitive clauses** (labelled Cli), ***ing*-clauses** (labelled Cling), and ***en*-clauses** (labelled Clen). We now show how these types combine with the classes of subordinate clauses given in 7.2.1–7.2.5. For example, an ***ing*-clause** can be further classified as an NCl, as an ACl, as an RCl, as a CCl, or as a PCl. We can easily combine the labels for these subclasses to make composite labels, e.g:

- NCling means '*ing*-noun clause', in other words, a noun clause (one that behaves like a noun phrase) with an –ing verb as its first or only verb, e.g. *Playing golf is her favourite activity*.
- AClen means '*en*-adverbial clause', in other words an adverbial clause (one that fills an adverbial slot in the main clause) with an -en verb as its only verb, e.g. *Accused of dishonesty by the media, the minister decided to resign*.

In looking at the following list of examples, remember that, usually, tenseless clauses do not have a subject.

7.4.1 Tenseless noun clauses

1. INFINITIVE NOUN CLAUSE (NCli):

    (45) [They advised him $_{NCli}^{Od}$[^{P}(to resign) ^{O}(his job) ^{A}(immediately)]].
    (46) [I want $_{NCli}^{Od}$[^{S}(all of you) ^{P}(to listen) ^{A}(carefully)]].

2. *ING*-NOUN CLAUSE (NCling):

    (47) [$_{NCling}^S$[^{P}(Seeing) ^{O}(a ghost) ^{A}(in your bedroom)] is a serious matter].
    (48) [We saw $_{NCling}^O$[^{S}(them) ^{P}(being threatened) ^{A}(by the gang)]].

7.4.2 Tenseless adverbial clauses

1. INFINITIVE ADVERBIAL CLAUSE (ACli):

    (49) [People work overtime $_{ACli}^A$[{$_{cj}$in order} ^{P}(to earn) ^{O}(extra money)]].
    (50) [$_{ACli}^A$[^{P}(To make) ^{O}(the film)], we applied for some money from the lottery].

We can often insert the conjunction *in order* before the infinitive in an ACli. This is a clue that the clause's meaning is that of an adverbial of purpose. Thus to make the meaning clearer, we could begin (50) with the words: *In order to make the film, ...*

2. *ING*-ADVERBIAL CLAUSE (ACling):

(51) [$_{ACling}^{A}$[Not ^{P}(knowing) ^{O}(the enemy's intentions)], Flavius took evasive action].

(52) [The committee adjourned at 9 p.m., $_{ACling}^{A}$[^{S}(all further business) ^{P}(being postponed) ^{A}(until the next meeting)]].

Example (52) shows an ing-clause with a subject, *all further business*.

3. *EN*-ADVERBIAL CLAUSE (AClen):

(53) [$_{AClen}^{A}$[^{A}(Heavily) ^{P}(disguised) ^{A}(as human beings)], they frequented the quayside bars].

(54) [The criminal, $_{AClen}$[^{S}(his head) ^{P}(covered)], was hustled from the courtroom].

As in these examples, tenseless adverbial clauses generally describe some circumstance that elaborates on the event in the main clause.

7.4.3 Tenseless relative clauses

1. INFINITIVE RELATIVE CLAUSE (RCli):

(55) [This is $_{NP}$(the best car $_{RCli}^{M}$[$_{cj}$for ^{S}(you) ^{P}(to buy)])]

(56) [We need $_{NP}$(some tools $_{RCli}^{M}$[^{A}(with which) ^{P}(to do) ^{O}(the job) ^{A}(properly)])].

Like relative clauses in general, tenseless relative clauses give some additional information about the noun (or pronoun) preceding it. For example, (56) gives us some idea about the purpose of the tools. Notice, also, that (56) contains a relative pronoun, *which*, although most instances of RCli do not. It would be possible to replace the clause in (56) by a tensed relative clause: *some tools [with which one can do the job properly]*.

2. *ING*-RELATIVE CLAUSE (RCling):

(57) [We talked $_{PP}$(to the peasants $_{RCling}^{M}$[^{P}(working) ^{A}(in the rice-fields)])].

Here again, we can see how the tenseless RCling is equivalent in meaning to a tensed RCl: *We talked to the peasants **who were working in the rice-fields**.*

3. *EN*-RELATIVE CLAUSE (RClen):

(58) [$_{NP}$(The information $_{RClen}^{M}$[^{P}(given) ^{Oi}(us) ^{A}(at the post office)]) was not reliable].

7.4.4 Tenseless comparative clauses

These are less common: only the infinitive clauses (CCli) and the *ing*-clauses (CCling) are illustrated here.

(59)   [She is (more likely to act $_{CCli}^{M}$[*than to think*])].
(60)   [He is (better at sleeping $_{CCling}^{M}$[*than doing a job*])].

7.4.5 Tenseless prepositional clauses

The *ing*-clause (PCling) occurs in this category:

(61)   They escaped $_{PCling}^{A}$[$_{P}$by ^{P}(climbing) ^{A}(through a window)].

(Now try Exercise 7c.)

7.5 Direct and indirect subordination

When we introduced the rank scale of grammatical units (3.2) we assumed that the elements of a unit are always units of the next lower rank: for example, that clauses are composed directly of phrases. But we have now seen that this need not be so: a unit can be an element (a) of another unit of the same rank (e.g. an adverbial clause as an element of another clause), or (b) of another unit of lower rank (e.g. a relative clause as an element of a noun phrase). Subordination of type (a) may be called DIRECT SUBORDINA-TION, and subordination of type (b) INDIRECT SUBORDINATION.[7] We summarise these types, together with the kind of bracketing associated with them, in Figure 7.3.

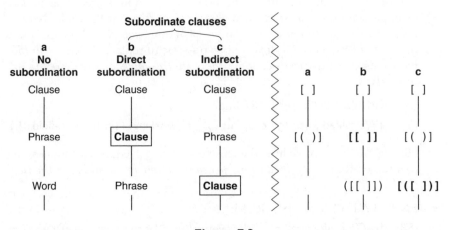

Figure 7.3

7.5.1 Direct subordination

There follows here a summary of the various types of subordination, the most important of which we have already dealt with (see Figure 7.3).

Clause-within-clause [[Cl]] : e.g. NCl as *O*; ACl as *A*.
Phrase-within-phrase ((Ph)): e.g. PP as *M* in an NP.
Word-within-word: e.g. *teapot, goldfish, rock-hard, fast-talking*. In COMPOUND WORDS, like these, one word (e.g. the noun *tea* or the adjective *hard*) occurs as part of another word (e.g. *teapot*). (See 2.4.1.)

7.5.2 Indirect subordination

The only type of indirect subordination worth noticing here is:

Clause-within-phrase ([Cl]): e.g. RCl as *M* in an NP or a PP.

It is generally agreed that the principle of subordination (also called embedding) is essential to grammar, but there is disagreement on how exactly subordination is to be applied to particular constructions. It is common, for example, to regard a PP as a phrase containing a preposition followed by a subordinate noun phrase, as in 1:

1. $^{PP}(_p$in $_{NP}$(the house))
2. $^{PP}(_p$in the house).

But we have preferred the simpler analysis 2. Although 1 is the better analysis from some points of view, it tends to make the PP appear more complex than it actually is. Similarly, it is possible to regard a genitive phrase as an NP subordinated within a word (a determiner) but, again, we have preferred an analysis which involves less subordination.

Whatever solutions one chooses to particular problems, an important point is that subordination can be repeated so as to make a sentence as complicated as we need to express complicated ideas:

(62) $_{NP}(_{GP}(_{GP}(_{GP}(_{GP}$(Cholmondeley's) wife's) father's) oldest friend's) farm).

In theory, there is no end to the possibilities of subordination within subordination – a fact which recalls the couplet:

Great fleas have little fleas upon their backs to bite 'em.
And little fleas have lesser fleas, and so *ad infinitum*.

7.6 Skeleton analysis

The complexity that subordination can introduce into sentences makes it useful to have a simplified notation for showing the layers and units of structure. This will be called SKELETON ANALYSIS. Tree diagrams, although they show structure clearly, tend to be bulky. Figure 7.4 shows this, yet it is not a tree diagram for a whole sentence but only for a single phrase.

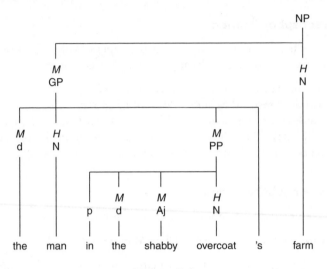

Figure 7.4

So it is convenient to summarise a structure like that shown in Figure 7.4 using bracketing, simply using the round brackets for what we may call SKELETON PHRASE ANALYSIS. This is what we have been doing so far, but, for simplicity, skeleton analysis can omit the form and function labels. For example, (63a) shows the same NP as Figure 7.4:

(63a)   ((the man (in the shabby overcoat)'s) farm)

Another version of skeleton analysis omits the words of the text, and uses only function labels:

(63b)   ((M H (p M M H)'s) H)

A further example of skeleton phrase analysis is the following analysis of the phrase *my uncle's farm in the north of Scotland*:

(64a)   ((my uncle's) farm (in the north (of Scotland)))

(64b)   (M H's) H (p M H (p H))

The point is that we can use just the kind of detail that is useful for our own purpose: we may wish to show just the words with phrases boundaries (64a), or to indicate the structure (64b) without the words.

7.6.1 Skeleton clause analysis

In a similar way we can use skeleton clause analysis to show the structure of a sentence in terms of main and subordinate clauses, using square brackets. These parses may show unnecessary detail:

(65)   [^{S}[$_{cj}$That ^{S}(I) ^{P}(could find) ^{O}(myself) ^{A}(in jail)] ^{P}(didn't bother) ^{O}(me)].

(66)   [^{S}(He) ^{P}(knew) ^{A}(very well) ^{O}[$_{cj}$that ^{S}(Tiger) ^{P}(had birdied) ^{O}(two holes)]].

We can simplify by omitting all the detail except for the square brackets, showing clauses:

(65a) [[That I could find myself in jail] didn't bother me].
(65b) [[That *S P O A*] *P O*]
(66a) [He knew very well [that Tiger had birdied two holes]].
(66b) [*S P A* [that *S P O*]]

But skeleton analysis is most useful when we are analysing more complex sentences containing a number of subordinate clauses:

(67) [Politicians always like [to think [that [what they want] is [what the country needs]]]].

In skeleton clause analysis, to represent INDIRECT subordination, we need to mark not only the [ ] (clauses) but the ( ) (boundaries of any phrase which contains a clause), so that we can see at a glance how that clause fits into the rest of the sentence. Suppose we are analysing a sentence containing a relative clause. The noun phrase containing the RCl as a modifier is signalled by ( ):

(68) [A miser is (a person [who never pays a gas-bill [unless threatened with prosecution]])].

Similarly with comparative clauses, the phrase containing the CCl (again an NP) is again signalled by ( ):

(69) [[Winning the lottery] gives people (more money [than they know [what to do with]])].

Any skeleton analysis is a way of saying, 'I am taking this short cut to save writing out structures which are in any case irrelevant to my purpose.' If you need to analyse the sentence structures in a whole paragraph or text, it can be helpful to use this short cut! (Now try Exercise 7d.)

7.7 Coordination

COORDINATION, like subordination, is a way of making a sentence as complex as we like. Through coordination (typically signalled by the conjunctions *and*, *or* or *but*), clauses, phrases or words (or indeed parts of these) can be conjoined to form a more complex construction which is, nevertheless, of the same rank and kind. In Figure 7.1 we showed how this worked in the case of coordinate main clauses. Here are examples of the coordination of subordinate clauses (Figure 7.5), the coordination of phrases – actually NPs (Figure 7.6) and the coordination of words – actually adjectives (Figure 7.7).

The usual idea for coordination, as we see here, is that the whole coordinate construction fills a single slot in the structure of which it is a part. However, the structure of the coordination itself has more than one unit of the next layer down. For example, in Figure 7.6 a single object slot is filled by two NPs, linked by a coordinator.

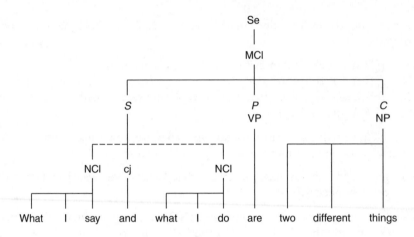

Figure 7.5

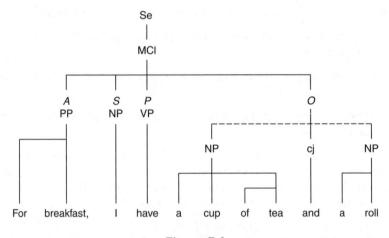

Figure 7.6

Again, however, it is convenient to save space and effort by using skeleton analysis for most purposes. In skeleton analysis and in labelled bracketing, we use ⟨ ⟩ (ANGLE BRACKETS) to enclose the two or more elements, or the COORDINATES, as we will call them, of a coordinate construction. Examples (70)–(72) repeat the structures of Figures 7.5, 7.6 and 7.7:

(70) [^{S}⟨$_{NCl}$[What I say] $_{cj}$and $_{NCl}$[what I do]⟩ ^{P}(are) ^{C}(two different things)].

(71) [For breakfast, I have ^{O}⟨$_{NP}$(a cup of tea) $_{cj}$and $_{NP}$(a roll)⟩].

(72) [She painted ^{O}(a ^{M}⟨$_{Aj}$large $_{cj}$and $_{Aj}$ugly⟩ ^{H}portrait)].

In skeleton analyses using function labels, it is convenient to use the '+' sign to indicate the coordinating conjunction:

(73) ⟨[Paul is a grouch], but [I rather like him]⟩.   ⟨[S P C] + [S A P O]⟩

(74) [You can pay ⟨(by credit card) or (in cash)⟩].   [S P ⟨(p M H) + (p H)⟩]

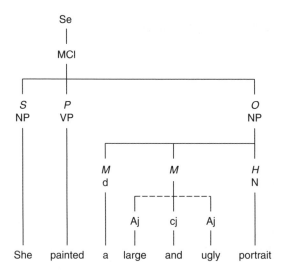

Figure 7.7

There can be ambiguity as to what is being coordinated; for example, *He was wearing old shoes and trousers* may or may not imply that the trousers are old. The two analyses are:

1. ⟨(old shoes) and (trousers)⟩
   (two coordinated NPs)

2. (old ^{H}⟨shoes $_{cj}$and trousers⟩).
   (one NP containing two coordinated nouns).

7.7.1 Omitting conjunctions

There may be more than two members of a coordinate construction:

(75) The primary colours are ⟨red and yellow and green and blue and black and white⟩.

But in such cases it is usual for the conjunction to be used only once, before the last coordinate, as in (76).

(76) Eggs can be ⟨boiled, fried, poached, or scrambled⟩.

Also, conjunctions can be omitted altogether. This can be called UNLINKED COORDINATION:

(77) Eggs can be ⟨boiled, fried, poached, scrambled⟩.
(78) ⟨You're not a man, you're a mouse⟩.

To represent unlinked coordination in a structural skeleton analysis, we can use a comma between the coordinates: (78) is analysed: ⟨[*S P* not *C*], [*S P C*]⟩.

7.8 Summary and conclusion

In this chapter we have introduced the following classes of subordinate clauses:

> noun clause (NCl); adverbial clause (ACl); relative clause (RCl);
> comparative clause (CCl); prepositional clause (PCl).

The abbreviations for these can be combined with the abbreviations for tenseless clauses (Cli, Cling, Clen) already introduced in 6.8, to form labels such as: NCling (*ing*-noun clause); ACli (**infinitive adverbial clause**); RClen (*en*-relative clause).

The ⟨ ⟩ (angle brackets) are used to enclose coordinate constructions, whether the coordinates (members) are clauses, phrases, words, etc.

We have introduced a method of analysis, **skeleton analysis**, which can be used to summarise a structure which it would be tedious to analyse in full. Skeleton analysis makes use of: ( ) for phrase boundaries, [ ] for clause boundaries and ⟨ ⟩ for boundaries of coordination. Labelling is not used, except where a separate summary of the structure in terms of function labels (*S, P, M, H*, etc.) is found useful.

The most 'skeletal' analysis is skeleton clause analysis, which is limited to the use of clause boundaries, shown as [ ], except where ( ) are used to show phrases which have a clause as a constituent, as in indirect subordination.

We now have the means to analyse the most complex sentences, and it will be fitting to end this chapter with an example of parsing (of a sentence from P. G. Wodehouse, *The Code of the Woosters*) which involves a variety of structures, including both subordination and coordination of clauses. First, here is the sentence in its original printed form:

> She laughed – a bit louder than I could have wished in my frail state of health, but then she is always a woman who tends to bring plaster falling from the ceiling when amused.

Now here is a version with full labelled bracketing. (Notice that we analyse *a bit* as a degree adverb, i.e. as a single word. Other analyses would be possible.):

$$\langle \,_{MCl}[\,_{NP}^{S}(\,_{pn}^{H}She)\ _{VP}^{P}(\,_{V}^{Mv}laughed) - \,_{AvP}^{A}(\,_{Av}^{M}a\ bit\ \,_{Av}^{H}louder\ \,_{CCl}^{M}[\,_{cj}than\ \,_{NP}^{S}(\,_{pn}^{H}I)\ \,_{VP}^{P}(\,_{v}^{Aux}could$$

$$\,_{v}^{Aux}have\ \,_{V}^{Mv}wished)\ \,_{PP}^{A}(\,_{p}in\ \,_{d}^{M}my\ \,_{Aj}^{M}frail\ \,_{N}^{H}state\ \,_{PP}^{M}(\,_{p}of\ \,_{N}^{H}health))])]\ _{cj}but\ _{MCl}[\,_{AvP}^{A}(\,_{Av}^{H}then)$$

$$\,_{NP}^{S}(\,_{pn}^{H}she)\ _{VP}^{P}(\,_{v}^{Mv}is)\ \,_{AvP}^{A}(\,_{Av}^{H}always)\ \,_{NP}^{C}(\,_{d}^{M}a\ \,_{N}^{H}woman\ \,_{RCl}^{M}[\,_{NP}^{S}(\,_{pn}^{H}who)\ _{VP}^{P}(\,_{V}^{Mv}tends)\ \,_{Cli}^{O}[\,_{VP}^{P}(to$$

$$\,_{V}^{Mv}bring)\ \,_{NP}^{O}(\,_{N}^{H}plaster)\ \,_{Cling}^{C}[\,_{VP}(\,_{V}^{Mv}falling)\ \,_{PP}^{A}(\,_{p}from\ \,_{d}^{M}the\ \,_{N}^{H}ceiling)]]]\ \,_{Clen}^{A}[\,_{cj}when$$

$$\,_{VP}^{P}(\,_{Ven}^{Mv}amused)]]\rangle\rangle$$

Everyone who follows our parsing method carefully should be able to achieve this analysis, but admittedly the impression it makes is frightening, even to the keenest grammarian! Hence skeleton analysis is a welcome alternative, when we are trying to summarise the syntactic patterns in texts. Here is a skeleton clause analysis of this example:

⟨[She laughed – (a bit louder [than I could have wished in my frail state of health])] but [then she is always (a woman [who tends [to bring plaster [falling from the ceiling]]] [when amused])]⟩

(Now try Exercise 7e.)

───────────── **EXERCISES** ─────────────

Exercise 7a (answers on pp. 219–20)
(i) Draw **full** tree diagrams (complete with form and function labels) of sentences (5) and (7) on pp. 105 and 106. (ii) Once you have done this, simplify the diagram by omitting phrase labels (both form and function). This is what we have called an **abbreviated** tree diagram (see 3.3.2).

Exercise 7b (answers on p. 220)
Each of the following sentences contains one subordinate clause (SCl). For each SCl:

(i)   What is its structure in terms of cj, S, P, O, C, A?
(ii) Is it a noun clause (NCl), an adverbial clause (ACl) or a relative clause (RCl)?
(iii) If it is an ACl, what is its meaning as time, condition, contrast, etc.?

1. [When the cat's away] the mice will play.
2. She stood near the door, [so that Prem would see her].
3. I've forgotten [what that little crooked-legged mule's name was].
4. The person [who gave us this present] was my great uncle Cedric.
5. Steinhacker had a large room [in which he kept gigantic frogs for his experiments].
6. [Why you bought that elephant gun] I cannot imagine.
7. [Although Paul is sometimes a grouch], I rather like him.
8. They tell me [he eats voraciously].
9. The magazine [she edits] is published every month.

Exercise 7c (answers on p. 220)
Identify the tenseless clauses bracketed in the following sentences as Cli, Cling or Clen, and say what function they have (e.g. S, O, A, M):

1. He regretted [making the comment about her paintings].
2. I am very sorry [to have caused you offence].
3. [For Max to pay his gas-bill on time] would be very surprising.
4. But I never heard [a shot fired in anger] until last night.
5. [Being at the top of the class], I sat directly underneath Mr Jackson's beaky nose.
6. I have several important things [to say to her].
7. [Duncan having retired for the night], Lady Macbeth put her sinister plan into effect.
8. [Judged by the standards of everyday life], university people seem oddballs.

Exercise 7d (answers on pp. 220–1)

The following sentences are grammatically ambiguous. Show the ambiguities by giving two different skeleton analyses for each sentence. In each case, add a comment to explain how the ambiguity arises.

1. I regret criticizing her bitterly.
2. I clearly remembered the time when I looked at my watch.
3. I told him that I had written the essay before he gave the lecture.
4. To speak the truth frankly is an unsafe policy.

For the following, three different skeleton analyses can be given:

5. The combatants agreed to sign a peace treaty in Geneva last week.
6. We must ask the farmer who owns the fields where we can camp.
7. I found the dog smoking a cigar.

Exercise 7e (answers on pp. 221–2)

Here are some further ambiguities, this time involving coordination. Again, distinguish the different interpretations of the same sentence by different skeleton analyses, using ⟨ ⟩ (angle brackets) to enclose coordinate structures.

1. We enjoyed an afternoon of honeyed scones and poetry.
2. Their officers always sport scarlet berets and moustaches.
3. She has passed her exams in French, German and English literature.
4. The manuscript is very old and difficult to read.
5. That evening we stayed indoors, reading and writing letters.
6. I was taught by the man who taught Mabel and the woman who taught you and Fred.
7. The neighbourhood is infested with stray cats and dogs of questionable parentage.
8. Mountjoy was a great lover and ardent student of language and literature.

Basic and Derived Structures

Chapters 3 to 7 have outlined a method of parsing English sentences. In this final chapter of Part B, we concentrate on some difficulties you are likely to meet when you apply this method to sentences you meet in texts. As we do this, we will sketch in an extra dimension to the study of grammar: that is, the study of what we may call BASIC and DERIVED structures. This will enable us to deal with a range of grammatical patterns which do not fit neatly into the view of grammar so far presented. But first, let's take stock of what has been done up to now.

8.1 Constituent structure grammar

In Chapter 3 (p. 33) we defined grammar, roughly, as a set of 'rules for constructing and for analysing sentences'. So far, we have been primarily interested in 'analysing' – taking a sentence to pieces – rather than 'constructing'. Essentially, we have been aiming at a parsing of sentences, and have been mainly concerned with the kinds of rules which enable us to identify the constituents of sentences, and their structures. For example:

- 'The structure of an NP is {*M**}*H* {*M**}' (specifying the structure of a class of constituent).
- 'An *O* can be an NP or an NCl' (saying what classes of constituent can fill a given functional slot).
- 'A subordinate clause can be either tensed or tenseless' (specifying the subclasses of a constituent).

These rules can be used in analysis, but if they were formulated precisely enough, they could also be used for **constructing** or **generating** grammatical sentences by rule. For example, we could use such rules to construct a sentence like *The question may arise*. But we could not use them to construct sentences such as:

(1) *The ask may arise.

(2) *The question arise may.

Why not? Because each of these sentences violates one of the rules of English grammar. In (1) *ask* is a V, not a N, and cannot therefore be used as head of a noun phrase. In (2) *may* is a modal auxiliary, and like all auxiliaries, can only occur **before** the main verb, not after it. Thus the rules that have been presented in a rather passive sense, as a means of analysis, can also be thought of in a more active, productive sense, as a MODEL of the English speaker's knowledge of grammar, whether it is used to analyse sentences, to produce sentences, or to judge whether sentences are grammatical or not.

The model we have presented can be called a CONSTITUENT STRUCTURE model of grammar, and it works pretty well. But there are some aspects of English grammar which it fails to explain. Some of them have been glimpsed already. Our response to them is not to throw away the whole model, but rather to see how the model can be improved or extended to cope with them. The tree diagrams of constituent structure grammar provide a two-dimensional view, and what we aim to do now is to make that grammar three-dimensional, by introducing the notion of BASIC and DERIVED structures. For this, we call on a further kind of grammatical rule, called a STRUCTURE-CHANGING RULE.[8] This is the kind of rule which relates two different constituent structures with essentially the same meaning. (Now try Exercise 8a.)

8.2 Basic and derived structures

It is often said that English has a fairly fixed word order, but that exceptional orders are allowed. Actually, when people discuss English word order, they almost invariably refer to what would be more correctly called 'phrase order' – the order of elements in the clause (the order of words in phrases being more or less fixed). We have already assumed a neutral, basic order of clause elements – *S, P, O, C, A* – which applies to normal declarative clauses. We have already implied, though, that some other clause types – e.g. questions, relative clauses – can be explained as systematic deviations from this expected order. Here are some more examples:

(3)	[(I) (adore) (cocktails)].	BASIC ORDER	*S P O*
(3a)	[(Cocktails) (I) (adore)].	DERIVED ORDER	*O S P*
(4)	[(He) (looks) (a weirdo)].	BASIC ORDER	*S P C*
(4a)	[(What a weirdo) (he) (looks)].	DERIVED ORDER	*C S P*
(5)	[(The rain) (came) (down)].	BASIC ORDER	*S P A*
(5a)	[(Down) (came) (the rain)].	DERIVED ORDER	*A P S*
(5b)	[(Down) (it) (came)].	DERIVED ORDER	*A S P*

We can now compose rough-and-ready rules to explain such variations of order (see Table 8.1). These rules can be called 'structure-changing' because they change one clause structure into another. The advantage of such rules is that they allow us to keep the idea of a 'basic' or 'neutral' ordering – an ordering that will be used unless there is some reason for doing otherwise – and at the same time account for acceptable departures from this order. We

Table 8.1

Rule	Basic structure	becomes	derived structure	under these conditions
Rule 1 'fronting'	S P O/C/A	⟶	O/C/A S P†	(a) in MCls, to give emphasis (b) when the shifted element is a *wh*- element like *what, which,* etc.
Rule 2 'S–P inversion'	A S P	⟶	A P S	In MCls, where A is an adverbial of place, where S is not a pronoun (cf. (5b)) and where P contains a *Mv* of position or motion

† *O/C/A* means 'either O or C or A'.

have already adopted such an approach, for example, in explaining questions (in 6.4.1) and relative clauses (in 7.2.3). Since constituent structure can be displayed in a two-dimensional tree diagram, Figure 8.1 shows how structure-changing gives an extra, third dimension to grammar. This diagram shows the relation between (3) and (3a) by means of the 'fronting' rule – **Rule 1**.

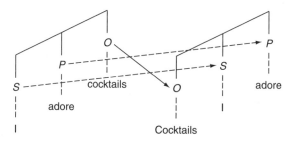

Figure 8.1

Structure-changing is either OPTIONAL or OBLIGATORY. Rule 1(a) is optional because either order is grammatical:

(6)* [^{S}(They) ^{P}(call) ^{O}(me) ^{C}(the Texas Ranger)].

(6a) [^{C}(The Texas Ranger) ^{S}(they) ^{P}(call) ^{O}(me)].

Rule 1(b), on the other hand, is obligatory, because only the derived order is possible:

(7) *I can't see [^{S}(I) ^{P}(am doing) ^{O}(what)].

(7a) I can't see [^{O}(what) ^{S}(I) ^{P}(am doing)].

In such cases we obviously cannot say that the basic order is the more likely one, yet in the context of English as a whole, the **S P O** order is usual.

Another way of expressing the same thing is to say that the **S P O/C/A** order is the **unmarked** order – i.e. the neutral or 'default' order that is used when there is no reason to use some other order – whereas the **O/C/A S P** order is marked. The derived, or marked, form is often, but not necessarily, the less frequent one, and the one which is stylistically more noticeable.

8.3 'Missing' elements

8.3.1 Omission of relative pronouns

Another phenomenon of grammar that we have encountered, and which the constituent structure model does not explain, is the existence of 'ghost' elements which do not occur in a given sentence, but are nevertheless 'understood' as part of the meaning of that sentence:

(8)   The stories [(which) (he) (invented)] were incredible.   [O S P]

(8a) The stories [(he) (invented)] were incredible.   [S P]

In accordance with Rule 1(b), the relative clause in (8) has its object (the relative pronoun *which*) in front position. But in (8a), which is like (8) in all other respects, this object is omitted. We would like to say, all the same, that the object in a sense 'is there' in (8a), because *invent* is a verb which cannot normally occur without an object: **He invented* is ungrammatical. But how can we say that the pronoun 'is not there' on the one hand, and 'is there' on the other? A way to make sense of this riddle is to treat (8a) as a derived structure, and to say that a rule of RELATIVE PRONOUN OMISSION converts (8) into (8a):

   Rule 3: 'A relative pronoun preceding the subject can be omitted.'[9]

8.3.2 Omission in comparative clauses

Like relative clauses, comparative clauses can be lacking in one or more of their elements:

(9)   [Bill is taller [$_{cj}$than ^{S}(he) ^{P}(seems)]].

The verb *seems* normally needs a complement: **[^{S}(He) ^{P}(seems)]* is incomplete, unless it is extended into something like [^{S}(He) ^{P}(seems) ^{C}(tall)]. So something must be missing after *seems*. But unlike the relative clause case, there is no option in the comparative clause whereby the 'missing' element actually occurs:

(9a) *[Bill is taller [than he seems tall]].

So this is an example where the omission is obligatory. But other omissions in the comparative clause are optional:

(10)   [Ann can knit mittens faster [than Pam can knit mittens]].   [cj S P O]

(10a) [Ann can knit mittens faster [than Pam can].   [cj S Aux]

(10b) [Ann can knit mittens faster (than Pam)].   (PP)

In (10b) so much of the basic structure of the clause has been omitted that what remains is merely a prepositional phrase (*than* behaves here like a preposition, rather than a conjunction). So omission can actually affect the rank of a constituent. In (10a) the auxiliary remains, but the rest of the clause is missing. This illustrates ELLIPSIS (see 13.4), the type of omission which helps us reduce grammatical complexity by avoiding repetition of words and structures used or understood elsewhere in the context. The construction of (10a) is derived rather than basic because, contrary to basic constituent structure rules, an *Aux* ('helping verb') here occurs without its *Mv*.

8.3.3 Omission in coordinate constructions

We have already seen how coordination of words and phrases often implies ellipsis:

(11)   [((Nena and *her sister*)) (are) (still) (at school)].

This has a meaning which can be spelled out as:

(11a)   ⟨[(*Nena*) (is) (still) (at school)] and [(*her sister*) (is) (still) (at school)]⟩.

Here again the notions of basic and derived structure are helpful. A sentence containing two coordinated phrases (here NPs) can be seen as deriving from a sentence with two coordinated clauses. The same is true of coordinated words:

(12)   [(The butler) (was ⟨*amazed* and *delighted*⟩) (by what he saw)].

means the same as:

(12a)   ⟨[(The butler) (was *amazed*) (by what he saw)] and [(the butler) (was *delighted*) (by what he saw)]⟩.

Notice that coordination, like ellipsis, is often a means of simplifying structure. We can easily think of (11) and (12) as being derived, by ellipsis, from the more complex sentences (11a) and (12a). But there is no difficulty in parsing them as they stand, once we allow coordinated words and phrases like ⟨*Nena and her sister*⟩. Less straightforward, though, are types of coordination where the coordinate parts are not whole constituents. For instance:

(13)   [(She) ⟨(got) (out of bed) and (went) (to the phone)⟩].

Here the elements coordinated are whole clauses except for the subject: S ⟨ P A + P A⟩. Still more tricky is:

(14)   [I('ll ⟨phone) (the hotel) and order) (some lunch)⟩].

where the coordinate parts are not even composed of clause elements: S *Aux* ⟨*Mv O* + *Mv O*⟩.

Such examples as (13) and (14) exemplify BRANCHING COORDINATION, and Figure 8.2, in which the coordinate structures branch out of a shared part of the clause, shows why this is an appropriate name.

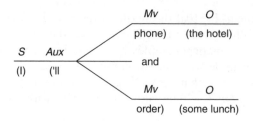

Figure 8.2

There is no easy way of deciding, in such cases, whether the sentence consists of one or two clauses. Perhaps it is most sensible to say that if the two coordinate parts have different main verbs, they are different clauses. On this basis, both (13) and (14) are complex sentences, each containing coordinate clauses.

These and the preceding examples can be explained by a rule of COORDINATION REDUCTION, very roughly as follows:

> **Rule 4**: 'Two or more coordinate clauses can be reduced in length by the omission of words and structures in one clause that are merely repetitions of what is in another clause.'

8.3.4 Tag questions

There are a number of conditions under which elliptical clauses such as [*than Pam can*] in (10a) occur. They occur, for example, in replies to questions:

(15)   Who would like some coffee?   [*I would*].   [S Aux]

Perhaps the most interesting type of elliptical clause is the TAG QUESTION – an interrogative clause, which is 'tagged' on to the end of a declarative clause, and which acts as a request for confirmation:

(16)   [We should go now], [*shouldn't we*]?   [Aux not S]?
(17)   [You aren't leaving], [*are you*]?   [Aux S]?

Such questions, which are common in conversation, are a rather eccentric feature of English. They change according to the form of the declarative clause, whereas similar tags in other languages (e.g. French *n'est-ce pas*, Italian *non è vero*, Japanese *ne*) are invariable. Tag questions are puzzling from the parsing point of view, not just because of their elliptical form, but because their relation with the preceding clause seems to fit the pattern of neither coordination nor subordination. Perhaps it is best, if a decision must be made, to treat these tags as cases of unlinked coordination (7.7.1):

(18)   MCl[You can drive], MCl[can't you]?
(19)   MCl[So he said that], MCl[did he]?

8.4 Split constituents

We have already met constituents which are split into two parts by an 'intrusive' element:

(20)   [^{S}(Jay) ^{P}(had ^{A}(certainly) taken) ^{O}(lessons on the role of Prince Charming)].

(21)   [^{P}(Could ^{S}(you) call) ^{O}(me) ^{A}(from the office)]?

Such discontinuities spoil the neatness of the constituent structure model, requiring tree diagrams with criss-crossing branches, as Figure 8.3 shows.

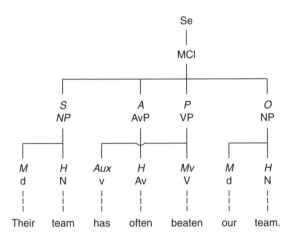

Figure 8.3

Once again, it helps to suppose that there is a simpler basic structure for these sentences, and that the splitting of phrases arises in derived structure. This is a reasonable view, since the language has clause structures in which these same elements can occur in a different order, without splitting:

(20a)   [^{A}(*Certainly*) ^{S}(Jay) ^{P}(had taken) ^{O}(lessons ...)].

(21a)   [^{S}(*You*) ^{P}(*could* call) ^{O}(me) ^{A}(from the office)].

So to account for (20) and (21), we can suggest (a) a rule which moves adverbials from final position to earlier positions in the clause, and (b) a rule which inverts the subject and tensed operator.

> Their team has beaten our team often ⟶ Their team has often beaten our team.
>
> You can't drive a car? ⟶ Can't you drive a car?

Here again, the point of introducing the notions of basic structure and derived structure is to enable us to make generalisations – i.e. to state rules – about aspects of English grammar which would otherwise seem puzzling. (Now try Exercises 8b and 8c.)

8.5 'Double analysis'

A final issue with a purely constituent structure model of grammar is that it sometimes leads to two conflicting analyses, neither of which is satisfactory on its own.

8.5.1 The passive reconsidered

A passive clause is a classic case of a structure which seems to require a double analysis:

(22)   [^{S}(Fido) ^{P}(bit) ^{O}(the cat-burglar) ^{A}(on the leg)].

(22a)   [^{S}(The cat-burglar) ^{P}(was bitten) ^{A}(on the leg) ^{A}(by Fido)].

The relation between these two sentences (and similar pairs) is obvious, and can be represented by a rule converting an active-type structure like (22) into a passive-type structure like (22a):

    Rule 5:   ('passive')
                  (optional)

Figure 8.4

In words, this means that the object of the active clause becomes the subject of the passive clause, and the subject of the active clause becomes the AGENT of the passive clause, i.e. the noun phrase introduced by the preposition *by*. Traditionally, *the cat-burglar* in (22a) has been called the 'grammatical' subject, but the 'logical' object of the clause. But how can an element be both S and O at the same time? In terms of a simple constituent structure model it cannot. But if we accept a distinction between basic and derived structure, it is perfectly reasonable to say that *the cat-burglar* is O in basic structure, but S in the passive derived structure. In this way, structure-changing rules allow us to have our cake and eat it: to say that two apparently incompatible analyses are both correct.

SPECIAL NOTE ON STRUCTURE-CHANGING TESTS

In 3.4 we introduced various tests (expansion, substitution, subtraction and movement) as ways of deciding the correct analysis of a sentence or part of it. We should now add to this list STRUCTURE-CHANGING TESTS, which use the ability to transform one structure into another as a basis for analysis. For example, an object (O) can be distinguished from other elements of clause structure partly by its ability to be changed into the subject of a corresponding passive clause. In (22), we can recognize *the cat-burglar* as an O because of its ability to act as the S of (22a).

8.5.2 Subject raising

Here is a slightly more complicated example of the same type. In English there is a common type of construction, called CATENATIVE ('chain-like'), where a sequence NP1 + VP1 + {NP2} + VP2 ... occurs. Here NP1 and NP2 are different noun phrases, and VP1 and VP2 are different verb phrases, VP2 being tenseless (see Table 8.2).

Table 8.2

	NP$_1$	VP$_1$	NP$_2$	VP$_2$	NP$_3$, etc.
(23)	Sir John	desired	his valet	to warm	his slippers.
(24)	I	'd like	you	to read	this letter.
(25)	They	required	him	to sedate	the gerbil.
(26)	Bob	considered	grammar	to be	a waste of time.
(27)	Vera	told	the chimp	to serve	the drinks.
(28)	Nobody	asked	you	to listen	to our talk.

Since there are two VPs, there must be two *P*s, and therefore two clauses – a tensed clause and a tenseless one. But the status of NP2 is unclear: is it an *O* in the main clause, or a *S* in the tenseless clause?

For (23) and (24), the better of these two analyses is to treat NP2 as the subject:

(23a) [^{S}(Sir John) ^{P}(desired) ^{O}[^{S}(his valet) ^{P}(to warm) ^{O}(his slippers)]].

The following arguments favour (23a):

1. The V in the main clause, *desire*, is the kind of verb which takes an *O* (e.g. John **desired** a bath).
2. We can change NP$_2$ + VP$_2$ + NP$_3$ into the passive without a change of meaning, thus suggesting that these three elements should be analysed as a clause, with the structure [*S P O*]:

    (23b) [Sir John *desired* [his slippers to be warmed by his valet]].

3. NP$_2$ + VP$_2$ + NP$_3$ is logically equivalent to a tensed NCl functioning as object:

    (23c) [Sir John desired [that his valet should warm his slippers]].

On the other hand, for (27) and (28) the best analysis seems to be different. It seems that NP$_2$ in this case belongs to the main clause, rather than the subordinate clause:

(27a) [^{S}(Vera) ^{P}(told) ^{Oi}(the chimp) ^{Od}[^{P}(to serve) ^{O}(the drinks)].

The arguments in favour of (27a) are:

4. The V in the main clause takes the pattern [*S P Oi Od*] (e.g. *They told me a story*), confirming NP$_2$ as an indirect object of the main clause.

5. NP$_2$ can become subject of a passive main clause, and so behaves like an O of the main clause:

    (27b) [The chimp was told [to serve the drinks] {by Vera}].

6. In this sentence, unlike (23), it is the VP$_2$ + NP$_3$ part that is logically equivalent to a tensed NCl:

    (27c) [Vera told the chimp [that he should serve the drinks]].

    BUT NOT:

    (27d) *[Vera told [that the chimp should serve the drinks]].

So we have found that clauses which appear on the surface to have the same kind of structure, like (23) and (27), actually require different analyses. The main difficulty comes, however, when we look at sentences like (25) and (26). For some purposes (e.g. for argument (3) above) they are like (23):

(26a) [Bob considered [that grammar is a waste of time]].

But for other purposes (e.g. argument (5)) they are like (27):

(26b) [Grammar was considered [to be a waste of time] {by Bob}].

Thus we have to entertain conflicting analyses of the same sentence:

(26c) [Bob considered [grammar to be a waste of time]].
(26d) [Bob considered grammar [to be a waste of time]].

This dilemma, like the one that arose with the subject of a passive clause, can be resolved if we allow both analyses to coexist, (26c) being the basic structure (the one which is appropriate 'logically speaking'), and (26d) the derived structure. To get from (26c) to (26d), we apply a rule which raises the subject of a subordinate clause and makes it the object of the main clause:

Rule 6: ('subject raising')

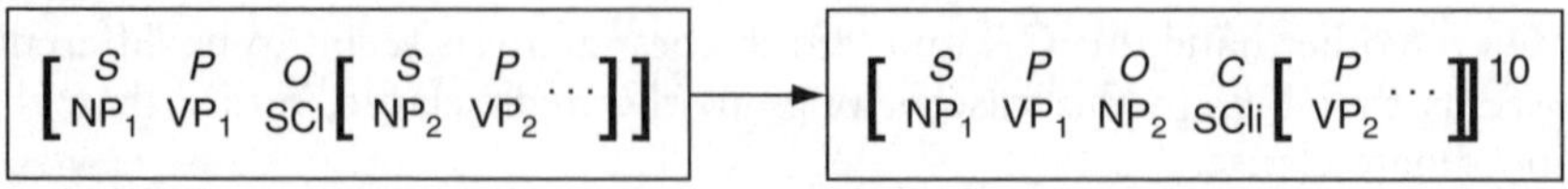

$$\left[\begin{smallmatrix} S \\ NP_1 \end{smallmatrix} \; \begin{smallmatrix} P \\ VP_1 \end{smallmatrix} \; \begin{smallmatrix} O \\ SCl \end{smallmatrix} \left[\begin{smallmatrix} S \\ NP_2 \end{smallmatrix} \; \begin{smallmatrix} P \\ VP_2 \end{smallmatrix} \cdots \right] \right] \longrightarrow \left[\begin{smallmatrix} S \\ NP_1 \end{smallmatrix} \; \begin{smallmatrix} P \\ VP_1 \end{smallmatrix} \; \begin{smallmatrix} O \\ NP_2 \end{smallmatrix} \; \begin{smallmatrix} C \\ SCli \end{smallmatrix} \left[\begin{smallmatrix} P \\ VP_2 \end{smallmatrix} \cdots \right] \right]^{10}$$

Figure 8.5

The term 'subject raising' clearly becomes appropriate when we look at (abbreviated) tree diagrams similar to (26c) and (26d). See what happens to NP$_2$ in Figure 8.6.

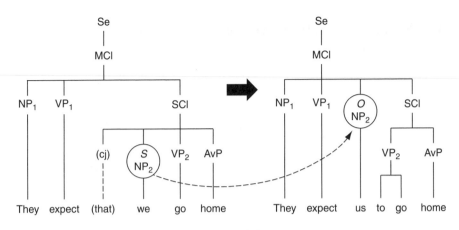

Figure 8.6

8.6 Back to parsing

Catenative constructions like (23)–(28) above are not easy to explain: they demonstrate more clearly than any of the examples so far the need for both basic and derived structures to be considered in the analysis of a sentence. But there is still a role for the 'two-dimensional' parsing of tree diagrams and labelled bracketing. It is very convenient to be able to break down sentences, or sequences of sentences in a text, into their visible or audible 'working parts'. And for this purpose, it is a parsing of the derived structure – the one that we 'see' on the page – that is required. We need a good method of analysing the sentence as it appears when written down, but this method must be rather more flexible than we allowed for in Chapters 3–7. We must even allow some improvisation in representing the structure of sentences. Consider these examples of derived clause structures:

(29)   [(You) (should (always) arrive) [before the boss does]].

(30)   [(Why) (must (you) (always) find) (something [to grumble about])]?

The main clause in (29) may be labelled [*S A P A*], showing the split predicator by the horizontal bracket. The subordinate clause may be analysed as [cj *S Aux*], in a way which mixes clause elements (*S*) with phrase elements (*Aux*) (cf. 8.3.3, 8.3.4), showing that ellipsis has deprived this clause of its main verb. In (30) the main clause has two 'intrusive' elements which split the predicator [*A S A P O*], and the subordinate clause has a stranded preposition: [to *P* p]. All these notations correctly render the structures of their clauses, even though none of them strictly conforms to the constituent structure model, whereby clauses consist of complete phrases and phrases consist of words.

8.7 Style and structure-changing rules

From the examples given, it will be clear that the structure-change from basic to derived structures leaves the content of a sentence largely unchanged. Hence many structure-changing rules – particularly those which move constituents around in the sentence – are primarily stylistic in function. That is, they serve the purpose of changing the way we say things – the way we package information for the reader – rather than what we have to say. For example, why should we prefer a passive sentence to an equivalent active one? The answer is suggested by the following, in which the final and communicatively most important elements (see 13.2.3) are italicized:

(31)   The heavy rains have destroyed *seventy houses.*

(31a) Seventy houses have been destroyed *by the heavy rains.*

(31b) Seventy houses have been *destroyed.*

One function of the passive, as in (31a), is to put the main emphasis on the 'basic subject' of the sentence – in this case, *the heavy rains* – by moving it towards the end. Notice, in this connection, the different emphasis of (31), where the main piece of information is that the rains have destroyed *seventy houses*, and (31a), where the main piece of information is that this was done by the *heavy rains*. (On the principle of 'end focus' operating here, see 13.2.3.) Another function of the passive, quite the opposite of this, is to allow the 'basic subject' to be omitted altogether, as in (31b), which lacks the optional agent phrase *by the heavy rains*. Although similar in structure and meaning, (31), (31a) and (31b) all have different communicative effects.

The last part of this chapter illustrates a number of other cases of stylistic structure-changing rules. In all of them the effect of the change of structure in general is either to move an element to the front of the sentence ('fronting'), or to move it towards the end ('postponement'). The function of postponement is generally to move the element to a position where it will attract attention as new information, whereas the effect of fronting an element is generally to stress its 'givenness' as the topic of the sentence – its connection with what has gone before in the text.

8.7.1 Clefts

It is often possible to form a number of different clefts (also called 'cleft sentences' or 'cleft clauses') from the same basic sentence:

(32)   John was wearing the pink socks last night.

(32a) It was *John* that was wearing the pink socks last night.

(32b) It was *the pink socks* that John was wearing last night.

(32c) It was *last night* that John was wearing the pink socks.

The following is a rough description of the rule for forming clefts:

1. Choose an element of the clause: it may be **S, O, C** *or* **A,** but not **P.**
2. Move that element (which we may call **X**) into the initial position, then prefix to it the 'dummy' subject *it*, and a form of the verb *to be* (e.g. *It is, It was*).
3. Introduce the rest of the clause by the relative pronoun *that* following **X.**

Thus in (32) the following structures are derived:

$$[S\ P\ O\ A] \longrightarrow \begin{cases} [\text{It be } S \text{ that } P\ O\ A] & \text{(32a)} \\ [\text{It be } O \text{ that } S\ P\ A] & \text{(32b)} \\ [\text{It be } A \text{ that } S\ P\ O] & \text{(32c)} \end{cases}$$

The **cleft** is so called because a single clause is 'cleft' or split into two separate clause-like parts. But these are better seen as forming a single clause with two predicators, rather than two separate clauses. Notice that the second part of a cleft (**that** *P O A* etc.) is similar to a relative clause. One sign of this is that we can replace the introductory word *that* by a relative pronoun such as *who*:

(32a)   It was John *who* was wearing pink socks last night.

8.7.2 Existential clauses

This type of clause is like the 'cleft' in that it begins with a special particle as subject, followed by the verb *to be*. The 'dummy' subject in this case is the EXISTENTIAL particle *there,* so called because it begins a clause postulating someone's or something's existence:

(33)   Nobody was around. ⟶ There was nobody around. ('Nobody existed in that area.')

(34)   A few people are getting promoted. ⟶ There are a few people getting promoted.

(35)   A whole box has been stolen. ⟶ There has been a whole box stolen.

The following is a rough approximation to the rule we can use for deriving existential sentences from a straightforward declarative clause:

[S be X] ⟶ [There be S X]

where **S** is a (normally indefinite) NP conveying new information, and **X** is anything which is added to complete the clause after the operator-verb *be*. Like other structure-changing rules so far mentioned, this one commonly has the function of postponing new information until the end ('end-focus').

8.7.3 Extraposition

This term is used for a construction in which a noun clause, usually one functioning as subject, is postponed to the end of the MCl, and is replaced in its basic position by the 'dummy' subject *it* (cf. 7.2.1):

(36) [[What you say to them] doesn't matter]. → [It doesn't matter [what you say to them]].

(37) [[That the dispute has been settled] is encouraging]. → [It is encouraging [that the dispute has been settled]].

(38) [[To move his arm] causes him considerable pain]. → [It causes him considerable pain [to move his arm]].

The clause is usually the most complex constituent, and extraposition postpones it in accordance with the principle of 'end-weight' which favours placing a heavy constituent at the end (see 13.2.3). So in this case it is the basic structure that is less common than the derived structure. The analysis of the changes in (36)–(38) is as follows:

(36) [S P] → [It P S]
    NCl   NCl

(37) [S P C] → [It P C S]
    NCl   NCl

(38) [S P Oi Od] → [It P Oi Od S]
    NCl   NCl

Three more types of stylistic structure-changing rules will be illustrated without much comment.

8.7.4 Fronting of subordinate clause object

It is convenient to take the extraposition construction of 8.7.3 as the basic structure for this example of fronting:

(39) It's a pleasure to teach her. → She's a pleasure to teach.

(40) It's difficult to play a saxophone. → A saxophone is difficult to play.

(41) It's fun to be with Margaret. → Margaret is fun to be with.

8.7.5 Substitution of PP for indirect object

(42) Tim sent Freda a telegram. → Tim sent a telegram to Freda.

(43) Moira knitted her mother a tea-cosy. → Moira knitted a tea-cosy for her mother.

(44) Bill is finding his brother a job. → Bill is finding a job for his brother.

8.7.6 Postponement of postmodifier

(45) The time to think of many things has come. → The time has come to think of many things.

(46)   A meeting of all the ratepayers was held. ⟶ A meeting was held of all the ratepayers.

(47)   I have less time than I used to have nowadays. ⟶ I have less time nowadays than I used to have.

This last structure-changing rule involves discontinuity. For example, *The time … to think of many things* is a split subject in the derived sentence of (45). (Now try Exercises 8d and 8e.)

8.8 Summary and conclusion

In this chapter we have touched on some of the more subtle areas of English grammar, making an important distinction between **basic** and **derived** structures. As far as parsing is concerned, these constructions invite us to introduce some freedom into the notations for grammatical analysis introduced in earlier chapters.

We have extended the use of ⌐___⌐ for showing a split constituent, and the practice of using named particles (e.g. **not, it, there**) in our labelling notation. We have also recognised the need for parsing with a mixture of phrase and clause elements (e.g. [*Aux S*] for tag questions) where ellipsis leads to derived structure with missing constituents.

We have explored stylistic structure-changing rules, and the means they provide of expressing the same content in different grammatical ways. This leads on naturally to the application of grammar to the study of style and composition: topics that will be developed later in the book.

═══════════════════ **EXERCISES** ═══════════════════

Exercise 8a (answers on p. 222)
Explain why these are not grammatical sentences in English:

1.   *The standing at the door girl was making.
2.   *My has got a job interesting.
3.   *He has very good reputation for.
4.   *To own an oil-well.
5.   *Has plenty of friends.

There may be circumstances in which 4 and 5 would be grammatical. Do you have any comments on this?

Exercise 8b (answers on p. 222)
Visit once again the groups of sentences given in Exercise 5g (p. 84). Formulate, as structure-changing rules, rules by which negatives, questions, emphatic sentences, tag questions and comparative clauses can be derived from the basic declarative structure. Add a special rule to deal with the auxiliary *do*. (You are not expected to formulate the rules in a particularly rigorous way, but of course the more precise you can make them the better. You can use either special symbols or ordinary words.)

Exercise 8c (answers on p. 223)

Bracket the following sentences containing branching coordination, using angle brackets as in examples (11) and (14) on p. 127.

(i)   As a first stage, you just need to insert the angle brackets into the sentences as printed below. Think about what **meanings** are linked by *and*, *or* or *but*. The elements which apply semantically to both coordinates should be outside the brackets. For example, in 1 below, *Every morning* applies to both Pat getting into her car and Pat driving to the office. So it should lie outside the ⟨ ⟩.

　　1.　Every morning Pat gets into her car and drives to the office.
　　2.　Have you been listening to the radio or watching television?
　　3.　I bought a puppet for Linda and a teddy-bear for Malcolm.
　　4.　At last the child went back to school and we had a rest.
　　5.　Unfortunately Jack Sprat likes lean meat, but his wife doesn't.
　　6.　With practice, your voice will grow more versatile, and your breathing more controlled.

(ii) As a second stage, combine the ⟨ ⟩ with the symbols [,], S, P, O, C, A, showing the structure of each clause, e.g., for the first sentence, [A S ⟨P A + P A⟩].

Exercise 8d (answers on p. 223)

1.　Invent two more examples of each of the stylistic structure-changing rules introduced in 8.7.4, 8.7.5 and 8.7.6. Give both the basic and the derived structures.
2.　Give as precise and general a description as you can of the relationship between the two structures. (You can formulate this as a structure-changing rule using and arrow (⟶), if you like.)

Exercise 8e (answers on p. 224)

Do a skeleton clause analysis (7.6.1) of the following sentences using the symbols S, P, O, C, A and cj to represent clause structures:

1.　It was odd that, although Rose had often been to her Aunt's in Ravenna, she had never talked alone with her cousins before.
2.　There was a sinister atmosphere about the deserted cottage, as if it was here that Gilpin had decided on his last, desperate course of action.
3.　If she does not come, should I conclude that she thinks I do not love her?

Part C

Applications

Working with Discourse: Speech and Writing

9.1 Introduction

Having worked carefully through Part B of this book, you should by now be equipped to analyse the structure of English sentences. In this chapter and the next we aim to show how this knowledge of grammar can be applied to the analysis and understanding of DISCOURSE – how people use language for communication – whether in dialogue, in monologue or in written texts.

Yes, the term DISCOURSE applies to both spoken and written language – and to literary and non-literary language – in fact to any sample of language used for any purpose. In Part B we mostly looked at individual sentences or clauses for analysis, and did not pay much attention to the context in which they might have occurred. We had to do this to focus on sentences and clauses as basic units of language structure, but now we expand our horizons to look at texts or extended text samples – chunks of language in actual use.

In 1.3.3 we briefly examined the categories of language use which affect language variation for all language users. These categories were TENOR, MODE and DOMAIN. The category of MODE is particularly important because it is related to the distinction between speech and writing. As we said in 1.3.3, mode 'has to do with the effects of the medium in which language is transmitted'. The obvious distinction for English is between the auditory and visual medium, that is, between speech and writing.

In 1.1 we made the point that grammar is at least as much involved in the study of speech as in the study of writing. Writing is essentially no 'better' or 'worse' than speech, but each performs different functions in society, uses different forms, and exhibits different linguistic characteristics. In this chapter we will compare speech and writing in detail, and our comparison will involve practice in the analysis of spoken and written discourse.[11]

9.2 Speech and writing: which comes first?

In 1.1 we said that the written language is 'secondary to its spoken form, which developed first'.

In the history of the human race, spoken language certainly came before writing. We have little evidence of the existence of a writing system of any kind before about 5,500 years ago, whereas we assume that spoken language existed many millennia before then. In the history of individual societies, spoken language also predates written language, and many languages spoken today have no written form. For the individual, too, spoken language comes first: children learn to speak before they learn to write.

On the other hand, in societies which do have writing systems (such as the Roman alphabet, used for English as well as many other languages), the written language is very important from a social and educational point of view. It would be impossible to imagine our own society functioning as we know it without the advantage that writing gives (see 9.3). Literacy is closely associated with civilisation and education. It is no wonder, then, that the written language traditionally has greater social prestige than the spoken language, and more official recognition. Speech is often evaluated socially according to its closeness to the written language, which explains why standard spoken English is probably closer to written English than is any other spoken variety. Written language is often viewed as more 'correct' than spoken language, and as more worthy of study. Also, from a legal point of view, written language takes precedence: a written contract, for example, is considered more binding than a verbal or spoken agreement. However, from a linguistic point of view we can only say that speech and writing are different; we cannot say that one is superior to the other.

9.3 Functions of writing and speech

The social prestige of written language is probably derived from the added functions which a written variety can fulfil for a society:

- Writing has the advantage of relative permanence, which allows for record-keeping in a form independent of the memories of those who keep the records, and capable of being checked and consulted by many different people.
- It also allows for communication over a great distance (by letters, newspapers, etc.), and to large numbers simultaneously (by publications of all kinds). Another advantage of written language is that not only is it permanent, but it also leaves visible traces. An important consequence of this is that it can be carefully planned and revised by the writer in a way that spoken language cannot.
- As far as the reader is concerned, written language can be processed at leisure, with parts of it reread and others omitted at will. This characteristic of written language promoted the development of literature, and intellectual development in general.
- The persistence of written language through historical time makes possible the creation of literary works of art in ways comparable with the creation of paintings or sculpture. It also promotes intellectual development by overcoming the limitations of human memory and allowing the incremental storage of visually accessible knowledge.

At the same time, speech retains its own functions that writing will never be able to fulfil:

- Speech achieves quick, direct ('on-line') communication with immediate feedback from the addressee.
- Speech is particularly important in integrating an individual into a social group, and those who cannot speak, even though they may be able to write (e.g. deaf people), often experience severe social isolation.
- Speech is used far more than writing; it is an everyday activity for almost everyone, whereas writing is not.

It is true that over the past 100 years modern technology has brought about big changes. The invention and evolution of sound recording, the telephone and the radio have helped to overcome the limitations of the **spoken** language regarding time, distance and numbers of addressees, but these are relatively recent developments in human history. More recently still, e-mail and chatgroups via the internet have extended the power of **written** language, giving it something of the interactive immediacy of speech. In terms of frequency of usage, internet communication and texting are altering the balance in favour of written language.

Ultimately, all we can say is that speech and writing are complementary in function: we cannot say that one is more important than the other. Ideally we need to be able to use both appropriately and adaptably as members of an English-speaking (and -writing) society.

9.4 The form of speech and writing

As well as being different in function, speech and writing differ in form as a result of the difference of medium. Features of speech which are absent in writing include rhythm, intonation and non-linguistic noises such as sighs and laughter. Since speech is typically used in a face-to-face situation, it can also be accompanied by non-verbal communication such as gestures and facial expression. None of these features can easily be conveyed by conventional writing systems, and those wishing to represent them have to devise special transcription systems. Writing, on the other hand, has several features which speech lacks, including punctuation, paragraphing and the capitalization of letters. Written language can be spoken probably more easily than spoken language can be written, but features of speech such as intonation have to be introduced by the speaker. Intonation can to some extent be conveyed by punctuation (especially commas, full stops and question marks), but only very partially. The intonation of the sentence *I'll take a taxi to the station* will differ according to whether the means of transport (taxi) or the destination (station) is the most important idea. This will be clear if you try reading the sentence aloud in different ways. The different meanings implied by differences of intonation would be difficult to convey in writing without changing the structure of the sentence.

9.5 Linguistic characteristics of speech and writing

After comparing the functions and forms of speech and writing, let's now compare their linguistic characteristics. For the sake of clarity we will outline the characteristics of 'typical' speech compared with 'typical' writing, though (as we shall see) there is actually some overlap between the two.

9.5.1 Inexplicitness

As speech is generally used in face-to-face situations, both the auditory and visual media are available. As a result, speech can be much less explicit than writing, because (a) we can convey extra information by 'body language' (e.g. facial expressions, gestures); (b) we can refer to the immediate physical environment, e.g. by pointing to objects or people; (c) our shared knowledge between individuals or local groups in a conversation makes explicitness unnecessary; and (d) in a conversation there is an opportunity for feedback from the hearer, so that the message can be clarified or repeated. Speech tends to make frequent use of pronouns such as *I, you, it, this* and *that*, all of which reflect its inexplicitness. Consider the following imaginary conversation (inadequately represented in writing – but notice the italicized pronouns):

(1)   A.   How did *it* go?
       B.   Not too bad. *I*'m just glad *it*'s over.
       A.   Was *it* the last *one*?
       B.   Yeah, for the time being.

We should also notice the occurrence of **ellipsis** (where grammatical structure has been 'understood' on the basis of context). For example, *Yeah, for the time being* omits the words that would presumably be needed to make this utterance into a fully structured sentence: *Yeah,* **it was the last one for the time being**. Not being participants in this conversation, we can only guess at what it might be about, e.g. a written examination or a tooth extraction.

9.5.2 Lack of clear sentence boundaries

The sentence, generally understood as the maximal unit of grammar, is essentially a unit of the written language. In speech, there are no full stops or sentence-initial capitals, and when we transcribe speech for linguistic purposes, it is probably better to avoid using punctuation, which gives a false impression of tidy sentence-like structures. Instead, in representing spoken examples, we propose here to avoid capital letters at the beginning of turns or utterances, to use | as a signal of an intonation prosodic boundary and to use a dash (–) as a signal of a pause. (A full transcription, taking account of stress, intonation, pauses of different length, and so on, would be a much more detailed and technical; we cannot attempt it here.) On this basis, example (1) could be rendered as:

(1a) A. how did *it* go
      B. not too bad | *I'm* just glad *it's* over.
      A. was *it* the last *one*
      B. yeah | for the time being.

If we stuck to the normal punctuation conventions of written language in transcribing conversation, we would continually come up against arbitrary decisions in placing full stops and other final pronunciation, for example:

(2) you always remember numbers | don't you | car numbers and telephone numbers and ...

The *don't you* here looks like a tag question, and could therefore be tacked on to the end of the previous clause *you always remember numbers*, as part of the same sentence (see 8.3.4). However, there is a problem if we add a full stop after *don't you*, treating the following noun phrase *car numbers* ... as a separate sentence. This noun phrase is a 'stand-alone' noun phrase, which does not fit into any slot for a noun phrase as recognized by our grammar: subject, object, complement, etc. Spontaneous spoken language is thickly sprinkled with such NON-CLAUSAL UNITS – phrases or words which cannot be said to be part of any clause. (For example, in (1a) above we find *not too bad* and *for the time being*, which appear to be adjective and prepositional phrases standing on their own. In these cases, it can be maintained that the missing clause structure, including a verb, has been omitted through ellipsis, but in many other cases there is no such ellipsis.)

To handle such phenomena of spoken grammar, Carter and McCarthy ('Grammar and the Spoken Language', 1995) and others have argued that spoken language has a radically different grammar from written language. Thus they maintain there are special structures in spoken grammar, determined in part by the lack of planning time available to speakers as they construct their utterances 'on-line'. Carter and McCarthy propose a three-part structure – in a broad sense, the spoken counterpart of the written sentence – in which a clause may be preceded or followed by 'satellite' elements such as noun phrases and tag questions – optional elements not integrated into clause structure. The pre-clause satellites are called 'topics', and the post-clause satellites 'tails', as in Table 9.1.

Table 9.1

Topic(s)	Body	Tail(s)	
north and south London	they're two different worlds	aren't they	in a way

Notice that a topic or a tail is linked in some tangible way to the main body of the utterance, though not by grammatical linkage. (The linkage may be by repetition or, in this case, by the use of the pronoun *they* referring back to *north and south London*.) This kind of pattern can also be seen in (2) above, where the tag question *don't you* and the repetitive phrase *car numbers* ...

are like tails referring back to the body element *you always remember numbers.*

However, such patterns only explain a small part of what occurs in the grammar of speech, and even they can be problematic. Consider this example:

(3)   they got one of the teachers that we always play jokes on | *one of the young women* | they got her to write it   (from J. Miller and R. Weinert, *Spontaneous Spoken Language.* Oxford: Clarendon Press, 1998)

The noun phrase *one of the young women* looks as if it could be a tail referring back to, and clarifying, *one of the teachers* in the preceding clause. But a similar argument could maintain that this phrase refers forward to *her* in the following clause. In other words, this noun phrase is poised between two main clauses, and could be treated either as topic of one or tail of the other.

Another difficulty about drawing sentence boundaries in speech is the status of coordination. In 7.7 we presented coordination using words like *and* as a device for linking grammatical units of the same status within a larger structure. Hence two coordinated clauses, as in [*Browne agreed*] *and* [*she walked away*] were treated as a single complex sentence. In writing, starting a sentence with a coordinating conjunction *and*, *or* or *but* has been frowned upon by the prescriptive grammar tradition, and serious writers tend to avoid it. But it does happen even in written texts (see the beginning of this sentence!). In speech, the practice of beginning a new utterance with words like *and* is common, and occurs in contexts such as the beginning of a turn, where no one could argue that the *and* is in the middle of a sentence:

(4)   *And* then they're open seven days a week | you say
(5)   *But* can you imagine being twenty years old and not knowing how to peel a banana.

Both these examples come at the beginning of a turn, in a way that is very characteristic of spoken dialogue. While, in written language, coordinating conjunctions are predominantly used to integrate a complex of ideas into a single sentence, in spoken language they can be looser connectors, difficult to distinguish from connective adverbs like *so* and *yet*.

From the observations in this section, it might be concluded that the grammar of speech is a degenerate form of the written grammar on which we focused in Part B, or even that speech is ungrammatical. The truth is more subtle than this. It is true that speech is generally more free and easy, in grammatical usage, than the edited written language that we see in print. But the primary reason for this is that speech is typically unedited and unplanned, having to cope with the pressures of on-line production. Every grammatical form of the written language can also occur in speech, but speech tends to operate with less integrated, less tightly connected structures at the higher levels of sentence and clause. One sign of this is the abundance in speech of non-clausal units, consisting of no more than a phrase or a word standing alone without being part of a clause or sentence. On the whole, the term 'sentence' is best avoided in discussing the grammar of the spoken language.

9.5.3 Simple structure

Spoken grammar is less complex than written grammar because of the short time available to produce and process it. Writing, on the other hand, can be redrafted and reread.

Naturally enough, there is a strong correlation between complexity and length (measured in number of words). Complexity is related to the discussion in the last section, where we argued that the written sentence is not an appropriate yardstick for the grammar of speech. The average length of a written sentence is about eighteen words. In contrast, the average length of an independent unit of grammar in speech is no more than five or six words. This is an arguable statement – depending on how we segment speech into independent units. But if we accept that clauses and stand-alone non-clausal units such as phrases and words are the operative units of spoken grammar, then the simplicity of the basic grammatical building blocks of speech is not surprising.

This is not to say that spoken grammar is always simple. Certain kinds of complexity, such as the subordination of noun clauses after *I think*, *did you know*, and so on, are very natural to speech:

(6)   [I think [you'll find [it counts towards your income]]].

The square brackets here show the subordination of one clause in another, but the sentence is not difficult to interpret, because the complexity is loaded towards the end of the utterance (see 13.2.3) – a very strong tendency in English, and especially in spoken English.

Example (6) illustrates, in a compact way, how complexity tends to build up in speech through the adding of one simple clause structure on to another in a linear way. This is shown more extensively in (7), where the speaker is telling a story about his dog:

(7)   The trouble is {{if you're}} if you're the only one in the house he follows you and you're looking for him and every time you're moving around he's moving around behind you ⟨⟨laughter⟩⟩ so you can't find him – I thought I wonder where the hell he's gone ⟨⟨laughter⟩⟩ – I mean he was immediately behind me.

Note: The brackets {{ }} show overlapping speech – the only example of disfluency in this passage; and the brackets ⟨⟨ ⟩⟩ signal non-verbal communication.

On the face of it, the grammar of (7) is quite complex, and this is confirmed if skeleton analysis (see 7.6) is used to show clause structure, including subordination:

(7a)   [The trouble is [[if you're the only one in the house] he follows you] and [you're looking for him] and [(every time [you're moving around]) he's moving around behind you [so you can't find him]]] – [I thought [I wonder where the hell he's gone]] – [I mean [he was immediately behind me]].

However, another way to look at this is to think of the passage as a process of adding one short, tensed clause-like unit on to another, in a sequential way which reflects the bit-by-bit way a speaker has to construct discourse on-line. Each clause-like 'chunk' marks a simple structure intelligible in its own terms, adding a stage in the progress of the story. These 'chunks' are marked by slant lines (/) in (6b), signalling the beginning of each new clause:

(7b) *The trouble* is / if *you*'re the only one in the house / *he* follows you and / *you*'re looking for him and every time / *you*'re moving around / *he*'s moving around behind you / so *you* can't find him – / *I* thought / *I* wonder / where the hell *he*'s gone –/ *I* mean / *he* was immediately behind me

This principle whereby spoken discourse develops by simple incremental steps can be called the ADD-ON PRINCIPLE. One factor which keeps each 'chunk' relatively brief is the simplicity of the grammatical subject (S) of each clause. In (7b) we have italicized each subject, and it is noticeable that all subjects are single-word pronouns, with the exception of *the trouble*, which is no more than two words.

The structure of spoken grammar is not necessarily simple in terms of subordinate and coordinate clauses, but its complexity is typically not of the kind that causes difficulty in the linear processing of the message (see 13.2). One-word subjects ensure that the stream of speech is not held up before the main verb, which provides the key to the interpretation of each clause. In contrast, written language, particularly of the more information-packed kind, tends to have complexity in phrase structure, particularly in the elaboration of noun phrases and prepositional phrases:

(8) (Despite the abnormal morphogenesis observed in such grafts), (the range of differential tissues formed in such an 'experimental teratoma') *can be used* to provide (an estimate of the developmental potential of the transferred tissue).

The brackets here mark the boundaries of main noun phrases and prepositional phrases (leaving unmarked the phrases that are part of other phrases). It is clear that the vast majority of words in this sentence belong to these phrases, and that the verb phrase (in italics) is delayed to a late position, burdening the memory of the reader who tries to process the sentence from left to right. In practice, readers are able to scan and rescan a sentence visually, so they are less dependent on sequential processing than in processing speech.

9.5.4 A repetitive repertoire

Because of the lack of permanence of speech, it is more repetitive than writing. Important information has to be repeated since the addressee cannot refer back to what has gone before. This is noticeable, for instance, in the amount of repetition that occurs in television commercials, and (for that matter) in unplanned dialogue:

(9) A. and that is about *what happens when someone leaves a job of their own accord – so what happens when someone leaves a job of their own accord | what happens* to their unemployment benefit

    B. {{*suspended*}}

    C. {{*suspended* pending}} enquiries

    D. yeah

    A. but not | *it's suspended* | *it's suspended* but *it's* not disallowed

Note: As before, {{ }} signals overlapping speech.

In this extract from a professional tutorial, the repeated elements are in italics.

Another way to think of this is in terms of redundancy. Whether through immediate repetition or more generally through the more frequent use of a limited vocabulary, spoken discourse tends to be less densely packed with information per word than written texts. One way this shows up is in the strong contrast between speech and writing in the usage of nouns and pronouns. Nouns, words that tend to be rich in specific information, are especially high in frequency in written texts, while pronouns, poor in information, are especially high in speech. Another indication of the lower information load of speech is the tendency for speech to rely heavily on highly frequent and formulaic multi-word expressions, such as *I don't know why . . .*, *so I said well . . .* and *you don't have to . . .* .

9.5.5 Normal disfluency

Far from being an aberration, lack of fluency is normal in spontaneous speech. It results from the unprepared nature of speech and includes phenomena such as hesitations, unintended repetitions (e.g. *I've I've . . .*), false starts, fillers (e.g. *um, er*), GRAMMATICAL BLENDS and unfinished sentences. A blend occurs where a sentence 'swaps horses' (see 12.7), beginning in one way and ending in another, for example in *He's a closet yuppie is what he is*. This utterance begins as a normal declarative clause *S P C*, but then finishes like a clause with inversion and fronting of the complement: *C P S* . It is as if two different complete clauses, *He's a closet yuppie* and *A closet yuppie is what he is*, have somehow been merged together. This is slightly different from a 'false start', where a sentence is broken off midway as a result of a change of mind, for example *You really ought – well do it your own way*. These disfluencies are edited out of written language. This even applies to the apparent fluency of the fictional speech that appears in literature.

9.5.6 Monitoring and interaction features

These features represent the social dimension of speech. They are more likely to occur in dialogue, with a physically present addressee, rather than in monologue. MONITORING features indicate the speaker's awareness of the addressee's presence and reactions, and include adverbs and adverbials such as *well, I mean, like, sort of, you know*. INTERACTION features invite the active participation of the addressee, as in questions, imperatives, second-person pronouns, and interjections (*no, okay, oops*, etc.) Two constructions with particular interaction potential are tag questions (8.3.4) and first-person imperatives with *let's*:

(10)   it's delicious *isn't it*
(11)   okay *let's* clean it up

Of course writing generally lacks these features – although with the recent upsurge of electronic modes of communication (e-mail, chat groups, virtual worlds, texting) dialogue features are taking a firm foothold in the written language of 'netspeak'.

9.5.7 Informality of style

The situations in which speech is used are generally less formal than those in which writing is used. Therefore, the linguistic characteristics of informality (such as the use of contractions in VPs – *it's, don't*, etc. – see below in 10.2) generally appear in speech, while those reflecting formality appear in writing.

We can go further and extend 'informality' here to include all the features of spoken grammar that make it casual, intimate, and the opposite of formal. Then we have to include such phenomena as non-standard and dialect grammar, 'chummy' use of vocatives like *mate, dude*, and *lovey*, and taboo language (swearing).

9.5.8 'Typical' speech, 'typical' writing, and in-between cases

We can summarize the above discussion by listing the characteristics of 'typical' speech and writing (see Table 9.2).

Table 9.2

	'Typical' speech	'Typical' writing
1.	Inexplicitness	Explicitness
2.	Lack of clear sentence boundaries	Clear sentence boundaries
3.	Simpler, looser structure	More complex, integrated structure
4.	Repetitive, restricted choice of vocabulary	Less repetitive, less restricted
5.	Normal disfluency	Fluency
6.	Monitoring features	No monitoring features
7.	Interaction features	No interaction features
8.	Features reflecting informality	Features reflecting formality

However, although these are characteristics of 'typical' speech and writing, there is some overlap. For example, a less 'typical' use of speech occurs on the telephone, where the visual medium is not available. The result is that the language needs to be somewhat more explicit. Also, although speech is generally unprepared, it may be prepared for a lecture or debate, and we can expect greater fluency as a result. Sometimes speech is prepared word for word in advance, as in the script of a television news bulletin. This speech will be atypical not only in fluency but in other ways, such as in lacking monitoring and interaction features. Conversely, writing can sometimes display the characteristics of speech, as in a text message or e-mail message, which may well have monitoring and interaction features. Here is an example of an e-mail message with extremely informal features:

(12)   What's up Dave. Just wanted to shoot you an email to see how you've been. Things have been going fine on my side, I just got a new job last week with this new company overseas. I think they've got some things you might like.

Tell me what you think and get back to me. ⟨⟨website address inserted⟩⟩

Thanks,

⟨⟨name⟩⟩

Private, personal letters will also have features reflecting a lesser degree of formality than is typical for writing.

So instead of seeing written and spoken language as watertight categories of mode, we have to recognise that there is some overlap or interpenetration, depending on the circumstances of language use. We might think of mode of discourse as a continuum from 'typical' speech to 'typical' writing, with in-between examples. The continuum could be represented very impressionistically as below:

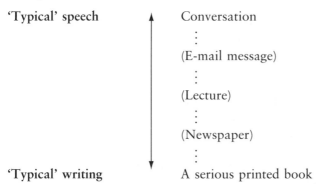

'Typical' speech   Conversation

                      (E-mail message)

                      (Lecture)

                      (Newspaper)

'Typical' writing   A serious printed book

9.6 An analysis of spoken and written discourse

Up to now we have tried to provide the background needed for an analysis of spoken and written discourse. For this purpose we will use a transcript of part of an actual conversation about a summer holiday. We will compare this with an imaginary version written in the form of a personal letter.

Since the following is a transcript of a conversation, there is no punctuation, but vertical lines indicate boundaries of the major units of intonation, and dashes indicate pauses. Laughter is indicated thus ⟨⟨*laughs*⟩⟩ and the material in brackets indicates the responses of the person not speaking at the time. You may wish to try (a) reading the transcript aloud, and (b) writing it out in conventional orthography, using capital letters and punctuation. This may help to identify for you some of the features which characterise it as speech: these features will be discussed below.

(I) Transcript of conversation	Line

B. so what how did you map out your day | you had your   1
    breakfast in the kitchen | 2

A. we had our breakfast | ⟨⟨*laughs*⟩⟩ in the kitchen | – and   3
    then we sort of did what we liked | and er got ready to   4
    go out | (m |) we usually went out quite soon after   5
    that | – erm the children were always up | at the crack of   6
    dawn | (m |) with the farmer | – and they went in the   7
    milking sheds | and helped him feed the pigs | and all   8
    this | you know we didn't see the children | – and er   9
    then we used to go out | we – we had super weather –   10
    absolutely super | – and so we went to a beach | usually   11
    for er but by about four o'clock it we were hot and we   12
    had to come off the beach (m | m |) – so we'd generally   13
    go for a tea somewhere | just in case supper was delayed   14
    you know | (⟨⟨*laughs*⟩⟩) ⟨⟨*laughs*⟩⟩ and then we'd get   15
    back | and the children would go straight back on to the farm ...   16

(from D. Crystal and D. Davy, *Advanced Conversational English*. London: Longman, 1975, simplified transcription)

(II) Imaginary letter version	Line

Dear B,   1
I thought I would write and tell you about our   2
summer holiday, which we spent on a farm.   3
Every day, the children were up at the crack   4
of dawn with the farmer. They went to the milking   5
sheds with him and helped him feed the pigs, so that we   6
barely saw them at all.   7
Then we would have our breakfast in the   8
kitchen. After breakfast, we usually did what we liked   9
for a short while, and then went out.   10
We had absolutely super weather, and so we   11
usually went to a beach. But by about four o'clock we   12
were hot and had to come off the beach. Then we'd   13
generally go and have tea somewhere just in case supper   14
was delayed. When we got back, the children would go   15
straight back on the farm ...   16

We will analyse the above samples in terms of the characteristics listed, in Table 9.2, as identifying 'typical' speech and 'typical' writing, and numbered

1–8. However, we should remember that while the conversation is close to 'typical' speech, the letter is some distance from 'typical' writing on the speech-writing continuum.

1. The **inexplicitness** of (I) is reflected, for example, in *that* (line 6), which occurs at some distance from its presumed antecedent, *breakfast*. *Breakfast* is repeated for greater explicitness in (II), where there is no chance for the addressee to ask for immediate clarification. Also, *and all this* in (I) (lines 8–9) is a vague, inexplicit reference to the farmer's tasks; it is eliminated in (II). The time sequence is made more explicit in the structure of the discourse of (II) than it is in (I), where events at dawn are mentioned after the description of breakfast. Lack of chronological reference to events is more common in speech than in writing, though it can occur in the latter.

2. If you have attempted a conventional orthographic transcription of (I), you may have had difficulty in deciding where the **sentence boundaries** should be. For example, do the occurrences of *and* indicate coordinated clauses, or new sentences? This is difficult to resolve for (I), whereas in (II) sentences are clearly marked by capital letters and full stops.

3. The **clause structure** of (II) is generally more complex than that of (I), especially in its greater use of subordination where (I) uses coordination. Examples of subordinated clauses in (II) are *which we spent on a farm* (line 3), *so that we barely saw them at all* (lines 6–7), and *when we got back* (line 15). The last is embedded at the beginning of the main clause, which is less typical of speech than being embedded at the end. The noun phrase structures of the two samples, however, seem to be about equally complex.

4. The **repetitiveness** of speech is reflected in (I) in the paraphrasing of *we usually went out quite soon after that* (lines 5–6) to *then we used to go out* (line 10), and in the repetition of *the children* (lines 6 and 9), *super* (lines 10 and 11) and *beach* (lines 11 and 13). In (II) there is some repetition, but less than in (I), and no paraphrasing.

5. **Disfluency** features in (I) include *er, erm, we – we* (line 10), *for er but* (line 12), and *it we were* (line 12). The latter two are false starts, where the speaker, in midflow, appeared to change her mind about what she was going to say. These features do not appear in (II) (although there might be deletions of errors in the original handwriting).

6. An obvious **interaction** feature in (I) is B's question, which is missing in (II). In (I) we also find responses from B while A is speaking, in the form of m and laughs. In line 15 A's laughter is in direct response to B's. In (II) there is only one conventional interaction feature: the address form *Dear B*.

7. The **monitoring** features in (I) are *sort of* (line 4) and *you know* (lines 9 and 15). It is interesting that the *you know* in line 15 elicits a laugh from the listener, immediately imitated by a laugh from the speaker. She seems reassured by the listener's reaction. There are no monitoring features in (II), where there is no physically present addressee.

8. The **informality** of both (I) and (II) is reflected in the simple (non-parenthetical) structure and non-technical, accessible vocabulary. Informal contractions are used in both: *didn't* and *we'd*.

In all, we can say that although both (I) and (II) have the same speaker and addressee and cover the same topic, and although they are not too far apart on the continuum between 'typical' speech and 'typical' writing, (I) nevertheless exhibits more of the characteristics typical of speech, and (II) more of those typical of writing. One would expect to find even more characteristics of 'typical' writing in discourse which does not really have a spoken equivalent. See, for example, the legalistic discourse in Exercise 9a [1] below.

9.7 Conclusion

In this chapter we have exemplified the category of mode with special reference to spoken and written discourse. We hope to have shown that speech and writing generally reflect complementary language habits, but that there can be some overlap, depending on what they are used for, and in what situation. In fact, the characteristics of spoken and written discourse can be better accounted for if we also consider the effect of the two other categories of use, TENOR and DOMAIN. These two categories will be dealt with in the next chapter.

─────────────────── **EXERCISES** ───────────────────

Exercise 9a

Analyse the following samples of discourse as in 9.6, paying special attention to the linguistic characteristics which reflect mode.

1. The times shown on the flight coupons of this ticket are the departure times of the aircraft. Check-in times, as shown on this page or in the airline's timetable, are the latest times at which passengers can be accepted for travel, allowing the necessary time to complete all formalities. Flights cannot be held up for passengers arriving late, and no responsibility can be accepted in such cases.
   (A paragraph from an IATA Passenger Ticket and Baggage Check)
2. SPOKEN DIALOGUE IN A SHOE SHOP:
   Transcription adapted to match the conventions of 9.6(I).

   A. Don't like them
   B. No | neither do I |
   A. to be quite honest |
   B. Let's looking you're looking for comfortable shoes aren't you |
   A. They're smart | they're a bit – I don't like those – they go slippy slidey all over the place with those – but these are nice |
   B. It's a shame they don't do the grey ones in black 'cause they looked comfortable as well
   A. Those? – Yeah – they do

B.   Sorry?

A.   Yeah they look – they do look comfortable but

B.   Sorry

A.   I mean I don't have to wear black shoes but – they do suit

B.   I think I've put my foot in it don't you |

(From the British National Corpus)

Exercise 9b (For discussion)

Modern electronic communications such as e-mail and texting often seem to bridge the gap between 'typical speech' and 'typical writing'. For example, their interactive immediacy and speed of execution (sometimes with no editing out of disfluencies) make them closer to spoken dialogue than are other kinds of written, visual communication.

Find your own examples of these kinds of communication, examine their language, and discuss how far they align themselves with 'typical speech' or 'typical writing', using the eight characteristics (inexplicitness v. explicitness, etc.) in Table 9.2. Some of the most obvious characteristics of these media are to do with the writing system – use of special abbreviations, smileys (☺), etc. While not ignoring these, in this exercise try to concentrate particularly on aspects of grammar.

Working with Discourse: Tenor and Domain

10

10.1 Introduction

In the last chapter we looked closely at the effect of **mode** on language, and we noticed in particular how speech and writing differ from one another. This chapter explores how discourse differs on other dimensions of register (see 1.3.3). Just as we saw how people vary their language according to whether they are speaking or writing, we will now see how they vary it according to factors such as

- who they are speaking to
- the situation
- the kind of activity the language is being used for.

This will involve us in investigating the effect of the dimensions of language use we called TENOR and DOMAIN in 1.3.3. Although we are considering the effect of each of the categories separately at first, we must recognise that they have a combined effect on any discourse. We will illustrate this combined effect in 10.6.

10.2 Tenor

In 1.3.3 we said that tenor 'has to do with the relationship between a speaker and the addressee(s) in a given situation, and is often shown by greater or less formality'. To illustrate this, if the relationship between the ADDRESSER (speaker or writer) and the ADDRESSEE is distant, public and official, as in a legal or quasi-legal document, the tenor will be FORMAL, whereas if it is close and intimate, as in a conversation between family members, the tenor will be INFORMAL (compare passages 1 and 2 in Exercise 9a). These two examples in fact represent extremes of formality: as we found with **mode** in 9.5.8, it is more realistic to think of a scale or continuum, from the most formal at one extreme to the most informal at the other. The tenor of a conversation between a lawyer and client, for example, has an intermediate degree of formality.

Other factors closely relating to formality are those of POLITENESS and IMPERSONALITY, which, like formality, reflect the relation between addresser(s) and addressee(s). If the addresser and addressee are not well known to one another but a good rapport between them is important, they will tend to use **polite**, respectful language:

(1) Dear Mr. Leech
     I'm terribly sorry to keep asking you for more information, but I'm afraid I need the expiry date for your card in addition to the details you supplied this morning.
     I have processed your order already, so this shouldn't delay the process in any way. However if you could send me these details at your earliest convenience I would be most grateful.
     Many thanks,

     David McKee

As is evident in this private business e-mail, politeness shows in the use of formulaic expressions, often standing alone in grammatical isolation (*Many thanks*), or at the beginning of a complex sentence: *I'm terribly sorry ...*, *I'm afraid ...* . Also, polite utterances such as thanks and apologies are often intensified (***Many thanks***, ***terribly*** *sorry*, ***most*** *grateful*). In making demanding utterances such as requests, on the other hand, a speaker or writer prefers indirect toning-down strategies such as the use of *would* and other hypothetically-slanted verbs: *If you could ... Would you ...?* This whole conditional sentence introduced by *if* is itself a device of polite indirectness, placing the addressee's compliance in the realms of conjecture rather than reality.

An **impersonal** style will result where the roles of the addresser and addressee are in the background, as in written documents with no specific author or addressee – or where, even if we knew who the author was, this would make little or no difference to our interpretation of the document. A good example of an impersonal style has already been given in the last chapter, example 1, p. 154, and here, for further illustration, we give another paragraph from the same document (an IATA Passenger Ticket and Baggage Check):

(2) **Notices and Conditions**
     Air transportation provided is subject to the individual terms of the transporting air carriers, which are herein incorporated and made part of the contract of carriage.

This legalistic style is totally impersonal, in avoiding reference to the addresser and the addressee. The addresser is 'airbrushed' out of the picture by the use of past participle (*provided*) and passive (*are ... incorporated*) constructions. A more personal style might begin *The air transportation we provide ...* . Also, no reference is made to the addressee. Some official documents these days try to achieve a more friendly rapport with the reader by a wording involving *you*, such as this: *The service we give you* .... But this could misrepresent the status of impersonality important for many legal documents: the 'we' of the document, for example, might not be identical with the party legally responsible for providing services to the passengers.

Table 10.1   Four related dimensions of tenor

Formal	Informal
Full forms, e.g. *there is, it has not, they will*	Contractions, e.g. *there's, it hasn't, they'll*
Polysyllabic, Romance/classical vocabulary, e.g. *enter, investigate, extinguish, decipher*	Monosyllabic, native Anglo-Saxon vocabulary, e.g. *come, old*; especially prepositional and phrasal verbs, e.g. *look into, put out, make out*
Structures beginning with a preposition + *wh*-word, e.g. *those to whom we wrote*	Structures ending with a preposition, e.g. *the people we wrote to*

Polite	Familiar
Respectful terms of address, e.g. *Sir, Mrs P., Dr. H.*	Familiar or intimate terms of address, e.g. *Tom, love*
Indirect requests, e.g. *Would you mind ... Could you ...*	Direct imperatives, e.g. *Give me ..., Let's do it*

Impersonal	Personal
Third person NPs, etc., e.g. *the reader, passengers*	First and second person pronouns, e.g. *I, me, you, we*
Passive clauses, e.g. *The problem has been solved*	Active clauses, e.g. *We've solved the problem*
Impersonal *It*, e.g. *It is evident that* (extraposition, 8.7.3)	Personal attributions, e.g. *I think ..., Did you know that ...*

Specialist	Popular
Complex structure, especially in NPs and PPs	Simpler structures, shorter sentences
More abstract language, e.g. abstract nouns like *system, development, research*	Vivid language involving activity, metaphor, etc. E.g. *Have a crack at*
Rare, technical vocabulary, e.g. *hindbrain, indigent*	Common, familiar vocabulary, e.g. *cash, big, take*

Table 10.1 illustrates four interrelated scales of **tenor**, listing two or three typical linguistic contrasts in each case. The extent to which a situation is formal, impersonal, etc., is obviously reflected in the type of language used.

The fourth factor of tenor, reflecting another aspect of the relationship between addresser(s) and addressee(s), is **specialist audience** vs. **popular audience**. A writer for a popular audience, for example, will try to engage the interest and involvement of the reader with vivid use of language, and a colloquial style associated with conversation. The specialist/popular distinction also correlates strongly with simplicity vs. complexity of style, understood in both a grammatical and a lexical sense. On the whole, the more complex the style of a text is, the more it makes demands on the reader

– and the less readable or accessible it is. A text aimed towards a **popular** mass readership will be written in simple language so as to be accessible to a very wide range of readers. A text directed towards a **specialist** readership, on the other hand, will be written in more complex and technical language, and will therefore be accessible to a limited range of readers. Accessibility applies as much to spoken language as to written language, by the way, but for convenience we have focused here on the written medium.

How do we measure complexity of language? In grammar, we can measure the number and complexity of grammatical units – or, as a rough-and-ready measure, we can simply count the number of words per sentence. It is also important, though, to find out what **kinds** of grammatical complexity exist (see 7.6, 9.5.3). In vocabulary, another rough-and-ready measure is the length of words, counted in terms of the average number of morphemes, syllables or letters per word. (In comparisons, the results will be much the same whichever unit is chosen.) But there are other factors involved in accessibility, such as the frequency or familiarity of words and their meanings. For example, although the nouns *accommodation* and *extravaganza* are of roughly equal length, *extravaganza* is a rarer and more specialized word than *accommodation*, and is in that sense more difficult.

10.3 Tenor and discourse

We now illustrate the general effect of simplicity–complexity, as well as of tenor in general, by examining two samples of discourse from radio news broadcasts. The mode and domain of the two are identical, so in many ways we might expect the language to be fairly similar. However, the tenor of the two is a little different. Both samples of discourse come from BBC Radio news broadcasts on the opening of the Olympic Games in Athens, covering the same general topic. However, the first is from *Newsbeat*, the Radio One news programme, and the second from *The World Tonight*, the Radio Four news programme. Radio One is aimed at a young audience primarily interested in popular music, while Radio Four is aimed at an older age range of people with an interest in current affairs. We have actually taken the written form of these broadcasts, on the internet.

(3)   (From Newsbeat, BBC Radio 1, Web version, 13 August 2004)
      Olympic Games open
      The Olympic Games have officially kicked off. Tony Blair and Princess Anne were among the thousands in the stadium at Athens. Meanwhile, two of the host country's top athletes have been given until Monday to explain why they didn't turn up to a drugs test. Kostas Kenteris and Katerina Thanou could now be booted out of the games. They're now both in hospital after a motorbike crash.

(4)   (From BBC Sport, Radio 4, Web version, 13 August 2004)
      The 28th Olympic Games have begun in lavish style in Athens.
      The Olympic Stadium hosted the opening ceremony in front of 72,000 spectators and an estimated global audience of four billion people.

Greek President Konstandinos Stefanopoulos declared the Games open after a spectacular theatrical celebration and procession of athletes.
The opening extravaganza marks the end of a rocky seven-year build-up and kicks off 16 days of sporting action.
Preparations have been blighted by controversy and the ceremony was played out against a backdrop of a drugs scandal involving Greece's top athlete Kostas Kenteris.

Using the rough-and-ready measure of length, we find that the Radio 4 report is considerably more complex than the Radio 1 report: an average of 12 words per sentence for the former passage contrasts with an average of 18.6 words per sentence in the second one. This figure 18.6 is, in fact, around average for written texts as a whole, so the Radio 1 passage stands out as remarkably simple in comparison.

Moving on to word length (measured in syllables), we find that the average word length of Passage (3) is 1.49 syllables, while the average word length of Passage (4) is 1.74 syllables – demonstrating again that (3) is considerably simpler than (4). As a crude generalization, we can say that in the Radio 1 passage monosyllabic words like *have* predominate, whereas in the Radio 4 passage there is a tendency to use more complex, polysyllabic words.

A third way to look at complexity is to undertake a skeleton grammatical analysis of the two passages, this time showing both clause boundaries (marked [ ]) and phrase boundaries (marked ( )). As always, ⟨ ⟩ shows the boundaries of a coordinate construction.

(3a) **(Olympic Games) (open)**

¹ [(The Olympic Games) (have (officially) kicked off].

² [⟨(Tony Blair) and (Princess Anne)⟩ (were) (among the thousands (in the stadium (at Athens)))].

³ [(Meanwhile), (two (of (the host country's) top athletes)) (have been given) (until Monday) [(to explain) [(why) (they) (didn't turn up) (to a drugs test)]]]].

⁴ [⟨(Kostas Kenteris) and (Katerina Thanou)⟩ (could (now) be booted) (out of the games)].

⁵ [(They)('re) (now) (both) (in hospital) (after a motorbike crash)].

(4a) **[(The 28th Olympic Games) (have begun) (in lavish style) (in Athens)].**

¹ [(The Olympic Stadium) (hosted) (the opening ceremony) (in front of ⟨(72,000 spectators) and (an estimated global audience (of four billion people)))⟩)].

² [((Greek President) Konstandinos Stefanopoulos) (declared) (the Games) (open) (after a ⟨(spectacular theatrical celebration) and (procession (of athletes)))⟩)].

³ [(The opening extravaganza) ⟨(marks) (the end (of a rocky seven-year build-up)) and (kicks off) (16 days (of sporting action))⟩].

[4] ⟨[(*Preparations*) (have been blighted) (*by controversy*)] and [(*the ceremony*) (was played out) (*against a backdrop* (*of a drugs scandal* [*involving* ((*Greece's*) *top athlete* (*Kostas Kenteris*))]))]⟩.

These annotated versions of the texts show where the grammatical simplicity or complexity is located. Both passages have very little subordination of clauses: subordinate clauses turn up only in sentence 3 of (3a), and sentence 4 of (4a). Coordination is somewhat more important: notice, for example, the way the two coordinated clauses ⟨[S P A] + [S P A]⟩ make sentence 4 the longest of passage (4a). But by far the greatest complexity in these passages comes from phrase structure – particularly NP and PP structure, often containing further subordinate phrases or clauses. The main NP and PP phrases are in italics in (3a) and (4a). Note, for instance, that more than half of the last sentence in (4a) is found in the phrase beginning *against a backdrop*, which ushers in the seamier side of the festivities – a 'drugs scandal'.

Complexity of phrases is a dominant feature of 'typical writing', whether journalistic, academic or legalistic. NPs and PPs, in particular, reflect a preoccupation with dense packing of information which characterises this kind of writing, and distinguishes it markedly from speech. Thus if we want to know the name of the Greek president, passage (4a) gives it to us. It also tells us what he did, what happened at the opening ceremony, how many people were present, and how many people watched it on TV. This information orientation is less strongly marked, yet present, in the more popular news bulletin of (3a).

However, when we speak of 'informational orientation', this should not be interpreted narrowly as an insistence on neutral, objective reporting. Both bulletins, in a way typical of their kind, find means to titillate the addressee with scandalous aspects of the story. These aspects show up more clearly in vocabulary than in syntax: note the words *blighted, controversy* and *scandal* in the last sentence of (4a).

In one respect passage (3a) shows more complexity than (4a): this is in verb phrases such as *have ... kicked off, have been given, didn't turn up, could ... be booted* – containing perfect, passive, negative and modal constructions. These suggest that the passage is not concerned just with neutral reporting, but with a more humanly-involved picture of what has happened, what didn't happen although it should have done, what could possibly happen, and so on. Passage (4a), on the other hand, except for its last sentence, is more concerned with factual reporting.

If we still look at the VPs, both passages show a penchant for the passive (*have been given, have been blighted*, etc.) and also for phrasal verbs (*kicked off, turn up, kicks off, played out*). These lead us back to other factors of tenor: impersonality and informality. News bulletins by tradition are impersonal, in keeping with their responsibility to be factual, so personal pronouns like *I* and *you* are not expected. The passive shows that they can be impersonal in a second way, by excluding certain kinds of personal information. Focusing on the main characters in the drama, they bypass the need to name the people – no doubt nameless officials – who would take disciplinary measures against the athletes. On the other hand, both passages are (to different degrees) rather informal, a tendency which has increased in broadcasting and journalism in recent years. We see this in the use of phrasal verbs like *kick off* instead of *start*. We also note, as a sign of informality in (3), the use of verb contractions (e.g. *They're* in sentence 5) and of shorter, more informal phraseology, such as *motorbike crash* rather than *motorcycle accident*.

We have not mentioned a further dimension of tenor – politeness – as this is largely irrelevant to the public and impersonal discourse we meet in news bulletins. Looking at both passages, we can say that they are similar in register, except for the greater simplicity and informality of passage (3). The similarities between them are due to the fact that they belong to the same **domain** – news reporting – and so it is to domain that we now turn.

10.4 Domain

As we said in 1.3.3, domain 'has to do with how language varies according to the human activity in which it plays a part'. Or, in other words, language varies according to the **function** it is fulfilling in communication.

A useful lead into the topic of domain will be to look briefly at the features that make passages (3) and (4) above representative of the domain of news reporting. Here we repeat these passages, italicizing some features that deserve comment:

(3b) **Olympic Games open**[a]
      The Olympic Games have officially *kicked off*[b]. Tony Blair and Princess Anne were among the thousands *in the stadium at Athens*[c]. Meanwhile, two of *the host country's top athletes*[d] have been given *until Monday*[c] to explain why *they*[f] didn't turn up to a drugs test. *Kostas Kenteris and Katerina Thanou*[g] could now be booted out of the games. *They*[f]*'re now both in hospital*[c] *after a motorbike crash*[c,h].

(4b) **The 28th Olympic Games have begun in lavish style** in Athens[c].
      The Olympic Stadium hosted the opening ceremony *in front of 72,000 spectators*[c] and *an estimated global audience of four billion people.*
      Greek President[h] Konstandinos Stefanopoulos declared the Games open *after a spectacular theatrical celebration*[e,g] and *procession of athletes.*
      The opening extravaganza[d] marks the end *of a rocky seven-year build-up*[e] and kicks off *16 days of sporting action*[e].
      Preparations have been blighted by controversy and the ceremony was *played out*[b] against a backdrop of a drugs scandal involving *Greece's top athlete Kostas Kenteris*[d,h].

Let's now address the different linguistic features of news reporting identified by the superscript letters a–h in (3b) and (4b):

a. News headlines are often written in a special abbreviated syntax known as 'headlinese'. For example, words of low information content such as the article *the* and the copula *to be* are omitted, so in (3b) the more orthodox syntax of *The Olympic Games are open* is reduced to *Olympic Games open*. Obviously this special syntax helps to save space on the page or on the computer screen, and the size of the type used can be accordingly magnified.

b. As noted above, news reporting, particularly in more popular styles, favours phrasal verbs. This is partly for informality, and partly for liveliness of style. Many phrasal and prepositional verbs, like *kick off* and *booted out of*, bring a vivid metaphorical touch to the page, with a suggestion of violence.

c. News reporting, as already noted, has an informational orientation, and some of the most common information-bearing units, as we see here, are prepositional phrases of time and place, giving circumstantial information about the events being narrated.

d. News reporting aims to pack a lot of information into a small space: both time and space, in the mass media, are precious. This leads to a favouring of certain NP constructions, such as the use of genitive phrases before the noun: X's Y. The genitive construction is particularly common in news texts, and is more compact than the equivalent: the Y of X.

e. More generally, news reporting favours the more complex NPs and PPs, where the complexity is found especially in combinations of premodifiers, particularly adjectives, genitives, and nouns (rather than PPs and RCls, which follow the noun head).

f. In contrast, pronouns (NPs that are maximally simple and uninformative) tend to be relatively infrequent. *They*, used twice in (3b), is the sole example of a personal pronoun in these two passages.

g. While pronouns are little used, another device for cross-reference to another part of the text is popular: this is 'elegant variation' (see 13.6) – saying the same thing in different words. This means, more precisely, substituting an alternative descriptive phrase which refers to the same thing, event or person: thus *a spectacular theatrical celebration* refers to the same event as *the opening ceremony* in (4b).

h. Another common construction for compression of information is the use of NPs in apposition, as in *Greece's top athlete Kostas Kenteris*. *Greece's top athlete* is an NP referring to the same person as *Kostas Kenteris*.

This list of points is enough to show how similarities of grammar between passages (3) and (4) reflect their similarity of communicative function, in spite of differences of tenor.

It is a commonplace to say that the function of language is communication. But what kind of communication? Language can be used to convey information, express feelings, persuade someone to do something, maintain contact with someone else, write poetry, or talk about language itself. Following a well-known analysis by the great linguist Roman Jakobson, these functions have been called respectively: referential, expressive, conative, phatic, poetic and metalinguistic. Language is often used to fulfil more than one function simultaneously. For example, *I feel like a cup of coffee* could be

Table 10.2

Domain	Function	
	Dominant	Subordinate
Journalism	referential	expressive, conative
Advertising	conative	referential, poetic
Religion	expressive	conative, poetic
Law	referential	metalinguistic, conative
Literature	poetic	expressive, referential
Conversation	phatic	referential, expressive

simultaneously referential, expressive and conative. It conveys information, expresses a feeling, and tries to persuade someone to provide a cup of coffee. In general, however, language used in a given type of activity has a dominant communicative function, with others subordinate to it, and we can initially characterise the domains of language according to their **dominant** functions. Table 10.2 is a list of some domains with the dominant and subordinate functions typically associated with them.

In fact, like the varieties of tenor and mode, the varieties of domain do not lend themselves to clear-cut distinctions. There are, for example, possible subcategories of domain with no clear separation between them: journalism involves **reporting** the news, and also **commenting on** the news, but it is notoriously difficult to separate these two. Also, domains vary in the extent to which they influence language use. It is not even clear, for example, whether conversation and literature should be called domains. This is because such a wide variety of language is possible in each case. People have more choice of topic and language behaviour in conversation and literature than in other domains. So, once again, language and situation are to some extent mutually determining. The language chosen can itself define the domain, for example joke-telling (as a subdomain of conversation) or poetry (as a subdomain of literature). This issue will be taken up again in 11.1.4 with reference to literature.

10.5 Domain and discourse

The concept of domain is best further illustrated by the analysis of actual discourse from a particular domain, that of advertising.

The following is the main part of a press advertisement for a car:

(5)   The Vauxhall Chevette has always offered a great combination of comfort, economy and enthusiastic performance.
But this year, by realigning the rear-seat, we've conjured up extra legroom in the back.
The result is even more space and greater comfort for passengers.
Drivers, on the other hand, will notice that, in most respects, it remains unchanged.

The Chevette is every bit as sure footed and sporty a performer as ever it was.

One surprise, though, is that it's now even more economical to run.

Because our engineers have managed to wring further fuel savings of around 4% from the already frugal 1256 cc engine.

Think of that as around 5p off every gallon of petrol you use and you'll appreciate its value.

In fact, recent Government figures show the Chevette saloon returning 44 mpg at 56 mph and 31.3 mpg at a constant 75 mph.

Other thoughtful touches for 1980 include side window demisters and optional automatic transmission.

Restyled flushline headlights accent the car's already aerodynamic lines.

If advertisements are to achieve their purpose, which is to sell a product, they have to be easy to read. The sentence structure must therefore be fairly simple. In this advertisement each sentence starts a new paragraph, and there is an average of 15 words per sentence, which is relatively short. The clause structure of the sentences is quite simple, with more use of co-ordination than subordination. The second sentence *But this year...* is probably the most complex, as it has a subordinate adverbial clause and a parenthetical structure. We can summarise it thus:

[But (this year), [by realigning the rear-seat], (we)('ve conjured up) (extra legroom) (in the back)].
[cj A, [p *P O*], *S P O A*]

This structure in fact creates a special effect. The adverbial *this year*, coming early in the sentence, stresses the newness of the model, and the rest of the main clause (*we've conjured up extra legroom at the back*), coming at the end, gives new information (see 13.2.3) about precisely what the new feature is. A special effect is also created by the seventh sentence, *Because our engineers* .... . This sentence is really a clause subordinate to the previous main clause, *it's now even more economical to run*. However, placing *because* at the beginning of a new sentence has the effect of giving separate emphasis to the explanation for the economy.

Below the level of the clause we can look at the structure of noun phrases. In advertising language, as in news reporting, they are often fairly complex, with particularly heavy use of premodifiers. This structure has the advantage of giving exact information, yet remaining concise. Premodifiers are often nouns in advertising, as in, for example, *recent **Government** figures, restyled **flushline** headlights, **side window** demisters. Other thoughtful touches for 1980* has both pre- and postmodifiers. The final noun phrase of the advertisement, *the car's already aerodynamic lines* has the use of the genitive *car's*, which is uncommon for inanimate nouns in many other language domains, but common in advertising. The premodifiers themselves in this case are subordinate phrases: ((*the car's*) (*already aerodynamic*) lines). This has the effect of conciseness and impact, as is clear if we compare an equivalent phrase with postmodification: *the lines* (*of the car*) (*which are already aerodynamic*).

As far as verbs are concerned, tense is used effectively to convey the advertiser's message. The simple present emphasises the features of the new model (e.g. *the result is*); the perfect shows what improvements have been made (e.g. *we've conjured up*), and the future cannily makes the assumption that the car will be bought (*Drivers … will notice*).

The vocabulary of the advertisement can be divided into two categories: (a) words (especially adjectives) which emphasise the positive aspects of the product, and persuade the consumer to buy (conative function), and (b) words which provide technical information about the car (referential function). The modifiers *great, extra, more, greater, sure, sporty*, and *thoughtful* fall into category (a); *realigning, returning 44 mpg, side window demisters, optional automatic transmission, restyled flushline headlights* and *aerodynamic lines* fall into category (b). *Aerodynamic* is a technical adjective used almost metaphorically, and calculated to impress.

A further characteristic of advertising language, contrasting with news reporting, is direct address: note the use of the second-person pronoun *you*, and the imperative *Think*, which acts as an appeal for notice. This point draws our attention to interconnections between domain, tenor and mode. Advertising language is typically very informal and personal, and even when it occurs in written form (e.g. in press advertisements) it shows some of the characteristics which we associate with spoken language. Notice this in the use of interaction features (see p. 150) and of verbal contractions as in *we've, it's* and *you'll*.

There are other characteristics of advertising language that could be picked out in this sample advertisement, but our analysis should serve to illustrate the effect of domain in discourse. The exercise at the end of this chapter will give you practice in working out the characteristics and effects of other domains of discourse.

10.6 Combining categories of use

So far we have looked separately at the effects of mode, tenor and domain in discourse. But in 10.5 we also noticed that a sample of discourse will be affected by all three categories simultaneously. All of the samples that we have analysed in this chapter and the last could be reanalysed, paying attention to all three categories of use instead of just one.

To illustrate the point more fully, we now analyse the effect of all three categories in the following sample of discourse:

(6) The 1980 Vauxhall Chevette is the same car it ever was.
Same lively performance.
Same light responsive steering.
Same level handling.
But there are a few new touches you might like.

Even better fuel economy from the 1256 cc engine.
Side window demisters.
More streamlined headlights.
And as an optional extra, automatic transmission plus lots more rear legroom.
The 1980 Vauxhall Chevette we have changed very little but improved quite a lot.

As you may have guessed, (6) is a script for a television advertisement for the same product as the press advertisement analysed in 10.5, and dating from the same year – 1980. We will analyse it briefly from the point of view of domain, mode and tenor.

Since the domain is advertising, the television advertisement shares several characteristics with its press equivalent. For example, there is vocabulary implying the positive aspects of the product, e.g. *responsive, new, better, extra*, and some of the same technical vocabulary conveying information, e.g. *1256 cc engine, side window demisters, automatic transmission*. There is also the direct address (*you*) which is generally characteristic of advertising, as is the liberal use of comparative constructions: *even better fuel economy*, etc.

However, because of the impermanence of the spoken mode and the constraints on time, less information can be conveyed. Because of this, memorability of the important points has to be aimed for. This is achieved partly by repetition. For example, *The 1980 Vauxhall Chevette* appears at both the beginning and end of the script (both times in a prominent position at the beginning of the sentence), and *same* appears three times in parallel NP structures, as the first premodifier followed by one or two more.

One characteristic which the script shares with much spoken language (see 9.5.2) is that we cannot divide it neatly into sentence units. There are only three grammatical units with clear sentential structure, at the beginning, middle and end of the script. The other units lack verbs – most of them are just NPs and are rather like slogans, functioning as a list of the attributes of the product. This particular structure is more characteristic of advertising language than of spoken language in general, and is no doubt due to the shortage of time and the importance of conveying essential information in a concise, dramatic way.

This sample of discourse also differs from other types of spoken language (see 9.5.5) because it is prepared, and so is unusually fluent. It has none of the monitoring or interaction features we find in normal conversation, for these depend on the immediate presence of an addressee (although some advertisements use such features to create the feeling that the viewer is actually there). This sample is also more explicit than spoken language in normal conversations, because the addressees are unknown and unable to give direct feedback. Another point is that it is supplemented by visual images and written language on the screen, which are not recorded here, but which help to determine the nature of the spoken language used. For example, the use of parallelism and incomplete sentences may be explained by the accompanying picture sequence.

Both spoken language and advertising language tend to reflect informality of tenor. The combined effect of these two categories in the script makes the language quite informal – in fact more so than in the press advertisement discussed above (10.5). The grammatical structure is extremely simple, with few subordinate or coordinated clauses. The vocabulary is generally concrete and accessible, and more colloquial than in the written advertisement (e.g. *new touches, plus lots more, quite a lot*). It is also quite personal (e.g. *you might like, we have changed very little*).

It is worth pointing out, however, that advertisements are not written to a formula, but to some extent have their individual styles. This advertisement adopts a casual low-key approach to the listener, as if the advertiser wants to disclaim the brash foot-in-the-door technique of the 'hard sell'. The tentativeness of *might* (*like*), *a few* (*touches*), and *quite* (*a lot*) are to some extent atypical of advertising in their moderation and even modesty.

In preparation for the next chapter, it is also worth noting that advertising language shares some features with poetry. The parallelism of:

Same lively performance.
Same light responsive steering.
Same level handling.

with its reiterated first word is characteristic of both poetry and public oratory, but the alliteration of the adjectives (*lively, light, level*) is a more specifically literary device.

We have given only a brief example of an analysis using all the categories of use. By doing the exercises at the end of this chapter, you will gain direct experience of how all these categories affect discourse simultaneously.

───────────────── **EXERCISES** ─────────────────

Exercise 10a

For the following samples of discourse, (i) identify the major factors of the tenor, mode and domain, and (ii) show how these categories of use are reflected in the use of language. Remember to look at different aspects of grammar, including clause and phrase structure, as well as vocabulary.

Note that some of these samples are spoken. However, all except the last have been written in conventional orthography so that you will have to identify the mode on linguistic grounds alone.

1. **SONY**
    Bigger everything. Bigger dogs, bigger trees, bigger children. Bigger screen on the back. The **2.5 inch LCD** screen makes everything look bigger. It'll look sharper, too. The **Carl Zeiss Vario-Tessar lens** and **Real Imaging Processor** makes each of the **5 effective megapixels** seem more lifelike and realistic. Fortunately, the camera itself is still nice and small. Cyber-shot W1

    'Sony' and 'Cybershot' are registered trademarks of the Sony Corporation, Japan
    www.sony-europe.com   You make it a Sony

    (Language content of an advertisement for a digital camera, *Telegraph Magazine*, 13 August 2004, p. 24)

2. EXCLUSIVE
    RACHEL DUMPS ROBBIE
    Superstar 'too paranoid'
    STUNNING Rachel Hunter has dumped pop superstar Robbie Williams
    because she can no longer cope with his 'paranoia', The Sun can reveal.

    Model-turned-actress Rachel, 33, told the mega-rich singer their
    romance was over last night, the eve of his 29th birthday.

    Ex-cocaine addict Robbie is battling depression with pills.

    And Rachel, right, the estranged wife of Rod Stewart, told pals she had
    been ground down by the former Take That star's tormented state of mind.

    (From p. 1 of *The Sun*, 13 February 2003)

3. We value every life; our enemies value none – not even the innocent, not
    even their own. And we seek the freedom and opportunity that give
    meaning and value to life.

    There is a line in our time, and in every time, between those who believe
    all men are created equal, and those who believe that some men and
    women and children are expendable in the pursuit of power. There is a line
    in our time, and in every time, between the defenders of human liberty and
    those who seek to master the minds and souls of others. Our generation
    has now heard history's call, and we will answer it.

    (From a speech by US President George W. Bush, 9 November 2002)

    (Look out for parallelism in this example.)

4. This Electromagnetic pet door is designed to selectively admit only pets
    wearing a collar carrying a magnet. Normally the flap is prevented from
    opening into the house by an electromagnetic catch, thus preventing stray
    pets from entering your house. However, when your pet approaches
    wearing the magnet, a detector sited in the outer edge of the body moulding
    senses the magnet and the electromagnetic catch is automatically depressed.
    Your pet may then push open the flap with its nose to enter the house. As
    soon as your pet has passed through the flap the electromagnetic catch
    returns to its normal position, so that following pets without a magnet are
    prevented from entering. Pets may exit from the flap without wearing a
    magnet.

    (From instructions for purchasers of a cat-flap or door to allow pets entry
    to a home)

5. **Sand Opera**
    While the Olympics offer a chance to see raw, unbridled power and
    athleticism, the games have also come to be known for showcasing and
    celebrating the sexy athleticism of the human form.

    And beach volleyball, which debuted as a medals sport in 1996 Atlanta
    Olympics, has become one of the most popular spectator sports – in part
    due to the bikinis worn by women players and the muscle-baring singlets
    for the men.

The sport was a big attraction at Sydney 2000. On Bondi Beach, it attracted the fifth largest TV audience of the 28 sports.

This time too, the bikini-clad teams were a sell-out. So has the media gone overboard? But, naturally.

(From the *Times of India* website, 29 August 2004)

6. Father eternal, giver of light and grace,
we have sinned against you and against our neighbour,
in what we have thought,
in what we have said and done,
through ignorance, through weakness,
through our own deliberate fault.
We have wounded your love
and marred your image in us.
We are sorry and ashamed
and repent of all our sins.
For the sake of your Son Jesus Christ,
who died for us,
forgive us all that is past
and lead us out from darkness
to walk as children of light.
Amen.

(From Confession, Common Worship)

7. Under the doctrine of estoppel by representation of fact: where one person ('the representor') has made a representation of fact to another person ('the representee') in words or by acts or conduct, or (being under a duty to the representee to speak or act) by silence or inaction, with the intention (actual or presumptive) and with the result of inducing the representee on the faith of such representation to alter his position to his detriment, the representor, in any litigation which may afterwards take place between him and the representee, is estopped, as against the representee, from making, or attempting to establish by evidence, any averment substantially at variance with his former representation, if the representee at the proper time, and in the proper manner, objects thereto.

(From the following legal textbook: P. Feltham, D. Hochberg and T. Leech, *Spencer Bower: The Law Relating to Estoppel by Representation*, 4th edn. London and Edinburgh: LexisNexis UK (2004), p. 4)

8. A. good afternoon Virgin trainlines Sandra speaking for which journey do you wish to purchase a ticket
   B. it's er – Stockport erm – Watford Junction
   A. Stockport to Watford Junction
   B. yes please
   A. now do you hold a current debit or credit card
   B. yes
   A. and how many people's travelling
   B. one

A. and what date is it you're travelling out

B. tomorrow

A. now i'm going to have to arrange for you to collect your tickets tomorrow at the train station

B. that's fine

A. so what time do you like to depart Stockport at

B. i'd like this to be processed before 2 if i could – erm – Stockport departing er er if i could get a super advance return that'd be great

(Extract from a corpus of The Trainline telephone dialogues, to be found at the website (www.comp.lancs.ac.uk/ucrel/).)

Exercise 10b

Passages (5) and (6) on pp. 164–5 and 166–7 illustrate grammatical characteristics of advertising style in the year 1980. Try to find suitably matching contemporary examples of advertising language to compare with them, and discuss whether the style of advertisements in the press and on television have changed since that time.

Also, if you live not in the UK but in another country where English-language publications and TV commercials are produced, compare these advertisements with advertisements from your own country. Are any of the linguistic differences you notice due to the contrasts between the regional varieties of English – i.e. between UK English and the English of your own country?

Working with Literary Discourse

11

In 2.2 we spent some time looking at the language of a short poem. Now we will examine a passage of prose, to show in more detail how grammar can contribute to the study of literature. We in fact refer to three extracts from novels in this chapter. The first, from D. H. Lawrence's *The Rainbow*, will be the main subject of study, and the second passage, from Dickens's *Bleak House*, will be used for further illustration. The Dickens passage and a further passage, from Virginia Woolf's *The Waves*, will provide material for the exercises at the end of the chapter. The three passages are given on pp. 179–80, 181–3.

Style, viewed as the particular choice of language made by an author, in a sense embodies that author's achievement, and way of experiencing and interpreting the world. This is why the study of style has often been seen as opening a door to fuller literary appreciation. The excellence of literary artists must be evident, ultimately, in their choice of language. But we cannot study this choice of language without some knowledge of how to discuss and analyse the language itself, including its grammar.

11.1 How to analyse style

There is no foolproof technique for analysing literary style – in fact, a method will fail if it is too rigid. Each analysis of style is like an adventure of discovery, in which we combine our knowledge of language and our response to literature in order to appreciate more clearly what the writer has succeeded in saying to us. But it is useful to have a flexible method of study, in which we:

1. First of all read the passage carefully twice or more.
2. Then identify and list features of style under various headings.
3. And then, finally, synthesise these features of style in an interpretation of the meaning and effect of the passage.

Stage 2 is where the real analysis of language takes place, and this is where it is helpful to provide a classification of features of style. We will note these features under one or other of the following major headings: LEXIS,

GRAMMAR, FIGURES OF SPEECH, COHESION AND CONTEXT. Although grammar is represented by only one of these categories, we will notice that it plays its part in the identification of features in the other categories as well.

11.1.1 Lexis

Under this heading we notice features of vocabulary. For example, how far is the vocabulary formal or informal, complex or simple, polysyllabic or monosyllabic? Does the passage contain unusual words, e.g. technical, archaic or dialect words? Do words co-occur in either habitual or unusual **collocations** (word-combinations)?

It is useful to make lists of words belonging to the major word classes, and to note which categories (in terms of form and meaning) they belong to. We might notice, for example, that a passage has many more abstract than concrete nouns, or that it contains many verbs of movement, or adjectives of colour. Although this sounds a mechanical exercise, it can in fact provide a great deal of insight into style.

Style features, whether lexical or grammatical, tend to be a matter of frequency, or more precisely a matter of **relative** frequency. We need to compare a passage with some standard of what is usual or 'normal' if we are going to recognise what is special about its style. This is why it is particularly helpful to compare a number of different passages of approximately the same length. We have chosen three such passages, so as to make the comparison of styles easier.

As lexis is the simplest level of style, and the one which is easiest to notice and discuss, we will say no more about it.

11.1.2 Grammar

Under this heading we look at the sentences and see how they are constructed. How complex are the sentences? What kinds of complexity are found (see 9.5)? Does complexity vary notably from one sentence to another? Are there marked uses of coordination or subordination, of linked or unlinked coordination (see p. 119)? Is there anything to say about the kinds of clause structure or phrase structure favoured? For instance, the writer may favour [*S P*] rather than [*S P O*] patterns, premodifiers rather than postmodifiers, and so on.

To see what role grammar can play in the effect of a passage, let's look at the first and last sentences of the *Bleak House* passage (pp. 181–2) (the sentence numbers in square brackets are those marked in the texts):

[1]   Fog everywhere.
[10]   And hard by Temple Bar, in Lincoln's Inn Hall, at the very heart of the fog, sits the Lord High Chancellor in his High Court of Chancery.

The first sentence is very short and to the point. In fact, it is not a complete sentence at all in the strict grammatical sense: it has no verb, and is simply a noun followed by an adverb of place. It expresses, in a nutshell, what the rest of the passage elaborates in detail – the ubiquity of the fog (and the dense murky fog of London was notorious at that time). It also sets a grammatical pattern that is continued through the first two paragraphs (*Fog up the river ... fog down the river*) where noun phrases, not clauses, become the main units of the text. Why does Dickens omit the tensed verbs? Two plausible answers are these: first, the repetition of *fog* becomes in this way more forceful and dramatic; secondly, the connections between the noun phrases become associative, rather than logical – the reader's eye seems to move from one disconnected scene to another, catching only glimpses of what lies within the fog. This is grammar communicating at an impressionistic level where explicit declarative sentences, with their implications of truth and precision, are not relevant.

The last sentence [10] , on the other hand, is quite long, and leads us to an appropriate climactic conclusion of the train of thought begun with *Fog everywhere*. The High Court of Chancery is for Dickens the *very heart of the fog*, a satirical symbol for the obfuscation of the law. Notice how he works us up to it in stages, as if we are making a journey to the very midst of obscurity. Sentence [9] leads us as far as *Temple Bar*, and sentence [10] completes the journey, taking us from *Temple Bar* to the *Court of Chancery*. This sentence is a good example of the principles of end-focus and end-weight (13.2.3), leading the reader from given to new information. It is important for the effect that the weighty phrases *the Lord High Chancellor in his High Court of Chancery* come at the end as a sort of denouement, and to ensure this there is an inversion of S and P: *sits the Lord High Chancellor*. The role of the first three adverbials (all adverbials of place) in building up the suspense must also be noted: *And hard by Temple Bar, in Lincoln's Inn Hall, at the very heart of the fog*. The order of elements in the clause is quite unusual: [cj A A A P S A].

So both sentence [1] and sentence [10] illustrate, in their different ways, a special descriptive effect that is brought about by unusual grammatical structure: in [1] the P-less sentence, and in [10] the inversion of S and P.

11.1.3 Figures of speech: irregularities and regularities

The traditional figures of speech (metaphor, etc.) are found in both everyday language and in literature. But in literature we often see figures of speech as particularly important: as special linguistic effects which are exploited in literature for their special communicative power. These effects take the shape of special irregularities or regularities.

Of the traditional figures of speech, those most often discussed, such as metaphor, irony and paradox, involve communication at a non-literal level. They usually arise from some 'irregularity' of language – for example, an incongruity of meaning between elements of the same grammatical structure. This example is from the Lawrence extract (p. 179):

[14]   She saw [^{S}(the moonlight) ^{P}(flash) ^{O}(question) (on his face)].

In the subordinate clause, the S, P and O are strangely ill-assorted from a literal point of view. The steady gleam of 'moonlight' cannot normally 'flash' anything, and (besides) a 'question' is not something that can be literally 'flashed', nor can a 'question', literally, be on anyone's face. And perhaps the oddest feature of all, grammatically, is the use of *question* without a determiner, as a **mass** noun. Yet the combined effect of these incongruities is a strikingly vivid impression. The moonlight, the sudden movement of a face out of the shadow, and the questioning expression on the face seem parts of the same momentary experience.

These instances exploit what is **unusual** in language. But there are also figures of speech which involve exploiting extra regularities. These include various types of parallelism: repetitive patterns of structures and words, such as we see pervasively in the Dickens and Lawrence passages. A mild example is sentence [3] of Lawrence:

[3]   [^{S}(he) ^{P}(was drawing) ^{A}(near)], and [^{S}(she) ^{P}(must turn) ^{A}(again)]

Both clauses have the structure [S P A], so the sentence has a neat pattern [S P A] + [S P A]. We call this a 'mild' example of parallelism, because to some extent such patterns arise by accident in discourse, and this instance could easily occur unintentionally. But the sentence is more 'regular', more patterned, than that suggests. Note that in each clause, the phrases contain the same number of words [1, 2, 1] + [1, 2, 1], and that the subjects are both personal pronouns *he* and *she*. If such patterns were merely ornaments, or embellishments of literary style, we would not need to take much notice of them. But there is an important principle that **parallelism of form implies parallelism of meaning**, and here we can feel how the clauses, with their contrasted subjects, balance and oppose one another like the parallel movements of partners in a dance.

The image of a slow, ritual-like dance seems a particularly fitting one to associate with this passage. Look at the more striking parallelism of:

[7]   [[As he came], she drew away], [[as he drew away] , she came].

This sentence consists of a mirror-image pattern, as shown in Figure 11.1. As a matter of interest, the criss-cross pattern is called CHIASMUS after the Greek letter Chi (χ). Again, the movement of the boy and the girl is enacted

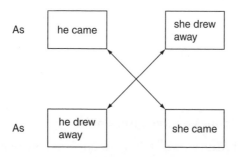

Figure 11.1

in the structure of the sentence. This example is a more striking case of parallelism than that of [3], because not only the structures but also the words which occupy those structures are repeated in the pattern.

In [7] the pattern has a MIMETIC function: it imitates the form of what it refers to – the interweaving movement of the boy and the girl. The effect of sound imitating sense, of form imitating meaning, is something we associate with poetry, but is perhaps an equally important aspect of prose writing. In prose, however, we rarely notice such effects unless we are looking for them. Who, for example, would notice the regular triple, dance-like rhythm of the following NP from Lawrence's opening sentence [1]?

[1] a rhythm, which carried their feet and their bodies in tune.
    x / x x / x x / x x / x x /
    (/ = stressed syllable; x = unstressed syllable).

Or who would notice that the parallelisms we have just observed in [3] and [7] are similarly reinforced by a pattern of regular duple rhythm?

[3] [/ x / x /] x [/ x / x /]
[7] [/ x / x / x /], [/ x / x / x /]

Written out like this, the mimetic quality of these patterns, suggesting the regular movements of the two harvesters, is apparent. But even if readers fail to notice such an effect, they can respond to it at a less conscious level.

If you have met the concept of mimesis in language before, it will probably have been in the more familiar form of ONOMATOPEIA, the use of imitative sounds (particularly vowel and consonant sounds), as in *buzz* and *cuckoo*. In Lawrence [3], for instance, the use of words like *swish* and *hiss* is clearly meant to conjure up the actual sound the oats would have made when picked up and carried. Elsewhere, such phonological suggestion is more subtle and indirect: there are examples in the first sentence of the Virginia Woolf extract (p. 182). But, to conclude, let's notice that repetition of speech sounds can have other functions, such as ironic emphasis. One of the salient effects of Dickens's sentence [10] above is the repeated *h* sounds (followed by similar vowel sounds) at the beginning of important words:

[10a] ... *hard* ... *Hall* ... *heart* ... Lord *High* Chancellor ... *High* Court of Chancery.

This helps the climax effect we have already noted in the grammar, especially through the emphasis it gives to that word *High*, which in this context is obviously ironic. Although *figures of speech* has often had a more limited meaning, we can interpret the term broadly enough to include all special devices like this.

11.1.4 Context (cohesion and situation)

We look finally at features which have to do with how sentences, and indeed whole discourses, are placed within a context. This term *context*, however, like *figures of speech* in 11.1.3, will be understood in a particularly wide sense. On the one hand, it can include the way a sentence fits into the wider context of the discourse, including its relation to preceding and following sentences. This is often called COHESION. On the other hand, it can refer to the way that parts of a discourse, and a discourse as a whole, presuppose a particular SITUATION in 'the world beyond the text'. But literature is a special kind of discourse. Whereas in other kinds of discourse (as in Chapters 9 and 10, especially 10.5) we fit our language to the situation, in literature, in general, we have to fit a situation to the language. That is, in literature, and particularly in works of fiction, we as readers find ourselves 'creating' a discourse situation, by implication from the text itself.

This means that for each novel there is an implied AUTHOR–READER SITUATION, which may be formal, informal, familiar, casual, etc., and through which the novel expresses a 'point of view' towards the characters and events in the fiction. A simple example of this is the use of the narrative present tense in the Dickens passage:

[9b] The raw afternoon *is* rawest, and the dense fog *is* densest, and the muddy streets *are* muddiest .... .

This usage is called the 'historic present': it means that the reader apprehends the goings-on in the novel as if they were happening now, at the very time of reading – a device for dramatic heightening. But in the *Bleak House* description of the fog, it has a further implication of timelessness. This is, indeed, very appropriate to the pettifoggery of the Court of Chancery, where lawsuits drag on interminably.

Another peculiarity of the discourse situation in fiction is that it is complicated by situations within situations. When fiction includes dialogue, it creates a CHARACTER–CHARACTER SITUATION which takes place within the author–reader situation. There are also CHARACTER–READER SITUATIONS (e.g. the dramatic monologue of the autobiographical novel), and possibilities of further complication by further embedding of one discourse in another, or switching from one situation to another, or representing the 'inner monologue' of a character's mind. So a novel may have quite an intricate discourse structure.

To illustrate the point that a novel implies its own discourse situation(s), let's look at the use of questions in the Lawrence passage:

[8]   Were they never to meet?

Questions imply an answer, and therefore evoke a situation in which someone is seeking some information, or the solution to a problem. When we meet this sentence, we are no longer interpreting the passage as part of the author-addressing-reader situation, but as part of a self-questioning situation which is going on in the mind of a character. The negative question (*never*), since it expects a negative answer, implies that character's sense of defeat and frustration.

This brings us to a set of grammatical choices which are intimately connected with the narrative point of view:

[8a] 'Are we never to meet?' he said.
[8b] He asked her if they were never to meet.
[8c] Were they never to meet?

The version which gives speech in quotation marks, [8a] , supplies the actual words supposedly spoken by the character. This is called DIRECT SPEECH, in contrast to the construction with the subordinate clause [8b], which is called INDIRECT SPEECH. A third possibility for reporting the speech of a character is that of [8c], known as FREE INDIRECT SPEECH. Here the main reporting clause is omitted, but the pronouns and tenses are those which are appropriate for indirect speech [8b]. The narrative functions of these three constructions are different. Roughly speaking, [8a] allows the character (the 'he' of Lawrence's narrative) to speak for himself, giving prominence to his point of view. In contrast, [8b] submerges the speaker's point of view in the narrator's (author's) point of view. And [8c] achieves a merger of these two effects. In modern fiction, though, much attention has been given to the rendering of the 'interior monologue' of the mind, not just of overt speech. So to [8a]–[8c] we should add three corresponding variants for reporting thought:

[8d] 'Are we never to meet?' he asked himself.
        (DIRECT THOUGHT)
[8e] He wondered whether they were never to meet.
        (INDIRECT THOUGHT)
[8f] Were they never to meet?
        (FREE INDIRECT THOUGHT)

The last of these, free indirect **thought**, is identical in form to free indirect **speech**: here again, we have to 'create' a situation to fit the words. Free indirect thought is a very common means of portraying the inner consciousness of a character. This is what (we assume) Lawrence is doing in [8].

With this preparation, we can return to the noting of features of style. Under the heading of **cohesion**, we note what use is made of various kinds of connection (e.g. by conjunctions like *and* and sentence adverbials like *therefore*); and of various kinds of cross-reference (e.g. by pronouns like *she*, *it*, *they*, by substitute forms, by ellipsis, by 'expressive repetition' and by 'elegant variation' – see 13.6). Sometimes, as in Dickens's description of the fog, it is the absence of normal devices of cohesion that is striking.

Turning to discourse **situation**, we should be aware of the role here, as in cohesion, of certain words and grammatical features enabling language to refer to aspects of its own situation. They include demonstrative words (*this*, *that*, *now*, *then*, *there*), first- and second-person pronouns (*I*, *you*, etc.), tense and aspect, and verbs like *come* and *go*. One of the fascinating things about the Lawrence extract is the way these items, as well as other indicators of situation, convey a shifting or ambivalent narrative point of view. First, the characters are denoted by the pronouns *he* and *she* throughout, without any variation at all. It seems as if Lawrence wants to maintain a strict objectivity and impersonality. But in [3] (*... he was drawing near, and she must turn again*) we clearly see things from the girl's point of view. This is implied in the phrase *drawing near*, and also in the verb phrases: both the progressive construction *was drawing* and the modal construction *must turn* suggest the subjectivity of her viewpoint. Later, in [7] (*As he came, she drew away, as he drew away, she came*) there is a strange ambivalence of viewpoint: *came* evokes the subjective position of one person watching the other approaching, but this position switches in the middle of the sentence. Perhaps we are seeing things from the centre point, the stook, as both she and he move towards and from it. But, later still, we are evidently experiencing things through the thoughts of the boy. The questions in the final paragraph can be interpreted only as free indirect thought from his viewpoint:

[17]   Why, as she came up from under the moon, would she halt and stand off from him?

To summarise, then: under the heading of COHESION we consider (a) connections and (b) cross-references between sentences; and under the heading of SITUATION we consider features which reflect (a) the author–reader situation and point of view; and (b) the presentation of speech and thought situations within the fiction.

11.2 Illustrative extract

D. H. Lawrence, *The Rainbow*, ch. 4

They worked together, coming and going, in a rhythm, which carried their feet and their bodies in tune.[1] She stooped, she lifted the burden of sheaves, she turned her face to the dimness where he was, and went with her burden over the stubble.[2] She hesitated, set down her sheaves, there was a swish and hiss of mingling oats, he was drawing near, and she must turn again.[3] And there was the flaring moon laying bare her bosom again, making her drift and ebb like a wave.[4]

He worked steadily, engrossed, threading backwards and forwards like a shuttle across the strip of cleared stubble, weaving the long line of riding shocks, nearer and nearer to the shadowy trees, threading his sheaves with hers. [5]

And always, she was gone before he came.[6] As he came, she drew away, as he drew away, she came.[7] Were they never to meet?[8] Gradually a low, deep-sounding will in him vibrated to her, tried to set her in accord, tried to bring her gradually to him, to a meeting, till they should be together, till they should meet as the sheaves that swished together.[9]...

He waited for her, he fumbled at the stook.[10] She came.[11] But she stood back till he drew away.[12] He saw her in shadow, a dark column, and spoke to her, and she answered.[13] She saw the moonlight flash question on his face.[14] But there was a space between them, and he went away, the work carried them, rhythmic.[15]

Why was there always a space between them, why were they apart?[16] Why, as she came up from under the moon, would she halt and stand off from him?[17] Why was he held away from her?[18] His will drummed persistently, darkly, it drowned everything else.[19]

(294 words)

(Between sentences [9] and [10] a short paragraph is omitted.)

11.3 Outline analysis (with questions for further study)

11.3.1 Lexis

In keeping with the subject, the vocabulary is simple and homely, but with a slightly literary or archaic flavour here and there: *drawing near, laying bare her bosom*, etc. What is the effect of this type of lexical choice?

Compare the frequency of nouns, verbs, adjectives and adverbs in this passage with those in the Dickens passage. You will discover some marked differences. What implications do these have?

11.3.2 Grammar

The sentences vary from extreme simplicity ([11]) to considerable complexity ([9]), but the complexity tends to be of a progressive kind through the repetition of coordinate, particularly unlinked, constructions:

[5] [He worked steadily, ⟨[engrossed], [threading . . .], [weaving . . .], [threading his sheaves with hers]⟩.]

Now try a skeleton parsing of sentence [9]. What is the most important feature of its structure? At word level, we notice, coordination tends to join elements in pairs: *coming and going* [1], *backwards and forwards* [5]. What other examples are there of pairing, whether by coordination or by other means? What is the relevance of all this pairing and coordination?

Clauses of [S P] or [S P A] structure predominate. There are few [S P O] structures. In this way, the passage tends to emphasise movements in themselves, rather than movements directed to a particular goal or purpose. It is significant that some of the clauses with objects that do occur have an inanimate subject and a human object – which is the opposite of what is normally expected: *the flaring moon laying bare her bosom* [4]; *the work carried them* [15] ; and a similar case is the passive *Why was he held away from her?* [18], where the **doer** of the action is left unspecified. What effect do these clauses have in the depiction of the harvest-making?

11.3.3 Figures of speech

What are the predominant metaphors of the passage, and how do they fit into the description of the 'ritual' mentioned above? (For example, in sentence [1] we suggest there are metaphorical uses of *carried* and *in tune*.) Metaphors are implied comparisons, whereas similes are overt comparisons. What similes occur in the passage (tell-tale words are *like, as, as if*), and how do they fit in with the metaphors?

We have already noticed, with reference to [3] and [7], that the passage contains grammatical and lexical parallelism. Look at the long sentence [9] from this point of view, and note the instances of unlinked coordination (see p. 119), coinciding with Lawrence's use of commas. What is the effect of repeating words and structures without using coordinating conjunctions like *and*?

One grammatical oddity of the passage is the use of an adjective form where normally an adverb in *-ly* would be called for: *the work carried them, rhythmic* [15]. Have you any ideas on why Lawrence should prefer this to the adverb form *rhythmically*?

11.3.4 Context and cohesion

We have already noted the repeated use of pronouns (*he, she*). Elsewhere it is part of Lawrence's technique to make repeated use of the same words, as if to make the most of their evocative or symbolic value. For example, the word *burden* is repeated in [2] ; *sheaves* is repeated a number of times; *threading* occurs twice in [5]. The clause *But there was a space between them* in [15] is largely repeated in the next sentence: *Why was there always a space between them?* In this way the passage insists on the symbolism of the 'space' – a physical distance evoking emotional distance. At the same time, the use of free indirect thought (p. 178) in the repeated, insistent *Why* questions makes the boy's longing the most dominant emotion of the passage.

Although Lawrence's language is relatively simple and accessible, he achieves intensity through the symbolism of natural or homely rhythms (the waves, the moon, the vibrating, the weaving), and the rhythmic repetitions and parallelisms of the language itself, imitating the to-and-fro movements of the harvesters.

11.4 Further illustrative extracts for discussion

11.4.1 Charles Dickens, *Bleak House*, ch. 1

Fog everywhere.[1] Fog up the river, where it flows among green aits† and meadows; fog down the river, where it rolls defiled among the tiers of shipping and the waterside pollutions of a great (and dirty) city.[2] Fog on the Essex marshes, fog on the Kentish heights.[3] Fog creeping into the cabooses of collier-brigs; fog lying out on the yards and hovering in the rigging of great ships; fog drooping on the gunwales of barges and small boats.[4] Fog in the eyes and throats of ancient Greenwich pensioners, wheezing by the firesides of their wards; fog in the stem and bowl of the afternoon pipe of the wrathful skipper, down in his close cabin; fog cruelly pinching the toes and fingers of his shivering little 'prentice boy on deck.[5] Chance people on the bridges peeping over the parapets into a nether sky of fog, with fog all round them, as if they were up in a balloon and hanging in the misty clouds..[6]

Gas looming through the fog in divers places in the streets, much as the sun may, from the spongey fields, be seen to loom by husbandman and ploughboy.[7] Most of the shops lighted two hours before their time – as the gas seems to know, for it has a haggard and unwilling look.[8]

The raw afternoon is rawest, and the dense fog is densest, and the muddy streets are muddiest near that leaden-headed old obstruction, appropriate ornament for the threshold of a leaden-headed old corporation, Temple Bar.[9] And hard by Temple Bar, in Lincoln's Inn Hall, at the very heart of the fog, sits the Lord High Chancellor in his High Court of Chancery.[10]

† Aits are small islands.

(276 words)

11.4.2 Virginia Woolf, *The Waves*, Penguin edn 1964, pp. 62–3

In the garden the birds that had sung erratically and spasmodically in the dawn on that tree, on that bush, now sang together in chorus, shrill and sharp; now together, as if conscious of companionship, now alone as if to the pale blue sky.[1] They swerved, all in one flight, when the black cat moved among the bushes, when the cook threw cinders on the ash heap and startled them.[2] Fear was in their song, and apprehension of pain, and joy to be snatched quickly now at this instant.[3] Also they sang emulously in the clear morning air, swerving high over the elm tree, singing together as they chased each other, escaping, pursuing, pecking each other as they turned high in the air.[4] And then tiring of pursuit and flight, lovelily they came descending, delicately declining, dropped down and sat silent on the tree, on the wall, with their bright eyes glancing, and their heads turned this way, that way; aware, awake; intensely conscious of one thing, one object in particular.[5]

Perhaps it was a snail shell, rising in the grass like a grey cathedral, a swelling building burnt with dark rings and shadowed green by the grass.[6] Or perhaps they saw the splendour of the flowers making a light of flowing purple over the beds, through which dark tunnels of purple shade were driven between the stalks.[7] Or they fixed their gaze on the small bright apple leaves dancing yet withheld, stiffly sparkling among the pink-tipped blossoms.[8] Or they saw the rain drop on the hedge, pendent but not falling, with a whole house bent in it, and towering elms; or gazing straight at the sun, their eyes became gold beads.[9]

(284 words)

=========== **EXERCISES** ===========

Exercise 11a

Comment in detail on the style of the passage from *Bleak House* (11.4.1), applying the general approach suggested in this chapter. Use grammatical analysis selectively, to make your commentary clearer and more explicit. The following aspects of style are among those worth examining:

1. LEXIS. Compare Dickens's vocabulary here with Lawrence's. Note any unusual or technical words. Compare the frequency of nouns, verbs, adjectives and adverbs with those of Lawrence.
2. GRAMMAR. Pairing of constructions by coordination. Contrast between the last two sentences and the other sentences. Use of ellipsis and grammatical omissions. Position and function of subordinate clauses, including -ing clauses.
3. FIGURES OF SPEECH. Use of similes and fanciful comparisons. Types and functions of parallelism and word repetition. Alliteration.
4. COHESION AND CONTEXT. Lack of connectives – coordinating conjunctions or linking adverbs – between sentences. (Are there any at all?) Use of the present tense.

Exercise 11b

Now try a similar stylistic analysis of the passage from The Waves (11.4.2). Comment in detail on the style of the passage, applying the general approach suggested in this chapter. Use grammatical analysis selectively, to make your commentary clearer and more explicit. The following aspects of style are among those worth examining:

1. LEXIS. Rich sensory qualities of vocabulary. Concrete nouns (referring to natural phenomena), descriptive adjectives (vision – especially colour – and sound), verbs of movement, adverbs – especially adverbs ending in -ly.
2. GRAMMAR. Complex sentences, coordination (linked and unlinked), tensed and tenseless subordinate clauses, adverbials.
3. FIGURES OF SPEECH. parallelism, alliteration, metaphors, similes.
4. COHESION AND CONTEXT. Linking of sentences, especially use of or. Use of the, that, a in relation to given and new information.

How does Woolf achieve such a vivid 'word painting'? How does she make us see things from the birds' point of view?

Grammar and Problems of Usage

In Chapters 9, 10 and 11 we examined how knowledge of grammar can be used to analyse language as used by others, whether in speech or writing, in non-literary discourse or literature. In this chapter and the next we investigate how we can apply what we know about grammar to the choices we make in our own use of language. So the focus changes from our roles as interpreters of language to our roles as speakers and (especially) writers.

12.1 Opinions about grammar

Our native language is such an important part of our social existence that, like other social institutions, it easily becomes a subject for argument. Language, moreover, is intimately connected with judgements about status, and about what is good or bad, right or wrong, beautiful or ugly. This is why it is so difficult for people to be unbiased and rational when they express opinions about their mother tongue. In this chapter, all the same, we shall try to say something impartial on problems of usage about which speakers of English can feel quite strongly. For example, some people (especially older people who have gone through a traditional education) feel quite strongly that we should not split our infinitives: for them, to separate *to* from the infinitive verb with which it belongs, as in *to flatly refuse*, can be little short of a crime.

What can we say about such opinions? In actual practice, split infinitives are quite common. So one reaction is to shrug one's shoulders and to say there is no point in arguing about matters of taste: people who dislike split infinitives are like people who object to loud ties or who cannot stomach kippers. Another view is the one we took in 1.2: in discussing prescriptive grammar we treated received opinions as to 'good' and 'bad' usage as sociological norms, like rules of etiquette. In some situations (particularly more formal situations such as writing a letter applying for a job) we will want to be on our best linguistic behaviour, and this means steering clear of pitfalls such as the 'split infinitive', if only to avoid usages which might give other people a negative image of us. Some precepts of 'good grammar' come to be regarded almost as shibboleths (discriminatory usages), distinguishing the educated from the uneducated. Other precepts do have a basis of common sense, and deserve serious discussion. But one thing is certain: people will not give up arguing about language usage, and it is as well to be aware of their attitudes. Knowledge of grammar can also help us to describe and understand these attitudes.

12.2 Prescriptive 'rules'

First, here is a test. If you had to choose, which of the following alternatives would you use in a letter applying for a job?

(1a) ... the post I am applying *for.*
(1b) ... the post *for which* I am applying.

(2a) *But* more recently I have been attending classes in German ...
(2b) More recently, *however,* I have been attending classes in German ...

(3a) I had to choose the *least* harmful of the two courses.
(3b) I had to choose the *less* harmful of the two courses.

If you want to improve your chances of creating a good impression, you will probably prefer the (b) sentence in each case, thereby obeying the following prescriptive 'rules':

- 'Do not end a sentence or clause with a preposition.'
- 'Do not begin a sentence with a coordinator such as *and* or *but*.'
- 'When comparing two things, use a comparative construction; when comparing more than two things, use a superlative construction.'

All these are typical prescriptive 'rules' in that they are assumed to work without exception. In practice, however, they are frequently broken by native speakers; this is why we enclose the word 'rule' in quotation marks. Moreover, if we try to apply them in every case, the result can be awkward and totally unEnglish. For example:

- *For what is it*? is not an acceptable variant of *What is it for*?
- *May the better man win* is abnormal and unidiomatic (say, when talking about two boxers) in comparison with *May the best man win*.

Such 'rules' may therefore have a problematic outcome, when, in an attempt to strenuously avoid a supposed offence, we fail to produce clear, idiomatic English. (As a case in point, notice that the split infinitive in the last sentence could not be happily replaced by *strenuously to avoid a supposed offence* or *to avoid a supposed offence strenuously*.) The safest course, in such cases, is to reword the sentence so that the possibility of breaking a prescriptive 'rule' does not arise: for example, *in a strenuous attempt to avoid* ... would solve the problem above.

We will not in general give solutions to problems of usage in this chapter, but we do offer one piece of advice, which is a generalisation of the evasive tactic just illustrated: when you are faced with the dilemma of either disobeying a prescriptive 'rule' or awkwardly and conspicuously obeying it, reformulate the sentence so that the dilemma does not arise.

This may be called the PRINCIPLE OF GRAMMATICAL DISCRETION, because it avoids giving offence to your addressees, whether their attitudes to usage are authoritarian or permissive. This principle applies chiefly to formal written English – the type of English in which prescriptive grammar tends to matter.

Prescriptive 'rules' like that of the split infinitive can reasonably be called superstitions: people have learned to obey them out of blind faith in authority, and find it difficult to explain **why** they obey them. But when attempts are made to justify such 'rules', these are among the reasons often given:

- The 'rule' helps one to communicate clearly, etc. (a **practical** reason)
- The 'rule' is in accordance with logic.   (an **intellectual** reason)
- The 'rule' is in accordance with good taste.   (an **aesthetic** reason)
- The 'rule' is in accordance with tradition.   (a **historical** reason)
- The 'rule' is in accordance with Standard
  English.   (a **normative** reason)

But these reasons rarely carry conviction on their own. If we search for the origin of prescriptive 'rules', we find that many of them began in attempts made, especially in the eighteenth century, to describe English grammar in terms of the categories of Latin grammar. The prestige of Latin was so enormous that English constructions that differed from the Latin model were disparaged. In other cases, we find that the early grammarians, in their attempt to codify English and reduce it to rules, rationalized a situation which, in the language of their time, was variable and uncertain.

So it was with a 'rule' about the choice between the modal verbs *will* and *shall*. In a nutshell, this 'rule' said that (in referring to future happenings) *shall* should be used with a first-person subject (*I* or *we*), and that *will* should be used with other subjects (*she, you,* etc.). However, as use of *shall* is declining considerably nowadays, even with first-person subjects, this rule seems no longer viable. It seems best to accept that *will* can be used for all persons.

Nowadays, with the decline of traditional grammar teaching, these 'rules', if they exist in people's minds at all, are often no more than vaguely remembered folklore.

12.3 The priests of usage

Human nature can always justify prescriptive rules, in the last resort, by appeal to authority. We are inclined to obey the *Highway Code*, for instance, because it is backed by the authority of law. But the strange thing about prescriptive 'rules' of English grammar is that they are not upheld by any official authority. (In this respect English differs from French; the *Académie Française*, even now, is regarded as the official arbiter of usage in France.) The tradition of the English-speaking world is to rely on the judgement of unofficial lawgivers, whose authority is derived simply from their reputations as scholars and writers. Among this 'priesthood' we should place many grammarians of the past; but its most famous members have been lexicographers, notably Samuel Johnson, the eighteenth-century author of the *Dictionary of the English Language*. In the twentieth century, a somewhat similar position to that of Dr Johnson was occupied by H. W. Fowler, author of *A Dictionary of Modern English Usage* (first published in 1926, and revised for a third edition by Burchfield, as *The New Fowler's Modern English Usage*, 1998). '*Fowler*' became a household word, and the book is still consulted for guidance not only on matters of word usage, but on matters of grammar as well. We might call Fowler the 'high priest of usage', but there are many other writers in the same fraternity: we might mention Eric Partridge, author of the popular *Usage and Abusage*.

Like his great predecessor, Johnson, Fowler is more noted for his wit and wisdom than for consistency and rationality. His attacks on some prescriptive 'rules' can be as spirited as his defence of others; in still other cases he gives up his priest's mantle and tells his readers to make up their own minds. Whether we agree with him or not, we are likely to find his criticisms of usage entertaining and instructive.

The great demand for books like '*Fowler*' testifies to the existence of problems of usage, and the need that users feel for guidance on these matters. How do such problems arise? In part, they seem to result from a misconception about standard English. People tend to expect that a standard language – as is more generally true of spelling than of grammar – allows only one correct form, and that the standard can never change. So when faced with a choice between two ways of saying the same thing, they assume that one of them must be the correct one – or at least must be the preferable one. Prescriptive 'rules' help to satisfy this need for a decision procedure, but grammar can be so subtle that the 'rules' do not always lead to acceptable solutions. Hence usage problems arise: problems of when we should or should not follow the rule, or problems of which rule to follow. In the remainder of the chapter we discuss some examples of these problems.

12.4 Problems of personal pronouns

The main prescriptive 'rule' for subject and object pronouns runs as follows:

'Rule' A

1. 'Use the subject pronouns *I, he, she, we, they, who* in the function of subject or complement': *I am tired*; *It was **she** who spoke first*.
2. 'Use the object pronouns *me, him, her, us, them, whom* in the function of object or prepositional complement': *Sarah saw **them***; *His sister spoke to **us***.

But 1 is frequently broken when the pronoun is a complement:

(4) Who's there? It's only *me*. (not: It's only *I*.)

And 2 is frequently broken in the case of *who/whom*:

(5) *Who* do you like best? *Who* were you speaking to? (rather than: *Whom* ...)

Only someone very pedantic would insist on saying *It's I* these days. *Whom do you like best?* also sounds rather pedantic in speech.

12.4.1 Pronouns with ellipsis

This is another difficulty. In constructions with ellipsis, prescriptive grammar argues that the correct form to use is the one which would be appropriate if omitted words were restored: that is, (6a) and (7a) are correct, rather than (6b) and (7b):

(6a) Who sent this letter? *I*.
(6b) Who sent this letter? *Me*.

(7a) She's nearly as tall as *he*.
(7b) She's nearly as tall as *him*.

Compare:

(6c) Who sent this letter? *I did*.
(7c) She's nearly as tall as *he is*.

But (6a) and (7a) are obviously stilted and unidiomatic beside the 'incorrect' forms (6b) and (7b). According to our principle of grammatical discretion (12.2), the best thing to do – if you are using such forms in serious writing – is to evade the problem by using a construction without ellipsis, as in (6c) and (7c).

12.4.2 Pronouns with coordination

The prescriptive 'rules' are quite often broken in coordinate phrases like *you and me, him and her*:

(8a) *You and me* must get together.
(8b) *Him and my mum* have split up.

People who know the 'rules' find these quite blatant and excruciating violations. Such examples do, however, show the tangles and uncertainties in which native speakers find themselves over the case of pronouns. Examples like (8a) and (8b) occur naturally and spontaneously in casual speech. On the other hand, examples like (9) and (10), where the subject pronoun replaces the object pronoun, seem to arise from the user's mistaken assumption that, when coordinated, *I* is always more correct than *me*:

(9) The decision will have to be made by *Christine and I*.
(10) Susan has invited *John and I* to a party.

This assumption is presumably made because of frequent correction of cases like (8a). Such mistaken attempts to overgeneralise a 'rule' are called

HYPERCORRECTIONS. However, sentences like (1) seem to be getting quite common these days: perhaps in the future they will be recognized as 'okay'.

12.4.3 Possessive and object forms

Not all pronoun problems arise over choice between subject and object pronouns. There is also the problem of choosing between the object and genitive/possessive forms in the subject position of NCling clauses:

(11a)   He objected to [*our* winning both prizes].
(11b)   He objected to [us winning both prizes].

Here prescriptive grammar favours the genitive of (11a). Fowler himself, voicing the usage priest's common conviction that grammatical standards are declining, is quite biting on the question: 'It is perhaps beyond hope for a generation that regards *upon you giving* as normal English to recover its hold upon the truth that grammar matters.' But once again there is an awkward effect when we attempt to generalise the genitive construction to nouns, and especially to complex noun phrases, which would have to be made into genitives to correspond with the possessive determiner option:

(12)   He objected to *members of the same school's* winning both prizes.
(13)   The crisis was a result *of recent inflation's* having outweighed the benefits of increased exports.

The use of a genitive phrase in such cases is rare and feels cumbersome. Both these sentences would seem more natural if the *'s* were omitted.

12.4.4 Pronoun usage in formal and informal English

To conclude this section on pronouns, there is a considerable gulf between formal and informal English in the choice of pronoun forms. While formal written English tends to follow the traditional Latin-based rules, informal spoken English follows its own rules, which are simple enough in their own terms. According to these rules, the subject pronoun is used in the normal subject position, preceding all or part of the verb phrase, whereas the object pronoun is used in other positions in the clause. This means that the object pronoun is the UNMARKED, neutral form in the pairs *I/me, she/her*, etc., even being used, for example, in unattached 'absolute' positions such as:

(14)   How do you feel?   *Me?* I feel fine.

But with *who/whom*, it is the subject form which is unmarked, since the *wh*-pronoun normally precedes the predicator, behaving in this sense like a subject:

(15)   *Who* were you talking to?
(16)   I want to see you. *Who? Me?*

Difficulties of pronoun usage arise because of the conflict between these two sets of rules – the formal and the informal.

12.5 The problem of number concord

The prescriptive 'rule' of number concord is simply this:

'Rule' B

1. A singular predicator goes with a singular subject.
2. A plural predicator goes with a plural subject.

This is nice and logical. But in a range of cases the 'rule' is commonly disobeyed, particularly in British English, as in:

(17) The Government *agree* with this view.

(Of course the 'correct' singular verb *agrees* could also be used here.) With nouns like *government, committee, family*, we find not only a singular verb following a singular subject, but a plural one following a singular subject. Such nouns are COLLECTIVE NOUNS: they refer to collections of people or things, and this is reflected in the choice of a plural predicator. In some cases the singular predicator cannot be sensibly used at all:

(18) In no time the audience *were* tapping *their* feet and clapping *their* hands.
(19) The family *are* always quarrelling among *themselves* about which TV channel to watch.

(*The audience was tapping its feet and clapping its hands* and *His family is always quarrelling among itself* would be absurd.) Examples (18) and (19) show that there is also a problem of concord for pronouns; for example, in (19) *themselves* is exceptional in being a plural pronoun in agreement with a singular antecedent (*the family*).

It is useful, in fact, to distinguish GRAMMATICAL CONCORD – the strict rule 'singular goes with singular, and plural with plural' – from NOTIONAL CONCORD – from the agreement of a pronoun or predicator with the **idea** of number present in the **meaning** of the preceding noun phrase. Notional concord lies behind examples like (17)–(19). It also applies to some converse cases such as the biblical *The **wages** of sin **is** death*. Here, although *wages* is grammatically plural, the meaning it expresses (reward) is arguably singular.

Pronouns such as *none, any, either, neither, everyone* form another set of cases where notional concord often wins the battle against grammatical concord in ordinary speech:

(20) None of the parcels *has/have* yet arrived.
(21) His plays are popular in the West, but I doubt whether any *has/have* been performed in Japan.
(22) Everyone can vote as *they* wish.
(23) What happens when somebody leaves *their* job of *their* own accord?

As with the problems of grammatical case discussed in 12.4, such violations of prescriptive 'rule' are common enough in speech, but still tend to be frowned on in serious writing.

12.6 The problem of the generic masculine

If we wished to alter (22) above in order to obey grammatical concord, we might choose between the following sentences:

(22a) Everyone can vote as *he* wishes.
(22b) Everyone can vote as *he* or *she* wishes.

Of these, (22a) is an instance of the GENERIC MASCULINE, i.e. the use of the pronoun *he* to refer to either male or female persons. The generic masculine *he*, although traditional, is widely avoided because it is felt to perpetuate a masculine bias in the language. On the other hand, the coordination of masculine and feminine pronouns as in (22b) is often felt to be awkward, especially when it is repeated, or when it is combined with reflexive pronouns:

> You won't be the last holiday-maker to get *himself or herself* involved in a holiday romance.

Himself or herself is felt to be a bit of a mouthful, so that speakers and writers sometimes resort to an abbreviated version *him- or herself*, or even to a new singular pronoun *themself*. So by rejecting (22a) in favour of (22b), we jump from a problem of grammatical concord only to land in a snare of clumsy coordination. The generic masculine is still sometimes used as a matter of convenience, but the principle of grammatical discretion (12.2) would lead us to avoid the problem of singular pronoun choice. This can be done, for example, by reformulating the sentence in the plural:

(22c) All citizens can vote as they wish.

Also, recently there has been growing acceptance of singular *they, them*, etc. even in written English (e.g. student textbooks), so that (22) may eventually turn out to be the most acceptable variant after all. As a matter of interest, we have avoided the generic masculine *he* throughout this book, although it occurs in the legal passage (7) quoted on p. 170.

12.7 Problems of ellipsis

Many of the grammatical uncertainties which beset people in writing English have to do with ellipsis. Describing the rules of English in this area is not easy, and it is difficult to draw the line between prescriptive and descriptive grammar. Nevertheless, we can roughly state a 'rule' as follows:

'Rule' C

A sentence with ellipsis is acceptable only if the same sentence is acceptable after the 'deleted' words are restored.

To this an explanatory rider should be added:

The words which are 'deleted' in ellipsis must duplicate words occurring elsewhere in the context.

Here is a simple illustration of this 'rule':

Version with ellipsis: (The place where ellipsis occurs is marked by ^.)
The city can ^, and always will, *be proud of its achievements*.

Version with 'deleted' elements restored:
The city can *be proud of its achievements*, and always will *be proud of its achievements*.

And here are two examples which violate the 'rule':

(25)   The city has ^, and always will *be proud of its achievements*.
(26)   They are *revising* the book more thoroughly than it has ever been ^.

The fault is clear when we try to insert the words in italics in the spaces marked ^ in these examples. To make the resulting sentences grammatical, we should have to insert *been* instead of *be*, and *revised* instead of *revising*. Here is a parallel case involving ellipsis of a noun:

(27)   This car is one of the safest ^, if not the safest *vehicle on the road*.

The rule requires the insertion of a singular noun *vehicle*, whereas the grammar of the sentence requires a plural one *vehicles*. This mismatch is enough to make the sentence strictly ungrammatical, though (oddly) the requirement is less strict if the elliptical phrase follows its sister construction:

(28)   This car is one of the safest *vehicles on the road*, if not the safest ^ .

The more complex a sentence is, the more liable it is to mismatches of ellipsis. It takes some time to work out what is wrong with this example:

(29)   If only the litter laws were enforced, *the disgrace of our present rubbish-strewn high streets* would be eliminated overnight, and could even bring economies in the city's overstretched waste-disposal services.

The ellipsis of the subject of the second clause, after *and*, is only allowable if the second subject is meant to be identical to the first one (the phrase in italics). But it makes no sense to say *the disgrace of our present rubbish-strewn high streets could ... bring economies ... .* The intended meaning must surely be that *the enforcement of the litter laws could ... bring economies ... .* This is the kind of lapse which Fowler describes as 'swapping horses' – where the writer loses track of how the sentence began, and completes it as if it had had a different beginning.

12.8 Dangling tenseless clauses

The mismatch of ellipsis most often condemned by traditional grammars and handbooks is the quaintly-named DANGLING PARTICIPLE (more officially called the 'misrelated' or 'unattached' participle). In fact, what is said about the dangling participle can be extended to apply to adverbial tenseless clauses in general, whether they are Cling, Clen, or Cli clauses:

(30) [Leaning over the parapet], a water rat caught my eye.
(31) [Lying under the table], the secretary found a large pile of secret documents.
(32) The award went to the mountaineers who had rushed Mrs Weekes to hospital [after breaking her ribs].
(33) [Abandoned by his public], his loyal bulldog was alone the companion of his last hours.
(34) [To reach London in time], she sent the parcel by air mail.

The 'rule' flouted in these sentences may be expressed in a loose but serviceable form as follows:

'Rule' D

An adverbial tenseless clause which has no overt subject is *understood* to have a subject identical to that of the main clause to which it belongs.

On this basis, (30) implies that the water rat was leaning over the parapet, (31) that the secretary was lying under the table, and (32) that the mountaineers broke Mrs Weekes's ribs – implications which would clearly not be intended by the writers of these sentences.

The *ing*-clauses of (30)–(32) may be described as MISRELATED, in the sense that they can be interpreted according to the 'rule' but that the interpretation is the wrong one. The *ing*-clause of (35) illustrates, rather, the UNATTACHED tenseless clause:

(35) Walking along the crest of the hill, it was a glorious day and the view was beautiful.

There is no sensible way of interpreting this according to the 'rule'. In practice, though, we do interpret it, by 'stretching' the rule to mean something like *While she/we/they was/were walking* ... . In scientific writing, passive sentences which are interpreted in this way do not seem particularly objectionable:

(36) Using this new technique, more accurate results have been obtained.

There are also cases like (37) and (38), where the dangling clause is idiomatically accepted as a sentence adverbial, and where its subject is identified not with the subject of the main clause, but with the speaker of the whole sentence:

(37) To cut a long story short, they got married.
(38) Considering how much it costs, this machine is a failure.

Few people would object to this kind of unattached clause. Once more we find that problems of usage are not so simple as they appear. In the case of the dangling tenseless clause, there seem to be different degrees of acceptability, and some apparent infringements of the 'rule' seem quite normal.

12.9 Conclusion

We have continually enclosed the word 'rule' in quotation marks, as a reminder that these precepts of prescriptive grammar are not binding on either the speaker or the writer of English. But there are three good reasons why it is best to keep these 'rules' in formal writing, unless there is good reason to the contrary. In breaking a 'rule', you may:

1. offend against principles of good style, as discussed in Chapter 13 (for example, dangling participles can cause ambiguity);
2. produce an inappropriate usage, in terms of register (for example, *Him and my mum have split up* would be quite inappropriate in formal written English, although not in colloquial spoken English);
3. offend in the sense of breaking a rule of etiquette which some readers regard as important (for example, splitting an infinitive may be objectionable to some, rather as putting one's elbows on the table or eating peas with the underside of one's fork may be found objectionable).

It is best, then, to keep to these 'rules' in formal written English unless there are bad consequences of obeying them which outweigh the good consequences. In such a case, the principle of grammatical discretion (12.2) comes to the rescue once more.

─────────────── **EXERCISES** ───────────────

Exercise 12a (answers on pp. 224–5)

The following is a list of sentences which some speakers of English would condemn as being contrary to some 'rule' of prescriptive grammar. In each case, say whether the 'rule' concerns (A) pronouns forms, (B) number concord, (C) ellipsis, (D) 'dangling' tenseless clauses, or (E) some other topic. If criticised for using such a sentence in formal writing, how would you either (i) justify the sentence as it stands, or (ii) change the sentence so as to avoid the criticism?

1. It was argued that the President, in common with many other Western politicians, were ignoring the interests of the developing world.
2. Mervyn John's record is now as good, if not better than his compatriot Michael Steed.
3. The risk of infection can be avoided by bathing the cut in antiseptic.
4. What worried her parents most was him being a racing driver.
5. Twenty per cent could be knocked off the fuel consumption and yet be able to keep the price at its present level.
6. Have each of you opened your parcels?
7. I believe it would be wrong to even think of it.
8. Are you sure it was them? It might have been us.
9. Margaret and he will be playing against you and I.
10. Neither the publisher nor the author were aware of the printer's blunder.
11. While they were talking, us girls were listening at the keyhole.
12. This error has fuelled the nation's distrust of multinational corporations and of its determination to stand on its own feet.

13. The press published a story about some Congressman from the Midwest taking bribes from farmers.
14. When removed from their normal habitat, it is advisable to treat these animals with great care.
15. All lights should be extinguished on vacating these premises.
16. These sort of radios are very reliable.
17. Flying through the air at the speed of sound, a sudden thought struck me.
18. Which team has the best record, yours or theirs?
19. We will not object to your postponing the meeting.
20. She absolutely denies that any of her supporters have been disloyal.

Exercise 12b (partial answers on p. 225)

This is a more challenging exercise, the purpose of which is to stimulate discussion rather than to produce solutions. There are more types of problem involving ellipsis than were illustrated in 12.7. The following sentences are felt to be unsatisfactory in one way or another. They do not, however, violate 'Rule' C as it stands.

(i) Divide the sentences below into three or more different types, according to the types of elliptical construction they illustrate.
(ii) Try to describe what might be thought unsatisfactory about each type.
(iii) Try to revise the conditions of 'Rule' C so that the 'rule' does not allow sentences of these kinds.
(iv) Revise each sentence so as to avoid the difficulty.

(A CLUE: Note that all the sentences contain coordination. TIPS: (a) Insert a ^ (caret) where ellipsis occurs; (b) place in ⟨ ⟩ (angle brackets) (see 7.7) the elements which are yoked together by coordination.)

1. They captured and put him in prison.
2. Brad was young, good-looking, and enjoyed life to the full.
3. Either the children did not know what had happened, or were trying to protect their parents.
4. The spy was in his forties, of average build, and obviously wore a wig.
5. By giving the police a pay rise, the Minister hopes to improve and make the force more efficient.
6. Had the queen lived five years longer or had given birth to an heir, the subsequent history of Ruritania would have been very different.
7. You have to weigh, count and pack the parcels in large containers.
8. Not only did she arrive late, but woke up the entire household.
9. They collect and distribute food and clothing to the homeless.
10. I am fond both of dogs and cats.

Grammar and Composition

13.1 Grammar and writing

How can knowledge of grammar be used to improve our style of written English? If we know something about grammar, we can criticise and discuss our own writing, and learn to improve it. Here are four maxims of good writing which we will illustrate and enlarge upon in this last chapter:

1. Make your language easy to follow.
2. Be clear.
3. Be economical.
4. Be effective.

Practical principles such as these cannot always be fulfilled at the same time. Sometimes they compete with one another. One example of this occurs whenever we open our mouths to speak: we have to speak loudly enough and slowly enough to be understood ('Be clear'), but we also have to try not to waste effort by speaking too slowly for the purpose ('Be economical'). So to hit the right level of delivery, we have to weigh up the competing demands of principles 2 and 3.

Such principles are, in a way, precepts of good behaviour in the use of language. Although they apply to both spoken and written language, in spontaneous speech we have little time to give them consideration. But there is less excuse for ignoring them in writing, where we have the leisure to revise and redraft, and where the addressee does not have the immediate chance to reply and seek clarification. People understandably tend to be more critical of style in writing than in speech – which is one reason why we concentrate in this chapter on style in written composition.

13.2 'Make your language easy to follow'

Time tyrannizes over the way we compose and understand messages. We cannot say all that we have to say at one moment, in one fell swoop; we have to choose in which order to express things. Often grammatical choices are choices which affect order. This is notably true of choices discussed in 8.7:

structure-changing choices such as that between an active and a passive construction, for example between *The Chinese invented fireworks* and *Fireworks were invented by the Chinese*.

Our first principle, 'Make your language easy to follow', is designed to help the reader make sense of a text in linear form. It has three aspects, SENTENCE LENGTH, SUBORDINATION and ORDERING.

13.2.1 Sentence length

For the reader's sake, a text should be suitably segmented into units, so that it can be understood bit by bit. In grammar, the largest unit is the sentence, and it is important to avoid sentences which are too long or too short. It would of course be wrong to prescribe an 'ideal sentence length' for all purposes, but recent studies indicate that the average sentence in written English is about eighteen words long.

In general, the longer a sentence is, the more complex it is (see p. 159 for a discussion of complexity). Also, the more complex it is, the greater the burden it places on our attention and memory. On the other hand, if we go to the other extreme, repeatedly making use of simple sentences, the result can be monotonous, lacking in light and shade. As is true of so many things, a happy medium is often the best course. Consider:

(1) John Keats was fascinated by the art and literature of the ancient world. Just before his twenty-first birthday in 1816, he read George Chapman's translation of Homer. He wrote a famous sonnet on the subject. The next year, he visited the Elgin Marbles. The painter Benjamin Haydon accompanied him. This developed his enthusiasm still further. He wrote another notable sonnet after the visit. But his Greece was essentially a Greece of the imagination. It was the Greece of John Lemprière's *Classical Dictionary*. This he had read when young. He never visited Greece.

Although its meaning is clear and easy to follow, this passage suffers from the flatness of a 'short-breathed' style, with brief, one-clause sentences. On the other hand, we have:

(2) Although John Keats had been fascinated by the art and literature of the ancient world ever since he read George Chapman's translation of Homer (which produced a famous sonnet on the subject) just before his twenty-first birthday in 1816, and had that enthusiasm further developed by his visit to the Elgin Marbles with the painter Benjamin Haydon the following year (which also produced a notable sonnet), his Greece was essentially a Greece of the imagination, inspired by his early reading of John Lemprière's *Classical Dictionary*: he never visited Greece.

This passage is a much more difficult reading experience than the preceding one: crammed into one sentence is all the content of the eleven sentences of (1). But (2) has an advantage over (1) in that it indicates, through subordination and other grammatical relations, the relations of meaning between the different clauses. We see all the different ideas fitting into a single 'complex thought', with clear indications of how one idea is linked to another, how one idea is subsidiary to another, etc. Now here is a happy medium between the two styles:

(3)   Although John Keats was fascinated by the art and literature of the ancient world, he never visited Greece. His Greece was essentially a Greece of the imagination, inspired by his early reading of John Lemprière's *Classical Dictionary*. Just before his twenty-first birthday, he read George Chapman's translation of Homer, an experience which inspired one of his most famous sonnets. His enthusiasm was further developed, in the following year, by a visit to the Elgin Marbles with the painter Benjamin Haydon.

Although there are occasions when we will want to use simple sentences, as in (1), or very complex sentences, as in (2), the most generally serviceable style will be one which, like (3), avoids the disadvantages of both.

13.2.2 Subordination

It helps the reader if we not only segment our message into units of suitable size, but also indicate the relative importance of ideas within those units. As (2) and (3) have already shown, subordinate clauses are one way of making one idea less salient than another. Putting an idea in a main clause is like shining a spotlight on it; putting it in a subordinate clause, by the same simile, is like a placing it in the shadow:

(4)   [[Although Keats spent the last months of his life in Rome], he never visited his beloved Greece].
(5)   [[Although he never visited his beloved Greece], Keats spent the last months of his life in Rome].

The contrast between (4), which spotlights the point about Greece, and (5), which spotlights that about Rome, is easy to notice. Subordinate clauses often state ideas which are well known, or have been mentioned before. This 'backgrounding' effect is still felt if the subordinate clause is placed in a final position. Compare (4) and (6):

(6)   [Keats never visited his beloved Greece, [although he spent the last months of his life in Rome]].

Still further backgrounding results from placing an idea in a tenseless clause or in a phrase. Compare:

(7)   *After he had visited the British Museum*, Keats wrote his famous *Ode on a Grecian Urn*. (tensed clause)
(8)   *After visiting the British Museum*, Keats wrote his famous *Ode on a Grecian Urn*. (tenseless clause)
(9)   *After a visit to the British Museum*, Keats wrote his *Ode on a Grecian Urn*. (phrase)

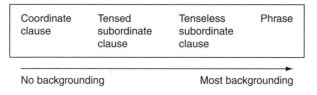

Figure 13.1

Coordination, on the other hand, gives equal importance to the clauses it links. We can contrast both (4) and (5) with (10) and (11), where the clauses are linked by the coordinating conjunctions *but* and *nor*:

(10)   Keats spent the last months of his life in Rome, but never visited his beloved Greece.

(11)   Keats never visited his beloved Greece, nor did he visit Rome until the last months of his life.

So there is a scale of 'backgrounding' roughly as shown in Figure 13.1. This scale is only an approximate indicator of importance; we should add that there are exceptions to it – for example, a noun clause in final position is often the most important part of a sentence to which it belongs: *Everyone thought* [*that I had made **a mistake**]*.

13.2.3 Ordering: end-focus and end-weight

In fact, ordering itself is a way of indicating the relative importance of two parts of a sentence. We can see this by reversing the order of the two clauses connected by *but*:

(12)   John Keats was fascinated by the art and literature of the ancient world, but he never visited Greece.

(13)   John Keats never visited Greece, but he was fascinated by the art and literature of the ancient world.

Although grammatically the two clauses are of the same status, in any construction X *but* Y, the main focus of attention seems to fall on Y. As we saw on pp. 17–18 (discussing a sentence by Samuel Butler), the final position is the most important in terms of information. Similarly, the main focus is often carried by a final subordinate clause. Compare in this respect (8) with (14):

(8)   After visiting the British Museum, *Keats wrote his famous Ode on a Grecian Urn.*

(14)   Keats wrote his famous *Ode on a Grecian Urn after visiting the British Museum.*

The emphasis typically carried by final position is best explained in terms of INFORMATION PACKAGING: as we read through a sequence of sentences in a text, we progressively add packages of ideas to the store of information with which we started. These packages correspond to grammatical units, especially clauses and phrases. Sentences we encounter in a text usually contain a mixture of GIVEN information (information we have met before) and NEW information (information we have not met before). In this sense, a written text is like a journey of exploration, where the reader is continually moving from familiar to less familiar territory. In general, **the reader is helped if given information is placed before, rather than after, new information**. This maxim, which may be called the maxim of END-FOCUS, applies not only to the ordering of clauses, but also to the ordering of clause elements. Which of the following is the easier to make sense of?

(15)   Instead of quinine, penicillin was given to the patient, who began to get better almost immediately. Within a week, she had completely recovered.

(16)   Instead of quinine, the patient was given penicillin, and began to get better almost immediately. Within a week, she had recovered completely.

The answer should be: (16) is easier to understand than (15). There are two reasons for this:

■ *Penicillin* (by its contrast *with quinine*) conveys the most important new information in the first clause, and should therefore follow the word *patient*, which is given information within this context.

■ *Recovered completely* is a better ordering than *completely recovered*, because 'recovery' has already been mentioned, and it is the adverb *completely* which brings in new information at this point.

As writers, then, we have to keep an eye on two kinds of emphasis: there is the 'spotlight' effect of main clauses, and the 'focusing' effect of final position. These two visual metaphors are compatible with one another, and enable us to treat the two kinds of emphasis, the structural and the sequential kinds, independently. For example:

(17)   The patient was given penicillin, and began to recover immediately.

(18)   The patient, who was given penicillin, began to recover immediately.

These two sentences differ not in terms of the order of the two main ideas, but in treating one as coordinate (in (17)) or as subordinate (in (18)) to the other. Although they are similar in one respect, they are different in another.

There is a third kind of emphasis. It is sometimes said that the first position in a clause or sentence is more important than the final position. While this is certainly not true with regard to information focus, an initial element does have its own kind of emphasis, because it is an element which first attracts the reader's attention, and which sets the scene for what follows. This is particularly clear when the initial element is a fronted object, complement or adverbial (see 8.2):

(19)   *Many of these questions* a computer can answer easily. [O S P A]

(20)   *Even more interesting* was their reaction to the Cuban crisis of 1962. [C P S]

An initial adverbial typically has a scene-setting role for what follows:

(21)   *Near Munich* a middle-aged woman was killed by a falling tree. [A S P A]

Notice that in these cases the first part of the sentence does not contain important new information – in fact, it tends to rely on what is already known. But its importance is rather that of providing a 'handle' by which to grasp what follows.

To the maxim of end-focus we now add a related maxim of END-WEIGHT: **place a 'heavy' constituent after a 'light' one, rather than a 'light' one after a 'heavy' one.** This maxim has to do with the weight, or complexity, of an element, rather than the amount of information conveyed, but the two measures of importance are interconnected. Naturally enough, a complex constituent (in practice, one that contains a large number of words) tends to contain more information than a simple one. Compare:

(22) The art and literature of the ancient world fascinated Keats.
(23) Keats was fascinated by the art and literature of the ancient world.

Sentence (23) is a 'happier' sentence than (22), because the complex phrase *by the art and literature of the ancient world* is placed at the end. Often it is a good idea to use a passive construction, as in (23), in order to put the 'weight' of the sentence in final position. A marked preference for the end-weight principle can be seen in sentences like:

(24) [(I) (admire) (greatly) (the courage of the men who dared to carry out that raid)].   [S P A O]
(25) [(One group) (had left) (open) (the possibility that they would carry weapons)].   [S P C O]

Here end-weight is so overriding that it leads the writer to rearrange the elements out of their normal order [S P O A], [S P O C]. It is in the light of the principles of end-focus and end-weight that we appreciate the usefulness of having, in English, a number of structure-changing rules (see 8.7) which allow elements to be moved out of their normal position in the clause.

13.3 'Be clear'

The principle of clarity is one of the obvious imperatives of written style. From the negative point of view, it means avoiding ambiguities (such as those grammatical ambiguities we noted on pp. 102 and 122) and also avoiding obscurity of expression which results not so much in outright ambiguity as in muddles and delays of interpretation. The following illustrate temporary, 'garden-path' ambiguities – they lead the reader up the garden path (or should we say a blind alley?), encouraging an analysis which as the sentence proceeds turns out to be wrong:

(26) The recruits *marched down that road* were never seen again.
(27) Though Birkett kept on watching *the film* frightened him.
(28) The woman shrieked at Ahmed *and his brother* started to cry.

In these examples, the constituent which is likely to mislead is in italics. In (26) the 'garden path' is the analysis of *marched down the road* as part of the main clause, instead of as a RClen relative clause ('who were marched . . .'). In (27) it is the analysis of *the film* as object of *watching* rather than as subject of *frightened*. And in (28) it is the analysis of *and his brother* as part of a prepositional phrase *at Ahmed and his brother*, rather than as the beginning of a new clause. In each case, there is an obvious remedy for the muddle: before the offending words, we can insert in (26) the words *who were*, and in (27) and (28) commas.

Another kind of delay of interpretation can occur in sentences with SPLIT phrases (see 8.7.6):

(29)   *Such accidents* have occurred in factories since 1974, *of which 44 have been fatal.*

The parts of (29) in italics constitute a single noun phrase. But what is the point of separating them? There are occasions when the demands of end-focus or end-weight strongly argue for discontinuity:

(30)   *The time* had come *for each of them to get on with their own lives in their own way.*

But there is no such pressing argument in (29), where the discontinuity simply adds to difficulties of comprehension, by splitting elements which belong together in meaning.

Notice that the reason for preferring (30) to (29) is a negative one: in (30) we need to sacrifice the principle of clarity for the principle of end-weight, whereas there is no such reason in the case of (29). In other words, (30a) is markedly awkward in comparison with (29a), and so needs to be reformulated:

(29a)   *Such accidents, of which 44 have been fatal,* have occurred in factories since 1974.

(30a)   *The time for each of them to get on with their own lives in their own way* had come.

In a similar way, the principle of clarity is often at odds with the principle of economy, as we will see in a moment.

13.4 'Be economical'

In grammar, the principle of economy can be paraphrased: 'Do not waste energy.' Avoiding unnecessary words is good because it means less work for the writer and for the reader. This underlies the common objection to REDUNDANT words and structures which could be omitted without loss of meaning from the sentence. Try omitting *generally* and *satisfactory* in:

(31)   As a rule, the negotiators *generally* manage to reach a *satisfactory* compromise which satisfies both parties.

Furthermore, a saving occurs whenever we avoid repetition, or avoid using words whose meaning could easily be inferred. The general phenomnon of grammar whereby we save words and hence simplify structures is called REDUCTION. We have already met three kinds of reduction:

■ The use of PRO-FORMS: personal pronouns (*he*, *she*, *it*, *they*, etc.) and other substitute words, such as (sometimes) *do, so, such, that*.
■ The use of ELLIPSIS, i.e. the omission of words which are predictable in that they merely repeat what is said in the nearby context.
■ The omission of *that* at the beginning of a zero *that-* clause or relative clause.

Both pro-forms and ellipsis are means of avoiding repetition:

(32) *My brother enjoys* squash more than *my brother enjoys* tennis. (REPETITION)
(33) My brother enjoys squash more than *he does* tennis. (PRO-FORMS)
(34) My brother enjoys squash more than ^ tennis. (ELLIPSIS)

As well as reducing length and complexity, pro-forms and ellipsis help to connect one part of a sentence or text to another. So *he* in (33) refers back to *my brother*, which is called the ANTECEDENT of the pronoun. The maxim we should follow, then, for economy and conciseness, is 'Reduce as much as possible'. This means, all other things being equal, 'Prefer ellipsis to pro-forms' (as in (34)), and 'Prefer pro-forms to repetition' (as in (33)). But often not all these alternatives are available. For example, we can say:

(35) *The intruders must have* smashed the glass and *the intruders must have* broken in. (REPETITION)
(36) The intruders must have smashed the glass and *they must have* broken in. (PRO-FORM + REPETITION)
(37) The intruders must have smashed the glass and ^ broken in. (ELLIPSIS)

But the use of the pronoun in (36), for example, also requires repetition of *must have*; there is no English sentence combining a pronoun with ellipsis, such as **The intruders must have smashed the glass and they broken in.*

13.5 'Be clear but concise': clarity versus economy

On the other hand, saving words can often lead to an unsuspected loss of meaning. So we should not reduce where economy conflicts with clarity. In (38), omitting the conjunction *that* after *proved* results in a 'garden-path' sentence. In (39), ellipsis leads to unclarity of constituent structure:

(38) Molesworth proved the theorem, on purely formal grounds, was false.
(39) They have been achieving their export targets and ^ increasing home sales every year.

Does *every year* apply (a) to the increase of home sales alone, or (b) does it also apply to the achievement of export targets? The second meaning is here more likely, because of the parallelism of the structure that expresses it:

(a) [S ⟨P O + P O⟩ A] in contrast to (b) [S ⟨P O + P O A⟩]

So if we intended to convey the first meaning we would have to restore the omitted elements of the second clause, adding a comma for extra clarity, as the coordination is now between entire clauses:

(40) They have been achieving their export targets, and *they have been* increasing home sales every year. ⟨[S P O], + [S P O A]⟩

Similarly, unclarity results when an ellipsis is too distant from its antecedent structure:

(41) A number of problems *will soon have been* solved, and the methods for ensuring more efficient legislative procedures in the coming session ^ clarified.

But the most obvious types of ambiguity and obscurity are those arising from the use of pronouns:

(42) The forwards shot hard and often but never straight till at last Hill decided to try his head. *It* came off first time.

Humorous examples like this point out the danger (increased here by the ambiguity of *came off*) of placing a pronoun too near to a 'false antecedent'. Normally the antecedent of a pronoun will be a preceding noun phrase which is either the nearest candidate, or the nearest candidate in a parallel function:

(43) *Joan* told *her sister* that *she* would have to leave home.

The nearest potential antecedent in (43) is *her sister,* but *Joan* is also a candidate because the function of *Joan* (subject) is parallel to that of *she.*

Apart from this type of ambiguity, there is the opposite danger of using a pronoun where there is no antecedent at all, or where the antecedent is too distant to be recognized:

(44) In the Elizabethan age, Roman Catholics were often under suspicion of treason, and *her* cousin Mary Queen of Scots was the chief *one.*

(Here, unless clarified by a previous sentence, the antecedents of *her* and *one* are not clear. To clarify, the second clause could read: *and Queen Elizabeth's cousin Mary Queen of Sots was the chief suspect.*) Yet another type of unclarity results from the repeated use of the same pronoun with a different antecedent:

(45) When the *headmistress* visited *Pam's* home to talk to *her mother, she* was afraid that *she* would tell *her* about *her* misconduct.

Having stressed these pitfalls, however, we should add that common sense knowledge frequently resolves a theoretical ambiguity. There would be little likelihood of interpreting (45), for example, as meaning that Pam would tell her mother about the headmistress's misconduct. The unclarity in such cases lies more in the possibility of a temporary tangle which will be resolved only by rereading. So to the maxim 'Reduce as far as possible', we must always add the rider 'unless unclarity results'.

13.6 'Be effective'

The three principles so far illustrated have to do with efficient rather than with effective communication. But to communicate effectively is to make good use not merely of the referential function of languages, but of all the functions of language (see pp. 163–4). This brings us back to the subject of literary style, and reminds us that the artistic sense of style can be found in quite ordinary texts: there is no gulf fixed between creative writing and practical writing. So, for example, the maxim 'Reduce as far as possible' can be overruled for the sake of EXPRESSIVE REPETITION

(46) John Brown was guilty of the crime, so John Brown would have to pay for it.

The repetition of *John Brown* here is not required for clarity, but suggests an emphasis ('that man and that man alone') which would be lost by reduction. On the other hand, 'ELEGANT VARIATION' – avoiding monotony by using alternative synonymous expressions – can be a reason for avoiding both repetition and reduction:

(47) That *fight* between Ali and Liston was the most sensational heavyweight *contest* since the Dempsey–Tunney *match* of 1926.

Variation for the sake of variation is often treated as a vice of style. Talking of so-called 'elegant variation', Fowler went so far as to say: 'There are few literary faults so widely prevalent, and this book will not have been written in vain if the present article should heal any sufferer of his infirmity' (Fowler, *A Dictionary of Modern English Usage,* 1926, 1965). Nowadays this opinion appears overstated, but it reminds us that some types of expression – such as proper names and technical terms – cannot usually be varied without artificiality, and are likely to be repeated in descriptive or explanatory writing. But elsewhere, e.g. in (47), variation can be a virtue that avoids both the tedium of overrepetition and the contrived switching from one synonym to another. Consider the italicized words in the following paragraph:

(48) The ancient civilization of India grew up in a sharply demarcated sub-continent bounded on the north by the world's largest *mountain range* – the *chain* of the Himalayas, which, with its extension to east and west, divides India from the rest of Asia and the world. The *barrier,* however, was at no time an insuperable one, and at all periods both settlers and traders have found their way over the high and desolate passes into India, while Indians have carried their commerce and culture beyond her *frontiers* by the same route. India's isolation has never been complete, and the effect of the *mountain wall* in developing her unique civilization has often been overrated.

(A. L. Basham, *The Wonder that was India,* p. 1)

Variation here is not so much a negative practice of avoiding repetition, as a positive search for different words which may appropriately highlight different aspects of the same thing. From different metaphorical viewpoints, a mountain range can be both a *chain* and a *wall*. It can also be a *frontier* when we are thinking of it as a boundary between peoples. So variation can be a strength, and we can argue more generally that linguistic variation of all kinds is to be welcomed in writing, so long as it is consistent with other goals. This includes not only variation in lexical choice, but variation of grammatical structure, such as:

- Variation in length or complexity of sentences.
- Variation in position and type of subordination.
- Variation between subordination and coordination.
- Variation in type and position of adverbials.
- Variation in type and position of modifiers.

If we keep an eye open for the opportunities of variation, we will make the most of the expressive range of the language and avoid the temptation to fall back on stereotyped formulas and clichés. Becoming aware of the manifold possibilities of English grammar, as outlined in Part B of this book, means becoming aware of how to use those possibilities, for varied effect, in our own writing.

―――――――――――― **EXERCISES** ――――――――――――

Exercise 13a   (answers on p. 225)

In view of the principles of style discussed in this chapter, all the following sentences can be regarded as less than successful. What is the stylistic weakness of each example, and how would you avoid it? (It will be useful to refer to the three principles examined in 13.2–13.5: a. Make your language easy to follow'; b. Be clear; c. Be economical.)

1. Mr and Mrs Smith bought a collar for their dog with studs all over it.
2. Once the war started, the powers that were needed human cannon fodder.
3. The pipe was leaking so badly that it ran all over the kitchen.
4. She argues in her latest book Ahdaf Soueif has produced a masterpiece.
5. In the long run, we shall one day eventually win the battle against poverty.
6. They have given their plans for improving the sports facilities up.
7. No one will ever know how Dickens meant *Edwin Drood,* the novel on which he was working when he died, to end.
8. The detective swore that he had seen the accused when he was checking in, which was evidence of his presence in the hotel.
9. The Inland Revenue does not allow you to give tax-free presents to your children of any size you like.
10. The desultory conversation in the drawing room among guests who had regarded Miss Manning's superb performance of the *Ave Verum* as a mere interruption revived.

Exercise 13b   (answers on p. 226)

Ambiguities, including those of the temporary, 'garden-path' type, can in many cases be eliminated by the insertion of commas or other stops. In other cases, they can be eliminated by changes in the grammar of the sentence, e.g. deletions, transformations, reorderings. How would you insert punctuation or otherwise clarify the structure and meaning of the sentences in the following cases? Provide an informal description of each ambiguity, an improved version of each sentence and a description of the change(s) you have made.

1. Before we started eating the table was absolutely loaded with delicacies.
2. It is best to reduce your overheads and work, as far as possible, alone.
3. As we soon discovered the ambassador was not interested in discussing armaments.
4. I fed the dog and Harry the budgerigar.
5. Inside the house looks almost as it did when Darwin died.
6. Her parents Lord and Lady Boothroyd refused to meet.
7. The party was attended by the Melchetts, some cousins of ours, and William, of course, arrived late.
8. Middlesex having already won the Schweppes Championship, looks like winning the Gillette Cup as well.

To conclude the exercises in this book, the following two supplementary exercises are designed to provide more wide-ranging material, for practice and discussion of written composition.

Supplementary exercise 13c

The following passage consists of short, repetitive sentences, which as they stand do not hold together as a reasonable piece of English prose. Make what grammatical and lexical changes you wish – including reordering by changing active into passive, etc., combining sentences by subordination or coordination, deletion, substitution of pronouns, etc. The goal is to make these sentences into three coherent paragraphs of an article or essay on Brook Farm. You may also add sentence adverbials. Be prepared to justify your changes, in terms of the principles outlined in this chapter.

Utopian communal experiments flourished in nineteenth-century America. The idealism and freedom of a young country inspired utopian communal experiments. Religious sects founded some utopian communal experiments. Other utopian communal experiments promoted radical sexual and marital arrangements. Few utopian communal experiments endured for more than a year or two. Brook Farm was in Massachusetts. Brook Farm was one of the more notable utopian communal experiments.

Brook Farm was one of the nobler failures of American social history. Brook Farm was begun by George Ripley and a small band of eminent followers. The followers were teachers and preachers, musicologists and writers. The writers included the celebrated novelist, Nathaniel Hawthorne. The founders included high-minded ladies and two experienced farmers.

Hawthorne signed his early letters from Brook Farm as 'Nathaniel Hawthorne, Ploughman'. Hawthorne was soon disabused about the glamour of farm work. Milking the cows seemed a comic occupation for a literary man. Hawthorne could joke about it in his letters to his family and in his letters to his fiancée. Mowing hay in the sweltering heat or shovelling in the manure pile proved to be exhausting work. At the end of the day, Hawthorne felt little inclination for writing stories. The always precarious financial situation of the community discouraged Hawthorne. Hawthorne left after seven months. Hawthorne chose not to remain through a long winter.

(Excerpts freely adapted from James R. Mellow, 'Brook Farm: an American Utopia', *Dialogue,* 13.1, 1980 pp. 44–52)

Supplementary exercise 13d

The following are two passages for comment. The first is an extract from a story by a 12-year-old girl. The second is from a letter written to a newspaper. Discuss each passage critically from the point of view of usage (Chapter 12) and from the point of view of good style (Chapter 13). If you were the author, and were asked to make revisions, what grammatical changes would you make to each passage?

1. As I was coming home one evening on the bus from school there in front were two children. One was shabby and thin looking and the other tubby and medium looking.

    These children were talking about a circus which had come to town which they had been to. The shabby girl's name was Sheila and she thought it was very funny. She liked the little short clowns and the giraffe-necked ladies and thought it was wonderful how all the animals were trained, especially the sea-lions, and thought how lovely they looked balancing the balls and for the first time in a circus she had seen giraffes taking part.

    But Anna, the posh, fancy, high-school looking girl had different ideas. She thought it was cruel to keep lions and elephants, polar-bears, grizzly-bears, sea-lions, seals, giraffes and all the other kinds of animals that used to roam on their own round ice-bergs in the sea and the jungle in a cage.

    (Quoted in James Britton, *Language and Learning,* Penguin, 1970, p. 252)

2. The major problem of socialism (and I am beginning to think it is insoluble) is to advocate liberal socialism in a capitalist society which has produced in the working class a form of acquisitiveness which uses capitalist blackmail in a way that could destroy capitalism without replacing it by a society where mankind could collectively control those of its members who have inordinate acquisitive instinct (and most people are not grossly greedy) without wholly suppressing man's normal self-interest, as has already been done in many large institutions.

    (From a letter to a newspaper)

Answers to Exercises

Exercise 1a

1. False. We can learn about grammar by studying Latin, but also by studying any other language.
2. True. (See 1.1.)
3. True. (See 1.1.)
4. False. Spelling has to do with the written representation of the sounds of a language, rather than with how whole words are put together to form sentences.
5. False. (See 1.1.)
6. False. Children learn how to speak grammatically without formal tuition, by listening to the speech they hear around them. (See 1.1.)
7. False. This would be a prescriptive approach. Studying grammar in fact involves describing how people **do** speak (and write).
8. False. Sentences quite often end in prepositions. Prescriptive notions of incorrectness are irrelevant to descriptive grammar. (See 1.2.)
9. False. American English is simply **different** from British English, and identifies its user as American. For example, the verb form *gotten* is used in American English, but not in British (where *got* is used instead). (See 1.3.1.)
10. True. Language varies according to the characteristics of the user. (See 1.3.2.)
11. False. (See 1.3.3.)
12. False. (See 1.3.2.)
13. True. (See 1.3.2, under 'Social-class membership'.)
14. False, at least in the context of grammar. (See 1.3.3.)
15. False. Speech and writing are equivalent in some ways, but not in others. (See 1.3.3 and Chapter 9.)
16. True. Doctors have specialised terms and language habits, barely comprehensible to patients, which they use when talking to one another.
17. False. (See 1.4.2.)
18. False. (See 1.5.)

Exercise 1b

1. **C**. Ambiguous as to who has the confidence.
2. **B**. Prescriptive grammar dictates that multiple negatives should be avoided. The form *ain't* is also regarded as 'bad grammar'. However, both these constructions are widely used in non-standard dialects.
3. **C**. Ambiguous as to whether there should be more teachers, or whether they should be more experienced.
4. **A**. The verbs *was, was* and *be* are used ungrammatically.

5. **B**. Prescriptive grammar would insist on *Jasmin and I*. But in casual speech, this use of *me, him* etc. occurs quite often. (See 12.4.2.)
6. **A**. This is actually a sentence produced by a foreign learner of English. It contains grammatical errors.
7. **C**. The sentence is not well balanced, and so is difficult to process. It could be better expressed: *The principal ... once gave the students a timely piece of advice.*
8. **A**. This word order is ungrammatical in English (but would be grammatical in German). (See 1.4.2).
9. **C**. The sentence is ambiguous: who has laid the eggs?
10. **B**. According to prescriptive grammar, the 'correct' form of this sentence should be: *Where are the books you told me about?*, or strictly (avoiding the final preposition) *Where are the books about which you told me?*

Exercise 1c

1. Informal; written; journalism.
2. Formal; written; religion.
3. Formal; spoken; politics.
4. Informal; written; advertising.
5. Informal; spoken; journalism.

(*Sources*: 1. The *Sun*, 13 February 2003; 2. *The Book of Common Prayer*; 3. a speech by American President Bush, 11 September 2002; 4. an MSN advertisement on the internet, June 2004; 5. BBC Radio One *Newsbeat*, 25 July 1980.)

Exercise 2a

1. The following words are complex. (Hyphens separating morphemes show why they are complex.) All the other words in these sentences are simple.

    a.   stori-es, decept-ion, terror-ist, associ-at-ion-s, brib-ery, embarrass-ed, com-promis-ed, execut-ive-s, Govern-ment, buck-pass-ing, un-preced-ent-ed, pro-portion-s
    b.   Real-ist-ic-al-ly, rough-est, tough-est, in-quir-y, under-tak-en, Brit-ish, Govern-ment.

2. Here are five examples: *(stori)(-es), (((associ)(-at))(-ion))(-s), (un-)(((preced)(-ent))(-ed)), ((((real)(-ist))(-ic))(-al))(-ly), ((under-)(tak))(-en).*

Exercise 2b

Answers to 1, 2 and 3: a *re-view-ed* (V), b *black-en-s* (V), c *kind-ness-es* (N), d *un-think-able* (Aj), e *over-turn-ing* (V), f *pro-act-ive-ly* (Av), g *magnet-iz-ing* (V), h *de-stabil-iz-es* (V), i *health-i-est* (Aj), j *inter-view-ee-s* (N). (N = noun, V = verb, Aj = adjective, Av = adverb.)

Exercise 2c

2. san-ity, reg-ion, re-cogn-ize, emphas-ize, qual-ify, clar-ify, curr-ent, con-fid-ent, hum-an, Americ-an, femin-ist.

Exercise 2d

A: *real-ly, probab-ly, certain-ly, usual-ly, clear-ly, quick-ly.* (These words are adverbs; they are derived from adjectives.)

B: *love-ly, queen-ly, friend-ly, cost-ly.* (These words are adjectives; they are derived from nouns.)

C: *natur-al, roy-al, norm-al, music-al, region-al.* (These words are adjectives; they are derived from nouns – note that *royal* has as its stem the French noun *roi*, 'king'.)

D: *tri-al, approv-al, withdraw-al, remov-al, arriv-al.* (These words are nouns; they are derived from verbs.)

Exercise 2f

PREFIX + STEM: *dis+appear, mis+match, inter+marry.*
STEM + SUFFIX: *straight+en, acquitt+al, real+ism, bright+est.*
STEM + STEM: *bath+room, life+long, broad+cast.*

Exercise 3b

1. See Figure A.1.

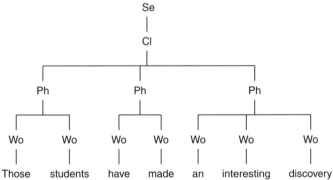

Figure A.1

2. See Figure A.2.

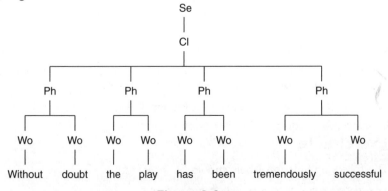

Figure A.2

(

(a) For abbreviated tree diagrams, leave out the labels Wo and Cl, joining up the vertical lines where these labels would have been.

(b) For unlabelled tree diagrams, leave out all the labels, including Ph, and join up the lines.

3. [(Tawny owls) (were hooting) (loudly) (in the wood)].

4. [(The critics) (have slated) (his plays) (without mercy)].

Exercise 3d

1. Cl[AvP(Av Typically), NP(N Aunt N Belinda) VP(v had v been v uttering) NP(N platitudes) NP(d all N evening)].

2. See Figure A.3.

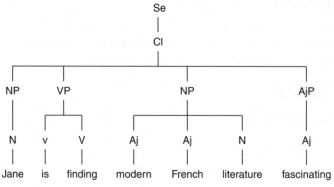

Figure A.3

3. Cl[A(H Next) S(M the H dancers) P(Aux will Mv perform) O(M a M vigorous H hopak)].

4. See Figure A.4.

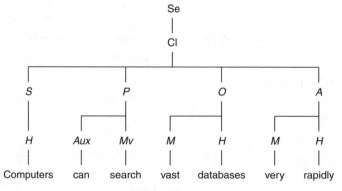

Figure A.4

Exercise 3e

The following function labels should be inserted:

1. S P   2. S P.   3. S P O.   4. S P O   5. S P.

Exercise 4a

1. Count nouns: *weed, laugh, employer, week*. The remainder are mass nouns.
2. a. For example, *paper*:
   COUNT NOUN: *news/examination/scholarly papers*;
   MASS NOUN: the material used for writing, printing, for newsprint, wallpaper, etc.
   b. For example, *grass*:
   COUNT NOUN: *In one hectare you can find hundreds of different* **grasses**.
   MASS NOUN: *The cows are feeding on the lush* **grass**.
3. For example:
   a. *woman ~ women; tooth ~ teeth.*
   b. *cactus ~ cacti; tempo ~ tempi.*
   c. *aquarium ~ aquaria; phenomenon ~ phenomena.*
   d. *sheep ~ sheep; series ~ series.*

Exercise 4b

1. Vo: the form given in the question. Vs: the Vo form with the *-s* suffix. Ving: the Vo form with the *-ing* suffix. Ved: *took, received, began, ran, slept, met*; Ven: *taken, received, begun, run, slept, met*. Of these, *receive* is regular.
2. Here are some of the most common irregular verbs apart from those already mentioned: *become, bring, come, feel, find, get, go, hear, hold, keep, know, leave, make, mean, pay, say, see, set, tell, think*. (You can spell out the different forms of each verb yourself.)

Exercise 4c

Kind, dirty and *careful* are the only gradable adjectives here. *Criminal* can be gradable, but not in the technical sense of *criminal law*.

Exercise 4d

Here are some examples. (Note that in the gradable case, the adverb *very* could be inserted.)

GRADABLE	NON-GRADABLE
a human failing	*a human life*
a guilty expression	*guilty of murder*
a musical family	*a musical box*
economic prices	*economic growth*
an original thinker	*the original owner*
a modern style	*modern languages*
a common mistake	*on common ground*
more royal than the queen	*the royal family*
free and easy	*a free offer*

Exercise 4e

1. 1 Aj, 2 Av.   2. 1 Av, 2 Aj.   3. 1 Aj 2 Av.   4. 1 Aj, 2 Av.   5. 1 Aj, 2 Av.
6. 1 Aj, 2 Av.   7. 1 Aj, 2 Av.   8. 1 Av, 2 Aj.

Exercise 4f

1. 1 N, 2 V.   2. 1 Aj, 2 N.   3. 1 V, 2 Aj.   4. 1 V, 2 Aj.   5. 1 V, 2 Aj.   6. 1 Aj,
2 V, 3 N.   7. 1 V, 2 N, 3 Aj.   8. *referee:* 1 N, 2 V. *match:* 1 N, 2 V.

Exercise 4g

Nouns:	*cruppets, spod, vomity, Podshaw, glup, whampet, mimsiness, manity, gooves.*
Verbs:	*whozing, priddling, yipped, brandling, gumbled.*
Adjectives:	*gleerful, groon, flupless, blunk.*
Adverbs:	*then, huffily, podulously, bindily, magistly* (it is perhaps possible to consider *magistly* a noun, but this is an unlikely interpretation).

Exercise 4h

1. [$_{cj}$But $_{ij}$alas, ($_d$the $_e$two $_{Aj}$ugly $_N$sisters) ($_v$had $_v$gone) ($_{Av}$home) ($_p$without $_{pn}$her)].
2. For example:
   a. [$_{ij}$OK, $_{cj}$although ($_{pn}$I) ($_v$am $_v$feeling) ($_{Av}$rather $_{Aj}$bored) ($_p$with $_d$these $_e$eleven $_N$classes)].
   b. [$_{cj}$And, $_{ij}$yes, ($_{pn}$he) ($_v$was ($_{Av}$brutally) $_v$murdered) ($_p$by $_d$the $_e$five $_{Aj}$bloody $_N$priests)].
   c. [($_{pn}$He) ($_v$did $_v$steal) – $_{cj}$and, $_{ij}$yes, ($_p$from $_d$the $_{Av}$securely $_{Aj}$hidden $_e$thirteenth $_N$chamber)].
   d. [$_{cj}$But $_{ij}$hey, ($_{pn}$she) ($_{Av}$really) ($_v$can $_v$move) ($_p$with $_d$those $_e$two $_{Aj}$old $_N$crutches).]

Acknowledgement: We owe examples a. and b. to Adrian Luescher, and c. to Judith Marchhart, first-year students at the University of Wales, Bangor.

Exercise 5a

See Figure A.5.

Exercise 5b

Main phrases: 1. (Mary), (had), (a little lamb). 2. (The fleece of the little lamb), (was), (as white as snow). 3. (Everyone in town), (admires), (the whiteness of the fleece of Mary's little lamb).
Subordinate phrases: 1. None. 2. (of the little lamb), (as snow). 3. (in town), (of the fleece of Mary's little lamb), (of Mary's little lamb), (Mary's).

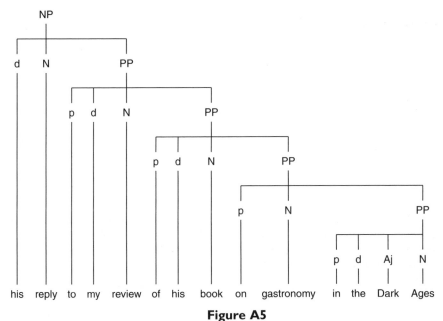

Figure A5

Exercise 5c

1. b. (her interest (in the coins (of Roman Britain))).
2. c. (the outbreak (of the revolution) (in Camelot)) or: (the outbreak (of the revolution (in Camelot))).
3. b. (the courage (of a stag (at bay))).
4. a. (a battle (of words) (in Parliament)).
5. a. (the fall (of Rome) (in 1527)).
6. a. (the highest rate (of inflation) (in Europe)).
7. c. (a father (of ten kids) (with a criminal record)) OR: (a father (of ten kids (with a criminal record))).
8. c. (a conference (on wild life) (in Canada)) OR: (a conference (on wild life (in Canada))).
9. b. (rap (for people (over sixty))).

Exercise 5d

A. We give only the most unmarked (or normal) orders: other, more marked orders are possible. To help in determining the premodifier ordering rules (B), we have indicated the class of each word.

1. $_{GP}$Cinderella's $_e$two $_{Aj}$ugly $_{N}^{H}$sisters.
2. $_d$A $_{Aj}$small $_{Aj}$green $_{Aj}$carved $_N$jade $_N$idol. OR:
   $_d$A $_{Aj}$small $_{Aj}$carved $_N$green-jade $_{N}^{H}$idol. (If 'green jade' is a substance.)
3. $_d$All $_d$those $_{Aj}$intricate $_{Aj}$old $_{Aj}$interlocking $_{Aj}$Chinese $_{N}^{H}$designs.
4. $_{Av}$Quite $_d$a $_d$few $_{Aj}$disgusting $_{Aj}$old $_{Aj}$Victorian $_{N}^{H}$drawings. OR:
   $_d$A $_d$few $_{Av}$quite $_{Aj}$disgusting $_{Aj}$old $_{Aj}$Victorian $_{N}^{H}$drawings.

5. $_{GP}$Moldwarp's $_{Aj}$brilliant $_{Aj}$new $_{Aj}$geological $_N^H$hypothesis.
6. $_{GP}$Morgan's $_e$second $_{Aj}$revolutionary $_{Aj}$cylindrical $_N$steam $_N^H$condenser.
7. $_d$An $_{Aj}$ancient $_{Aj}$grey $_{Aj}$Gothic $_N$church $_N^H$tower.
8. $_{Av}$Almost $_d$all $_d$the $_e$first $_e$hundred $_{Aj}$foreign $_N^H$tourists.
9. $_d$Her $_{Aj}$heavy $_{Aj}$new $_{Aj}$moral $_N^H$responsibilities.
10. $_d$My $_{Aj}$hectic $_N$London $_{Aj}$social $_N^H$life.

B. It is probably easier to start with the head N. In general, N modifiers come immediately before the head. Aj modifiers precede N modifiers if any. (An Aj can be preceded by its own modifier, an Av like *very*.) Enumerators (e) precede Aj or N modifiers if any. Determiners (d) or GPs precede all other premodifiers if any, except that certain adverbs can precede a determiner (e.g. *almost all* in 8 above).

The only exception to these statements is *London social life* in 10, where the adjective *social* follows the noun *London*. This is an unusual case, where the adjective is more strongly tied to the head, the group *social life* being treated almost as if it were a single head noun itself.

How about the ordering of adjectives if more than one occurs in front of the head? A general rule is that **classifying** adjectives, telling us what **category** of thing the H refers to, come nearer to the head than **descriptive** adjectives, which describe more broadly what the H referent is like. For example, in 5, *geological* (classifying) is nearer to the head than *new* (descriptive). A third type of adjective we can distinguish is an **evaluating** adjective, which is more subjective, telling us more about what the speaker **thinks** or **feels**. Evaluating adjectives tend to precede descriptive adjectives (e.g. *brilliant* precedes *new* in 5). Notice that evaluating and descriptive adjectives are normally **gradable**.

Exercise 5e

1. $(_{pn}^H$she). 2. $(_d^M$the $_N^H$skeleton $_{pp}^M$(in ...)). 3. $(_d^M$that $_{Aj}^M$strange $_N^H$feeling).
4. $(_d^M$half $_d^M$the $_N^H$people $_{Aj}^M$present). 5. $(_{GP}^M$(Stanley's) $_{Aj}^M$historic $_N^H$meeting $_{pp}^M$(with ...) $_{pp}^M$(at ...). 6. $(_d^M$all $_d^M$those $_{AjP}^M$(utterly fruitless) $_N^M$afternoon $_N^H$meetings $_{pp}^M$(of ...) $_{NP}^M$(last year)).

Exercise 5f

1. *I,* 2. *we,* 3. *you,* 4. *you,* 5. *he,* 6. *she,* 7. *it,* 8. *they,* 9. *me,* 10. *us,* 11. *you,* 12. *you,* 13. *him,* 14. *her,* 15. *it,* 16. *them,* 17. *myself,* 18. *ourselves,* 19. *yourself,* 20. *yourselves,* 21. *himself,* 22. *herself,* 23. *itself,* 24. *themselves,* 25. *my,* 26. *our,* 27. *your,* 28. *your,* 29. *his,* 30. *her,* 31. *its,* 32. *their,* 33. *mine,* 34. *ours,* 35. *yours,* 36. *yours,* 37. *his,* 38. *hers,* 39. *--,* 40. *theirs.*

The OBJECT form of the pronoun is in fact the form that occurs in the greatest variety of places in grammatical structure, for example (a) as O, (b) as head of a PP (i.e. after a p), (c) in one-word answers (*Who's coming?* **Me.**), (d) in most people's casual speech after cj (*John and* **him**), and (e) as C (*That's* **him**.). Other functions of the object pronoun will be seen later (See pp. 187–9.).

Exercise 5g

Briefly, (i) the construction types 2–6 require the existence of an operator verb as auxiliary in the ordinary declarative form (1). (ii) If there is no operator verb, the appropriate form of the dummy operator verb *do* is inserted, and is followed by the basic Vo form of the main verb, e.g. She works hard ⟶ She *does* work hard ⟶ *Does* she work hard?

Exercise 6a

2. [S P], 3. [S P A], 4. [S P O C], 5. [S P O A], 6. [A S P C],
7. [A S P O O A] (for the possibility of a second O, see 6.6).

Exercise 6b

2. [NP VP], 3. [NP VP PP], 4. [NP VP NP AjP], 5. [NP VP NP AvP],
6. [PP NP VP AjP], 7. [NP NP VP NP NP AvP].

Exercise 6c

1. [S P Oi Od] and [S P O C], 2. [S A P O] and [S A P O A] (A = *on the beach*),
3. [S P C] and [S P O], 4. [S P Oi Od] and [S P O C], 5. [S P A] and [S P O],
6. [S P A] and [S P A A].

Exercise 6d

1. [S P O], 2. This is a passive clause (see 6.5) – the passive clause pattern is [S P],
the corresponding active clause pattern is [S P O], 3. [S P], 4. [S P O C], 5. [S P O],
6. [S P C], 7. [S P Oi Od].

Exercise 6e

1. ^{A}(for a man ^{M}(with one eye)), or ^{A}(for a man) ^{A}(with one eye), where
   second A is a **manner adverbial**.
2. ^{A}($_{Av}$down), or ^{O}($_N$down).
3. *What* in the question was intended to elicit an O, but a C was given in
   answer.
4. (*the day* [*he was born*]) is an O, or alternatively an A of time.

Exercise 6f

(In the tree diagrams we have used the more general labels v, V, and *Aux*, rather than more specialised labels such as m, Ving, *Prog*, etc.)

1. See Figure A.6.

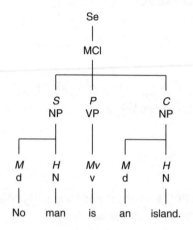

Figure A.6

2. See Figure A.7.

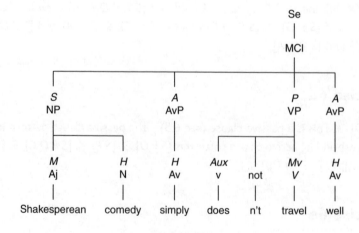

Figure A.7

3. See Figure A.8.

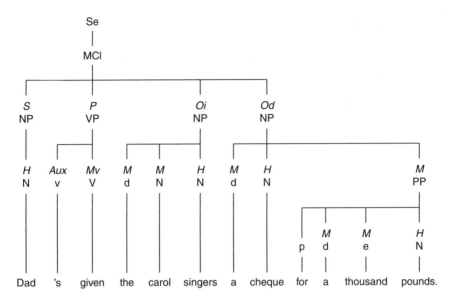

Figure A.8

Exercise 7a

(i) See Figures A.9 and A.10. For (ii), the answers are not illustrated.

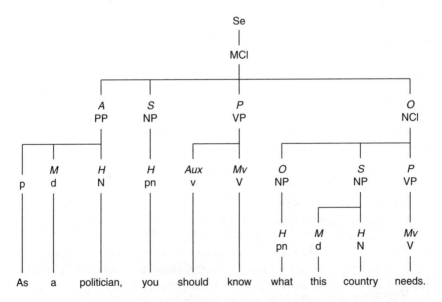

Figure A.9

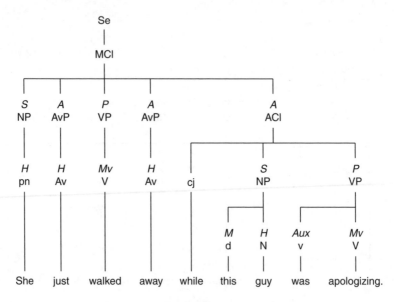

Figure A.10

Exercise 7b

1. ACl[cj S P C], time. 2. ACl[cj S P O] , purpose. 3. NCl[C S P]. 4. RCl[S P Oi Od].
5. RCl[A S P O A]. 6. NCl[A S P O]. 7. ACl[cj S P A C], contrast. 8. NCl[S P A].
9. RCl[S P].

Exercise 7c

1. $^{O}_{Cling}$, 2. $^{M}_{Cli}$, 3. $^{S}_{Cli}$, 4. $^{O}_{Clen}$, 5. $^{A}_{Cling}$, 6. $^{M}_{Cli}$, 7. $^{A}_{Cling}$, 8. $^{A}_{Clen}$.

Exercise 7d

(Examples 1 and 2 are shown with function labels as well as with the text. Only the text is given with the remaining examples)

1. [I regret [criticizing him] bitterly] OR: [I regret [criticising him bitterly]].
   [S P [P O] A] OR: [S P [P O A]].
2. [I clearly remembered (the time [when I looked at my watch])]. OR:
   [I clearly remembered the time [when I looked at my watch]].
   [S A P (M H [A S P A])]. OR: [S A P O [cj S P A]].
3. [I told him [that I had written the essay [before he gave the lecture]]]. OR:
   [I told him [that I had written the essay] [before he gave the lecture]].
4. [[To speak the truth frankly] is an unsafe policy]. OR:
   [[To speak the truth] frankly is an unsafe policy].
5. [The combatants agreed [to sign a peace treaty in Geneva last week]]. OR:
   [The combatants agreed [to sign a peace treaty in Geneva] last week]. OR:
   [The combatants agreed [to sign a peace treaty] in Geneva last week].

6. [We must ask (the farmer [who owns the field]) [where we can camp]].
    OR:
    [We must ask the farmer [who owns (the field [where we can camp])]]. OR:
    [We must ask (the farmer [who owns (the field [where we can camp])])].
7. [I found the dog [smoking a cigar]].
    [I found (the dog [smoking a cigar])].
    and finally one in which [*the dog smoking a cigar*] was the event which I
    found:
    [I found [the dog smoking a cigar]].

    This is a 'catenative' construction (see 8.5.2).

Exercise 7e

(Examples 1 and 2 are shown with function labels as well as with the text. Only
the text is given with the remaining examples)

1. [We enjoyed an afternoon of honeyed ⟨scones and poetry⟩].
    [S P O (M ⟨H + H⟩)]
    [We enjoyed an afternoon of ⟨honeyed scones and poetry⟩].
    [S P O ⟨(M H) + (H)⟩]
2. [Their officers always sport ⟨scarlet berets and moustaches⟩].
    [S A P ⟨(M H) + (H)⟩]
    [Their officers always sport ⟨scarlet berets and moustaches⟩].
    [S A P (M ⟨H + H⟩)]
3. [She has passed her exams in ⟨(French), (German) and (English
    literature)⟩].
    [She has passed her exams in ⟨French, German and English⟩ literature].
4. [The manuscript is ⟨very old and difficult [to read]⟩.]
    [The manuscript is very ⟨old and difficult [to read]⟩.]
5. [That evening we stayed indoors, ⟨[reading] and [writing letters]⟩].
    [That evening we stayed indoors, [⟨reading and writing⟩ letters]].
6. [I was taught by ⟨(the man [who taught Mabel]) and (the woman [who
    taught ⟨you and Fred⟩])⟩].
    [I was taught by (the man [who taught ⟨(Mabel) and (the woman [who
    taught ⟨you and Fred⟩])⟩])].
    [I was taught by ⟨(the man [who taught Mabel]) and (the woman [who
    taught you]) and (Fred)⟩].
7. [The neighbourhood is infested with ⟨(stray cats) and (dogs of questionable
    parentage)⟩].
    [The neighbourhood is infested with stray ⟨cats and dogs⟩ of questionable
    parentage].
    [The neighbourhood is infested with stray ⟨(cats) and (dogs of questionable
    parentage)⟩].
    [The neighbourhood is infested with ⟨(stray cats) and (dogs)⟩ of
    questionable parentage].

8. [Mountjoy was a ⟨(great lover) and (ardent student)⟩ of ⟨language and literature⟩].

[Mountjoy was a ⟨(great lover) and (ardent student of ⟨language and literature⟩)⟩].

Exercise 8a

1. (a) [*Standing at the door*] should **post**modify *girl*, instead of **pre**modifying it. (b) *Making* requires an *O*, but there is none.
2. (a) *My* should be **subject** pn *I*, and *has* should change to *have*, because of concord. (b) The adjective *interesting* should **pre**modify *job*.
3. (a) The NP (*very good reputation*) requires *a*, the indefinite article. (b) The preposition *for* should introduce a PP or a SCl.
4. A non-finite clause (here a Cli) is not usually a MCl in a sentence. (But it could occur as a SCl, or as an **elliptical** sentence, e.g. in reply to a question or as the heading of an article.)
5. A clause without a S is not usually a MCl in a sentence. (But such a clause might occur as an elliptical sentence, e.g. in very casual conversation, or perhaps in an advertisement, e.g. *Have gun, will travel.*)

Exercise 8b

1. 'DO SUPPORT': All the following transformations require a tensed operator verb, v = m, be, hv (see 5.5.2 and 6.4.1). If there is none, use the **dummy operator** *do*. It will be the tensed element, carrying tense and agreeing with S.
2. CLAUSE NEGATION: Place negative *not, n't* immediately after the first (tensed) v of P. If it is *n't*, attach it to this v.
3. YES–NO INTERROGATION: Place the first (finite) v of P before S.
4. CLAUSE EMPHASIS: Place the main stress on the first v.
5. TAGS: Add an unlinked second Cl (on unlinked coordination see 7.7.1), consisting of the first v of the P of the original Cl, with *n't* attached, followed by the subject pn that would stand for the S of the first Cl. (If the P of the first Cl is negated, the tag will not be negative, i.e. the tag is opposite in **polarity**, positive or negative, to the original Cl. There are also 'just-checking' tags, which have the **same** polarity as the original Cl (*You like cheese, do you?*).
6. ELLIPTICAL COMPARATIVES: There are a number of different kinds of elliptical CCl, but the kind represented by the data on p. 84 consists of $_{cj}$*than* followed by a S not identical to the MCl S, followed by a repeat of the first v of the MCl P (assuming the CCl would have a dummy operator if necessary; also, that the CCl would have a full v like *is*, and not a contraction like *'s*).

Note: (a) ^{Mv}*do* is not an operator v, hence it needs dummy *do* (*I didn't do it*). (b) ^{Mv}*have* is an operator v in some varieties of English, but is more often a full V these days: for example, *Have you a match?* is less common than *Do you have a match?*

Exercise 8c

(i)
1. Every morning Pat ⟨gets into her car and drives to the office⟩.
2. Have you been ⟨listening to the radio or watching television⟩?
3. I bought ⟨a puppet for Linda and a teddy-bear for Malcolm⟩.
4. At last ⟨the child went back to school and we had a rest⟩.
5. Unfortunately ⟨Jack Sprat likes lean meat, but his wife doesn't⟩.
6. With practice, ⟨your voice will grow more versatile, and your breathing more controlled⟩.

(ii)
1. [A S ⟨P A + P A⟩].
2. [Aux S Aux ⟨Mv A + Mv O⟩]?
3. [S P ⟨O A + O A⟩].
4. [A ⟨S P A A + S P O⟩].
5. [A ⟨ S P O + S Aux not⟩] (note that the dummy operator *does* 'stands for' $^{Mv}_{Vs}$likes)
6. [A ⟨S P C + S C⟩].

Exercise 8d

We give a fairly general description of the transformation, using symbols (you may have used a less abstract description), but we do not attempt to give the rather complex restrictions on the rule's application.

1. *Fronting of subordinate clause object*

   it be C $^S_{Cli}$[... Pi $^O_{NPI}$ ...] ⟶ $^S_{NPI}$ be C (... $^M_{Cli}$[...Pi...])

   For example,

   It is ^{C}(interesting) $^S_{Cli}$[^{Pi}(to study) $^O_{NP}$(grammar) in depth]. ⟶
   $^S_{NP}$(Grammar) is ^{C}(interesting $^M_{Cli}$[^{Pi}(to study) in depth]).

2. *Postponement of indirect object*

   S P $^{Oi}_{NPI}$Od ⟶ S P Od ^{A}(p + NPI), where p = *to* or *for*.

   For example,

   [^{S}(We) ^{P}(are teaching) ^{Oi}(you) ^{Od}(grammar)]. ⟶ [^{S}(We) ^{P}(are teaching) ^{O}(grammar) ^{A}($_p$to you)].

3. *Postponement of postmodifier*

   $_{NP}$(... H M) ⟶ $_{NP}$(... H .... M), where M must be a Ph or Cl.

   (This transformation is hedged about with restrictions: the postponed postmodifier should be a longish constituent, preferably a clause.) For example,

   $^S_{NP}$(The ^{H}road $^M_{PP}$(to a mastery of grammar) ^{P}(is) ^{C}(very thorny). ⟶
   $^S_{NP}$(The ^{H}road ^{P}(is) ^{C}(very thorny) $^M_{PP}$(to a mastery of grammar)).

Exercise 8e

1. [it be C [cj [cj S A P A] S A P A A A]].
2. [there be S A [cj it be A that S P A]].
3. [[cj S P] S P [cj S P [S P O]]]?

(No answers are supplied to the Exercises in Chapters 9–11, as these are textual analyses to which there are no specific answers.)

Exercise 12a

(The error-type is followed by a suggested revision.)

1. B. It was argued that the President … *was* ignoring the interests of the developing world.
2. C. Mervyn John's record is now as good *as*, if not better than, *that of* his compatriot Michael Steed.
3. D. (It is difficult to avoid the 'dangling' tenseless clause, which is in any case not seriously objectionable with the passive.)
4. A. What worried her parents most was *his/him* being a racing driver. (These days both the variants are acceptable, although the object form (*him*) is more informal.)
5. C. We could knock twenty per cent off the fuel consumption and yet be able to keep the price … .
6. B. Have *both/all* of you opened your parcels?
7. E. … it would be wrong *even to / to even* think of it. (There is nothing wrong with the 'split infinitive', which is arguably clearer than the 'corrected' version.)
8. A. (There is no obvious way of evading the object pronouns: subject pronouns would look extremely odd here.)
9. A. Margaret and he will be playing against you and *me*.
10. B. Neither the publisher nor the author *was* aware of the printer's blunder.
11. A. … *we* girls were listening at the keyhole.
12. C. … and its determination to stand on its own feet. (Delete *of*)
13. E. (The genitive … *some Congressman from the Midwest's* … would be extremely awkward here. Either leave the sentence as it is, or substitute a relative clause construction: … *about some Congressman … who had taken* … .)
14. D. When *these animals are* removed from their normal habitat, it is advisable to treat *them* with great care.
15. D. Put the lights out when you leave. (A simpler and more direct style is preferable, and avoids the usage problem.)
16. B. Radios of this sort are very reliable. This sort of radio is very reliable.
17. D. *As I was* flying through the air at the speed of sound, a sudden thought struck me.

18.   E. Which team has the *better* record, yours or theirs?
19.   E. We *will/shall* not object if you postpone the meeting. (Both *will* and *shall* are acceptable these days, although prescriptive tradition favours *shall* after *I* or *we*.)
20.   B. She absolutely denies that any of her supporters *has* been disloyal.

Exercise 12b

Examples 3 and 10 involve correlative conjunctions (see 4.3.5) *either ... or* and *both ... and*. Examples 6 and 8 involve inversion in the first coordinate. Examples 2, 4 and 7 involve three coordinates. The remaining examples show a mismatch between coordinated verbs and the elements O, C, A that follow them. Common to all these cases is a mismatch between coordinates.

We do not attempt a full explanation here, but recommend the following corrections to the examples:

KEY

Underlining indicates an addition to the original sentence; double underlining indicates a substitute pronoun, to avoid repeating the same expression; the ^ indicates a place where ellipsis occurs.

---

1.   They ⟨captured him and ^ put him in prison⟩.
2.   Brad was ⟨⟨young and ^ good-looking⟩, and ^ enjoyed life to the full⟩. OR: Brad ⟨was young, ^ was good-looking, and ^ enjoyed life to the full⟩.
3.   Either ⟨the children did not know what had happened, or they were trying to protect their parents⟩.
4.   The spy ⟨was in his forties, ^ was of average build, and ^ obviously wore a wig⟩.
5.   By giving the police a pay rise, the Minister hopes to ⟨improve the force and ^ make it more efficient⟩.
6.   ⟨Had the queen lived five years longer or had she given birth to an heir⟩, the subsequent history of Ruritania would have been very different.
7.   You have to ⟨weigh the parcels, ^ count them and ^ pack them in large containers⟩.
8.   Not only ⟨did she arrive late, but she woke up the entire household⟩.
9.   They ⟨collect food and clothing and ^ distribute it to the homeless⟩.
10.   I am fond both ⟨of dogs and ^ of cats⟩. OR:
     I am fond of both ⟨dogs and ^ cats⟩.

Exercise 13a

Problems

1.   b. There is a split object: *a collar with studs all over it.*
2.   b. 'Garden-path' ambiguity: *that were needed* reads like a passive relative clause.

3. b. *It* lacks an antecedent such as *water.*
4. b. Ambiguity: the adverbial *in her latest book* can belong to the main clause or to the noun clause.
5. c. Redundancy: *in the long run*, *eventually* and *one day* are all similar in meaning.
6. a. End-weight: *up* follows a long object.
7. a. End-weight: *to end* follows a long object.
8. b. Unclear antecedents for *he*, *which* and *his.*
9. b. There is a split object: *tax-free presents of any size you like.*
10. a. End-weight: the predicator *revived* follows a very long subject.

Suggested revisions

1. Mr and Mrs Smith bought their dog a collar with studs all over it.
2. Once the war started, the 'powers that were' needed human cannon fodder.
3. The pipe was leaking so badly that the water ran all over the kitchen.
4. She argues that in her latest book Ahdaf Soueif has produced a masterpiece.
5. In the long run, we shall win the battle against poverty.
6. They have given up their plans for improving the sports facilities.
7. No one will ever know how Dickens intended to finish *Edwin Drood*, the novel on which he was working when he died.
8. The detective swore that he had seen the accused checking in. This sighting was evidence of the presence of the accused in the hotel.
9. The Inland Revenue does not allow you to give your children tax-free presents of any size you like.
10. The desultory conversation revived in the drawing room among guests who had regarded Miss Manning's performance of *Ave Verum* as a mere interruption.

Exercise 13b

Description of ambiguities

(All are 'garden paths' except 4 and 6.)

1. *The table* is initially read as object of the adverbial clause, not as subject of the main clause.
2. *Work* is initially read as a noun coordinated with *overheads*, rather than as a verb.
3. *The ambassador* is initially read as object of *discovered*, rather than as subject of *was.*
4. EITHER *Harry the budgerigar* is a noun phrase coordinated with *the dog*, OR *Harry* is the subject, and *the budgerigar* the object, of an 'ellipted' verb *fed.*
5. *Inside* is read initially as a preposition, and *inside the house* as a prepositional phrase. In fact, *inside* is an adverb, and *the house* is subject of *looks.*

6. EITHER *Lord and Lady Boothroyd* is in apposition to *Her parents*, or *Her parents* is the 'fronted' object of *meet.*
7. *William* is read initially as coordinated with *the Melchetts and some cousins of ours*, rather than as subject of *arrived.*
8. *Middlesex* can be read initially as the subject of the adverbial *ing*-clause *Middlesex ... Championship*, rather than as subject of the main clause.

Suggested revisions

1. Before we started eating, the table was absolutely loaded with delicacies.
2. It is best to reduce your overheads, and to work as far as possible alone.
3. As we soon discovered, the ambassador was not interested in discussing armaments.
4. I fed the dog, and Harry fed the budgerigar.
5. Inside, the house looks almost as it did when Darwin died.
6. Lord and Lady Boothroyd refused to meet her parents. OR: Her parents, Lord and Lady Boothroyd, refused to meet each other.
7. The party was attended by the Melchetts, some cousins of ours; William, of course, arrived late.
8. Middlesex, having already won the Schweppes Championship, looks like winning the Gillette Cup as well.

Notes

1. (p. 37) But note that these conventions are not always followed, e.g. *I want to stay here. With you.* and *Did we despair? Not at all.* Here *With you* and *Not at all* are not complete sentences. In speech we often operate with units which are not fully-fledged sentences. Also, the boundaries of words, particularly of noun compounds (see the 'special note' on p. 22) are not always clear; e.g. we can write the sequence *piggy* + *bank* in three different ways: *piggy bank, piggy-bank* or *piggybank*. There is no easy way of deciding whether this is one word or two.

2. (p. 66) Actually in many systems of analysis a prepositional phrase has a noun phrase following the preposition, as a phrase subordinate to the PP (see 5.2.1). The preposition is then regarded as the head of the PP. In the present system, we find it better to simplify the analysis and the notation by avoiding this extra degree of subordination.

3. (p. 73) In the first edition of this book we used the more complex analysis, treating *my, their,* etc. as genitive phrases.

4. (p. 77) The terns 'tensed' and 'tenseless' are used here instead of the more traditional terms 'finite' and 'non-finite' used in this book's first edition. 'Finite' and 'non-finite' are more difficult labels, as it is not clear how these words, as normally used, apply to the grammatical constructions they represent.

5. (p. 80) We regard modal verbs as **tensed**, because (a) they have a contrast (between *can* and *would, will* and *would,* etc.) which is historically present versus past tense, and (b) they always behave like operators. However, the term 'tensed' here should not be taken too literally: sometimes we can use modals in ways that reflect tense (e.g. *She can't swim* ∼ *She couldn't swim*) whereas in other cases we cannot.

6. (p. 111) When we defined prepositions as particles in 4.3.8, we showed that they could be a 'floating' element in the clause, occurring sometimes stranded at the end of the clause, rather than as part of a regular prepositional phrase. We now see, in this section, that prepositions can occur as introductory elements to a clause – rather like conjunctions, in fact. This is another reason why prepositions are treated as particles, rather than as modifiers in phrase structure.

7. (p. 114) Notice that the use of 'direct' and 'indirect' as applied to subordination is not connected with the use of terms like 'indirect statement' and 'indirect question' in 7.2.1.

8. (p. 124) The concept of structure-changing rules has been developed rigorously in modern technical studies of English grammar (see, for example, Andrew Radford, *Transformational Grammar: A First Course,* 1988). Our aim is to make very informal use of this concept as a means of explaining significant relations between sentence structures.

9. (p. 126) Rule 3 in fact only applies to 'restrictive' relative clauses, which are not separated from the rest of the sentence by commas or other punctuation marks. Compare (8) with *The stories, which he invented, were incredible.* Here *which* could not be omitted.

10. (p. 132) The infinitive clause is here labelled as a complement because of its close parallel to the object complement in sentences like *Bob considered grammar a waste of time*.

11. (p. 141) Even new electronic media of communication such as e-mail and chat groups, which are often discussed as if amalgams of speech and writing, belong fundamentally to the written, visual medium. We give some attention to these later, in 9.5.8; for a more extended treatment, see David Crystal, *Language and the Internet*, 2001.

Further Reading

This list of references gives a selection of books to be consulted and studied by students following up some of the topics in this book, particularly from the viewpoint of English grammar.

The items are listed by author, in alphabetical order, and are also numbered consecutively for easy identification according to topic:

Topic	Reference numbers
Language and linguistics	5, 24, 31, 41, 45
Language variation	16, 18, 19, 28, 31, 38, 40, 49, 53
English language generally	1, 14, 22, 30, 36, 45
English grammar†	3*, 4*, 6, 11, 13*, 15*, 17, 23, 24, 27, 29, 34, 35*, 43*, 44, 45, 50
Speech, writing, punctuation	3, 4, 9, 10, 51, 54
Discourse and text analysis	7, 12, 25, 26
Analysis of literary discourse	33, 46, 48, 52, 55, 56
Authority, usage, correctness	2, 8, 20, 21, 32, 37, 39, 42, 47

†Under the topic of English grammar, there are many differences of terminology, theory and description. Both in the numerical list above and in the references below, we have used a * to identify publications with the same kind of system of analysis as this book, although there will be differences in detail.

References

1. Kim Ballard, *The Frameworks of English*. Basingstoke: Palgrave, 2001.
2. Albert C. Baugh and Thomas Cable, *A History of the English Language*, 5th edn. London: Routledge, 2002, ch. 9, 'The Appeal to Authority, 1650–1800'.
*3. Douglas Biber, Susan Conrad and Geoffrey Leech, *Longman Student Grammar of Spoken and Written English*. Harlow: Longman, 2002.
*4. Douglas Biber, Stig Johansson, Geoffrey Leech, Susan Conrad and Edward Finegan, *Longman Grammar of Spoken and Written English*. London: Longman, 1999.
5. Dwight Bolinger and Donald A. Sears, *Aspects of Language*, 3rd edn. New York: Harcourt Brace Jovanovich, 1981.
6. Kersti Börjars and Kate Burridge, *Introducing English Grammar*. London: Arnold, 2001.
7. Gillian Brown and George Yule, *Discourse Analysis*. Cambridge: Cambridge University Press, 1983.
8. R. W. Burchfield (ed.), *The New Fowler's Modern English Usage*, 3rd edn. Oxford: Clarendon Press, 1996.

9. G. V. Carey, *Mind the Stop: A Brief Guide to Punctuation*. Harmondsworth: Penguin, 1976.

10. Ron Carter and Mick McCarthy, 'Grammar and the Spoken Language', *Applied Linguistics* 16 (2), 1995, 141–58.

11. Sylvia Chalker and Edmund Weiner, *The Oxford Dictionary of English Grammar*. Oxford and New York: Clarendon Press, 1994.

12. Herbert H. Clark, *Using Language*. New York: Cambridge University Press, 1996.

*13. Susan Conrad, Douglas Biber and Geoffrey Leech, *Longman Student Grammar of Spoken and Written English: Workbook*. Harlow: Longman, 2002.

*14. David Crystal, *Rediscover Grammar with David Crystal*, 2nd edn. London: Longman, 1996.

15. David Crystal, *Language and the Internet*. Cambridge: Cambridge University Press, 2001.

16. David Crystal, *Cambridge Encyclopedia of the English Language*, 2nd edn. Cambridge: Cambridge University Press, 2003.

*17. David Crystal, *Making Sense of Grammar*, London: Longman, 2004.

18. David Crystal, *The Stories of English*, London: Allen Lane, 2004.

19. S. Eggins and J. R. Martin, 'Genres and Registers in Discourse', in Teun van Dijk (ed.), *Discourse as Structure and Process*. London: Sage, 1997, 230–56.

20. H. W. Fowler, *A Dictionary of Modern English Usage*, 2nd edn, revised by Sir Ernest Gowers, 1965. (See also Burchfield, 1996.) Oxford: Clarendon Press, 1926.

21. Bryan A. Garner, *Garner's Modern American Usage*, 2nd edn. New York: Oxford University Press, 2003.

22. Stephan Gramley and Kurt-Michael Pätzold, *A Survey of Modern English*, 2nd edn. London and New York: Routledge, 2004.

*23. Sidney Greenbaum and Randolph Quirk, *A Student's Grammar of the English Language*. London: Longman, 1990.

24. M. A. K. Halliday and Ruqaiya Hasan, *Cohesion in English*. London: Longman, 1976.

25. M. A. K. Halliday and Ruqaiya Hasan, *Language, Context and Text: Aspects of Language in a Social–Semiotic Perspective*. Deakin University, Victoria, 1985; republished by Oxford University Press, 1989.

26. M. A. K. Halliday and Christian Mathiessen, *An Introduction to Functional Grammar*, 3rd edn. London: Arnold, 2004.

27. Rodney Huddleston and Geoffrey Pullum, *Cambridge Grammar of the English Language*. Cambridge: Cambridge University Press, 2002.

28. Arthur Hughes and Peter Trudgill, *English Accents and Dialects*, 2nd edn. London: Arnold, 1987.

29. James R. Hurford, *Grammar: A Student's Guide*. Cambridge and New York: Cambridge University Press, 1994.

30. Samuel Johnson, *A Dictionary of the English Language*. London: Longman, 1755.

31. Graeme Kennedy, *An Introduction to Corpus Linguistics*. London: Longman, 1998.

32. Laurie G. Kirszner and Stephen R. Mandell, *The Holt Handbook*, 3rd edn. Fort Worth: Harcourt Brace Jovanovich, 1992, especially chs 6 and 7.

*33. Geoffrey Leech, Benita Cruickshank and Roz Ivanič, *An A–Z of English Grammar & Usage*, 2nd edn. London and New York: Longman, 2001.

34. Geoffrey Leech and Michael Short, *Style in Fiction: A Linguistic Introduction to English Fictional Prose*. London and New York: Longman, 1981.

*35. Geoffrey Leech and Jan Svartvik, *A Communicative Grammar of English*, 3rd edn. London and New York: Longman, 2002.
36. Tom McArthur (ed.), *The Oxford Companion to the English Language*. Oxford: Oxford University Press, 1992.
37. James Milroy and Lesley Milroy, *Authority in Language: Investigating Language Prescription and Standardisation*, 2nd edn. London and New York: Routledge, 1987.
38. James Milroy and Lesley Milroy (eds), *Real English: The Grammar of English Dialects in the British Isles*. London and New York: Longman, 1993.
39. W. H. Mittins et al., *Attitudes to English Usage*. Oxford: Oxford University Press, 1970.
40. W. R. O'Donnell and Loreto Todd, *Variety in Contemporary English*. London: Allen & Unwin, 1980.
41. William O'Grady, Michael Dobrovolsky and Francis Katamba, *Contemporary Linguistics: An Introduction*. London and New York: Longman, 1998.
42. Eric Partridge, *Usage and Abusage*, new edn, edited by Janet Whitcut, New York: W.W. Norton, 1997.
*43 Randolph Quirk, Sidney Greenbaum, Geoffrey Leech and Jan Svartvik, *A Comprehensive Grammar of the English Language*. London: Longman, 1985.
44. Andrew Radford, *Transformational Grammar: A First Course*. Cambridge: Cambridge University Press, 1988.
45. Andrew Radford, *Syntactic Theory and the Structure of English*. Cambridge and New York: Cambridge University Press, 1997.
46. Mick Short, *Exploring the Language of Poems, Plays and Prose*. London: Longman, 1996.
47. William Strunk and E. B. White, *The Elements of Style*, 4th edn. London: Longman, 2000.
48. Michael Toolan, *Language in Literature: An Introduction to Stylistics*. London: Arnold, 1998.
49. Gunnel Tottie, *An Introduction to American English*. Malden, MA: Blackwell, 2002, ch. 7, 'The Grammar of American English'.
50. R. L. Trask, *A Dictionary of Grammatical Terms in Linguistics*. London and New York: Routledge, 1992.
51. R. L. Trask, *The Penguin Guide to Punctuation*. London: Penguin, 1997.
52. Elizabeth Closs Traugott and Mary Louise Pratt, *Linguistics for Students of Literature*. New York: Harcourt Brace Jovanovich, 1980.
53. Peter Trudgill and J. K. Chambers (eds), *Dialects of English: Studies in Grammatical Variation*. Harlow: Longman, 1991.
54. Lynne Truss, *Eats, Shoots and Leaves: A Zero Tolerance Approach to Punctuation*. London: Profile Books, 2003.
55. Katie Wales, *A Dictionary of Stylistics*, 2nd edn. London: Longman, 2001.
56. Henry G. Widdowson, *Practical Stylistics: An Approach to Poetry*. Oxford: Oxford University Press, 1992.

Index

Notes

1 Major or defining page references are printed in bold type.
2 See pages xiv–xvi for symbols and conventions.